Berichte + Dokumentationen

Rezensionen

Liebe Lesende,

die materielle Wende ist in aller Munde. Dieser Eindruck drängt sich zumindest auf, wenn man auf jüngere Publikationsdiskurse diverser Geistes- und Kulturwissenschaften (darunter auch die Religionswissenschaft) blickt. Auch in der Interkulturellen Theologie finden sich zunehmend Arbeiten, die die konstitutive Rolle von materiellen Objekten und körperlichen Praktiken bei der Produktion von Identität und Bedeutung in den Fokus rücken. Das vorliegende Heft versammelt einige dieser Texte, um einen exemplarischen Überblick über Forschungsperspektiven, Fragestellungen und methodische Zugänge zu liefern, die verschiedene am *material turn* interessierte Autorinnen und Autoren aus dem Bereich der Religionswissenschaft und Interkulturellen Theologie ihren Arbeiten zugrunde legen. Um das Feld thematisch einzugrenzen, wurden Beiträge in das Heft aufgenommen, die sich schwerpunktmäßig in die Erforschung des globalen Christentums einordnen lassen. Dass die Beschränkung auf diesen Forschungsgegenstand indes keine Engführung bedeutet, zeigt der Umstand, dass sich das Themenfeld seinerseits durch eine große Bandbreite an Unterbereichen, weiteren Themen und Kontexten auszeichnet. Die in diesem Heft versammelten Texte legen das auf eindrückliche Weise dar.

Was aber ist unter dem *material turn* bzw. der materiellen Wende zu verstehen? Welche Forschungsfragen und -probleme adressieren entsprechende Ansätze, und was ist ihr Erkenntnisinteresse? Im Zentrum steht in der Regel die Hypothese, dass die materielle Präsenz von Objekten und Körpern die Produktion von Sinn und Bedeutung im Rahmen menschlich-kommunikativer Interaktion auf vielfältige Art und Weise prägt, wenn nicht gar konstituiert. In Abgrenzung zu Ansätzen, die sich vor allem auf die Analyse nicht-materieller Ideen und symbolischer Systeme konzentrieren, nehmen Arbeiten zum *material turn* primär ›Dinge‹, also physische Objekte und Artefakte, in den Blick und untersuchen deren Rolle in menschlichen Beziehungen, gesellschaftlichen Aushandlungsprozessen und Praktiken sowie bei der Konstruktion von Weltverständnissen, Bedeutung und Identität. Diese Perspektive wurde in den letzten Jahren noch dadurch erweitert, dass nunmehr auch die mit diesen ›Dingen‹ in Beziehung stehenden Körper, die sie umgebenden materiellen Assemblagen und räumlich-ästhetischen Arrangements sowie die Infrastruktur als Ausdruck vernetzter Sozialitäten in den Blick genommen werden. Daneben hat die Konzentration auf die materielle Dimension von Kultur dafür gesorgt, dass die in der Religionswissenschaft und Interkulturellen Theologie auch als *material religion* bezeichnete Forschungsrichtung – im Rückgriff auf sozial- und kulturwissenschaftliche Theoriebildung – ›Praxis‹ als zentrales Konzept in ihr theoretisches Inventar übernommen hat. Damit hat sich der Fokus gewissermaßen erweitert: vom Objekt hin zum handelnden Subjekt, sodass nun nicht nur »doing objects«, sondern ebenfalls »doing subjects« im Zentrum des Interesses stehen. Beobachten lässt sich in diesem Zusammenhang die (teilweise durchaus kritische) Auseinandersetzung mit diskurstheoretischen Ansätzen aus dem Bereich der poststrukturalistischen oder postkolonialen Theorie, indem Fragen nach dem Verhältnis von Sprache und Körperlichkeit, nach der Materialität von Diskursen, aber auch nach der Hegemonialität materiell konstituierter gesellschaftlicher Wirklichkeiten in den Blick genommen werden.

Die konstitutive Bedeutung von Materialität und Praxis für diskursive Aushandlungsprozesse und die Produktion von Bedeutung und Identität wird – unter Anwendung verschiedener Ansätze aus dem Bereich des *material turn* – von den Beiträgen des vorliegenden Heftes auf exemplarische Weise reflektiert.

So rückt Jessica A. Albrecht in ihrer ethnographischen Forschungsarbeit die zentrale Bedeutung der *Chapel of the Hope of the World* am *Ladies' College Colombo* (gegründet im Jahr 1900) in den Fokus. Die Kapelle spielt für die Genese eines lokalen christlichen Geschichtsbewusstseins sowie einer spezifisch srilankisch-anglikanischen Gender-Identität von Frauen eine bedeutende Rolle. In diesem Zusammenhang knüpft die Autorin vor allem an Konzepte des sogenannten *spatial turns* sowie der Infrastrukturstudien an.

Tanji Mas Beitrag zur sogenannten Nestorianischen Stele, die 781 n. Chr. als eines der frühesten Zeugnisse des Christentums in China in der Tang-Hauptstadt Chang'an errichtet wurde, beleuchtet die komplexen Diskurse, die seit dem 8. Jahrhundert bis heute um dieses Objekt geführt wurden. Dabei versteht er die Stele als palimpsestisches Diskursobjekt, dessen materielle Gegenwart zu verschiedenen Zeiten Prozesse der diskursiven Aneignung und hybriden Identitätsbildung in China selbst und darüber hinaus initiiert hat.

Wie umgekehrt Materialisierung durch Sprache vollzogen wird, illustriert Doris Günther-Kriegel in ihrer Analyse aktueller Publikationen zu *Fair Trade* aus dem Bereich der evangelischen Entwicklungsarbeit. Hier zeigt sie, wie vergeschlechtlichende Repräsentationen von Produzentinnen den Spalt zwischen Globalem Süden und Globalem Norden gleichsam real und objektiv reproduzieren und zementieren.

Der Beitrag von Thorsten Wettich zu *herchurch*, einer lutherisch-feministischen kirchlichen Gemeinschaft in San Francisco, knüpft an Birgit Meyers Konzept der *sensational forms* an. Wettich demonstriert, wie Sprache, Ikonographie und rituelle Praxis der *Ebenezer Lutheran Church* das Göttlich-Weibliche sinnlich erfahrbar machen und dabei eine affektive Öffnung zur Transzendenz erzeugen.

Dass auch die materielle Dimension von Texten religiöse Aushandlungsprozesse beeinflussen kann, zeigt Jan Gehms Artikel zur Textkultur orientalisch-orthodoxer Kirchen in Europa. Am Beispiel mehrerer Fallstudien aus den Bereichen der armenischen, koptischen und syrisch-orthodoxen Kirchen zeichnet er die Verflechtung von Tradition und Moderne sowie die dynamischen Entwicklungen religiöser Identitätskonstruktion in verschiedenen soziokulturellen Kontexten Europas nach.

Égide Pèlerin Muziazias Studie untersucht die Funktion des Rosenkranzes in der römisch-katholischen Frömmigkeit im Kontext der Demokratischen Republik Kongo. Der Autor rezipiert dabei insbesondere solche Ansätze, die sich der *agency*, also der Handlungsmacht, von Dingen verschrieben haben, und illustriert, wie der Rosenkranz seine religiöse und politische Wirkung durch die Aktivierung spezifischer kultureller Codes sowie die Mobilisierung kollektiver Vorstellungswelten entfaltet.

Einen spannenden Einblick in aktuelle Entwicklungen des Christentums in der Golfregion bietet abschließend der Beitrag von Claudia Rammelt und Gregor Etzelmüller zu Migrationskirchen in den Vereinigten Arabischen Emiraten (VAE), die in den letzten Jahren (von der Forschung bislang offenbar weitgehend unbemerkt) zum neuen Zentrum des arabischsprachigen Christentums avanciert sind. Der Beitrag knüpft an Feldforschungen vor Ort an und bettet die komplexe konfessionelle Landschaft in die infrastrukturellen und politischen Rahmenbedingungen der VAE ein.

Wir hoffen, dass die abgedruckten Beiträge nicht nur einen vielstimmigen Überblick über aktuelle Tendenzen bezüglich des *material turn* in Religionswissenschaft und Interkultureller Theologie eröffnen, sondern auch zu weiterer Reflexion und Diskussion ermuntern. Im Namen der gesamten Redaktion wünschen wir allen Lesenden eine anregende und ertragreiche Lektüre!

Ulrike Schröder & Yan Suarsana

Where History is Made

The Chapel of the Hope of the World – Ladies' College, Colombo – at the Heart of Collective Religious Identity

Jessica A. Albrecht

1. Introduction

In September 2021, I visited Ladies' College Colombo. Ladies' College is a semi-private elite girls' school – concerning class and academic prestige –, founded in 1900 by the Church Missionary Society (England) and belonging to the Church of Ceylon (Anglican) under the Diocese of Colombo. This visit was part of my PhD research on elite girls' schools in Sri Lanka.[1] Ladies' College is built in late-colonial architectural style, two to three storey buildings and spread across a large compound (4.32 hectares), surrounded by abundant greenery. Coming in through the official entrance – there is another one at the back end for the boarding house and the nursery/kindergarten – the first buildings one can see are classroom buildings. However, when entering the centre of these buildings and turning left, passing the large College Hall and library, the space opens up to the college chapel. The chapel, thus, lies directly on the connective path between the classroom buildings and the sports compound as well as the boarding house and the nursery. While not in the actual centre of the school premises, it lies at the connective pathway and is therefore, in the sense of social and experienced space, in the centre of the school life.

1 I was allowed to visit the school, even though it was officially closed due to the pandemic lock-downs, because one of my interlocutors then worked at the school and was an influential »Old Girl« of Ladies' College. It was also she who showed me around the campus.

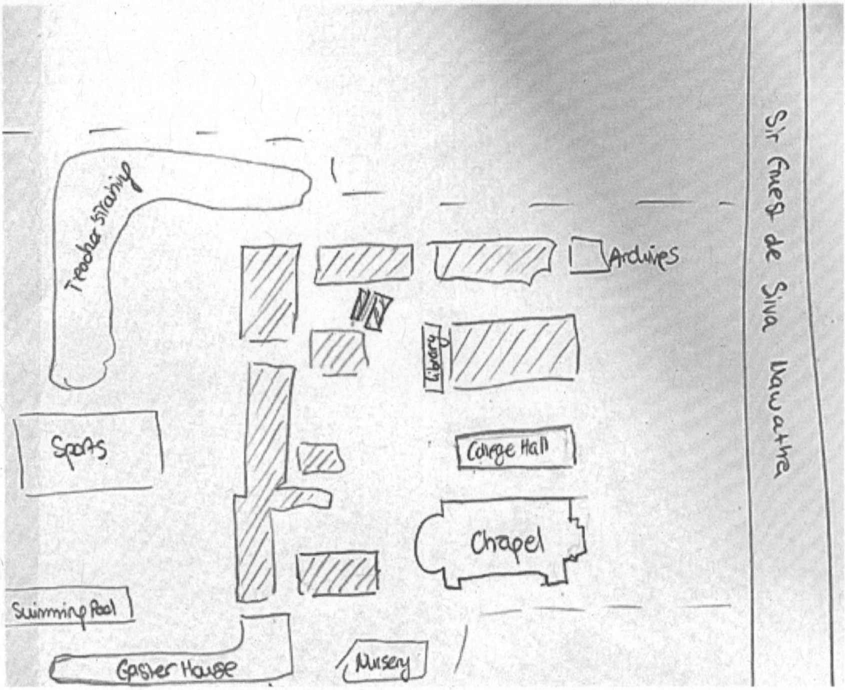

Figure 1: Sketch of the Ladies' College compound, ethnographc diary of the author, 2021, shaded buildings are educational buildings.

This article explores how the chapel, as a material and spatial site, contributes to the construction of history – and, by extension, to a specific Sri Lankan Christian identity centred on girls' education and the emancipation of women. Drawing on the findings of field research conducted in 2021 as well as archival research, this case study aims to bring the study and conceptualisation of global Christianity into dialogue with approaches from the spatial and material turns. Starting from the premise that spaces, always already shaped by cultures, in turn act as ontological structures and affordances for both human and non-human actors, I argue that infrastructural and spatial approaches can help dissolve the apparent boundaries between discourse theory and the material turn. By focusing on the construction of history – and thus also on the formation of Christian identity – I will demonstrate how practice and narration are always already entangled with the spatial conditions in which they emerge.

Figure 2: Chapel inside depicting the altar, picture taken by author in 2021

2. Material Religion, Space and Infrastructure

In recent years, the study of religion has seen a growing interest in material and spatial approaches, often summarized under the label of the *material turn*. The most influential scholars in this strand are Birgit Meyer (media, mediation, and the sensory dimensions of religion)[2] and David Morgan (visual culture, embodiment, and the sacred gaze).[3] They have emphasized that religion is not only com-

2 Birgit Meyer, »Religion Across Media«. Materielle Medien und religiöse Praktiken der Welterzeugung, in: Anke Offerhaus (ed.), Medienvielfalt – Religionsvielfalt. Facetten der Transformation von Medien und Religion, Wiesbaden 2023, 47–71; Birgit Meyer, Religion as Mediation, in: Entangled Religions 11 (2020), https://doi.org/10.13154/er.11.2020.8444; Birgit Meyer (ed.), Aesthetic Formations. Media, Religion, and the Senses, New York 2009.

3 David Morgan, The Sacred Gaze. Religious Visual Culture in Theory and Practice, Berkeley 2005; David Morgan, Mediation or Mediatisation. The History of Media in the Study of Religion, in: Culture and Religion 12 (2011), 137–152; David Morgan, Material Analysis and the Study of Religion, in: Tim Hutchings/Joanne McKenzie (eds.), Materiality and the Study of Religion. The Stuff of the Sacred, London 2016, 14–32.

municated through doctrines and beliefs but also experienced and made present through material forms, embodied practices, and affective engagements. The aim of material religion was to criticize the text- and faith-based methodologies in the study of religion. These multiple critiques reached from a more general highlighting of the exclusion of certain types of sources (materials, artefacts, and objects) and methodologies (embodiment, performativity, and ritual) to a more specific critique of the colonial and orientalist legacies of text-based approaches that are also embedded in and stem from Christian theological scholarship (as well as for instance historical and philological scholarship) in the nineteenth century.

Both Meyer and Morgan have shaped the material turn in Religious Studies through their focus on Christianity – Meyer through her work on Pentecostalism in Ghana and the sensory-material mediation of religious experience, and Morgan through his theorisation of the sacred gaze and the visual cultures of Western Christianity. Because of this, their contributions prove to be very insightful for the study of Global Christianity and missionary movements, in particular.[4] In the study of postcolonial Christianity in the Global South, such as here in Sri Lanka, the application of theories and approaches from material religion has to be done with care and constant reflexivity in relation to the underlying religious (or else) assumptions that build the grounds for these theories. Institutions like Ladies' College in Colombo are embedded in entangled genealogies: colonial Anglicanism, local translations that lead to Sri Lankan forms of Christianities, and elite educational practices intersect in ways that provide not only an empirical expansion, but also a theoretical testing ground for the material and spatial turns in Religious Studies.

While the spatial turn is now often discussed as part of the broader material turn in Religious Studies, spatial analysis has a much longer genealogy in fields such as geography, architecture, and urban studies, and only more recently entered religious studies through the lens of material religion, particularly through

4 In relation to other religions, this might, consequently, prove a problem. In particular, Morgan's conceptualization of mediation, which often builds on a Catholic model of materialization – where objects are understood to channel or contain the sacred – raises questions about the applicability of such frameworks to non-Christian religious traditions. In other words, one could argue that in his effort to critique the *Protestant bias* in Religious Studies to look at texts and individual beliefs rather than the materiality of religion, he turns over to a very Catholic framework that, likewise, bears its colonial marks, exclusions, and epistemic orders. Even in Meyer's work, where media and aesthetics are grounded in anthropological contexts, the conceptual scaffolding remains shaped by Christian assumptions about presence, transcendence, and the sensual.

the engagement with religion and infrastructure. While *space* has its own specific history in the study of religion, thinking back on theories and texts produced on *sacred space* during the twentieth century, the analysis of infrastructure as emerged within material religion is quite a new perspective in the study of religion[5] as well as missionary history[6] that detaches from such earlier approaches by mainly engaging with space through the lens of infrastructure and, thus, from a constructivist perspective. Before theorising space, I want to therefore explain my reason for coming from the perspective of infrastructure, as this informed my reading of spatial theories in this article.

Infrastructure refers to the underlying physical and organisational systems – such as buildings, roads, or technologies – that enable and shape social life, often invisibly structuring how people interact, move, and experience the world. It is thus a very direct bond between ontology, ideology, and epistemology. Ontology, because it structures the ways in which bodies can move, and information can be transmitted in this world. Ideology, because it directly links this ontological structure to politics precisely because this link is rendered invisible in everyday use. Epistemology, because the structuring of said space not only informs, but constricts and enables knowledge as such. As Isaiah Ellis has argued:

> »To understand the physical structures that facilitate movement and its meanings is to understand, ›the material conditions of possibility for life‹ – how the spatial worlds we inhabit came to be and how they might change. To understand infrastructure is therefore not just a matter of technical or historical knowledge, but of political possibility.«[7]

Nevertheless, agency and transformation are always present in these conceptions of infrastructure.[8] Infrastructure is, thus, a way to think about the relationship between the material and the discursive in ways that are methodologically

5 Isaiah Ellis, Infrastructure between Anthropology, Geography, and Religious Studies, in: Katie Day/ Elise M. Edwards (eds.), The Routledge Handbook of Religion and Cities, London 2020, 94–104; Benjamin Kirby, Religious Infrastructure. Designations, Transformations, Entanglements, in: State & Society 52 (2024), 96–113; Yanti Hoelzchen/Benjamin Kirby, Religious Infrastructure. Establishing a Research Agenda, in: Religion, State and Society 52 (2024), 88–95.

6 Steve Bradbury, Mission, Missionaries and Development, Cheltenham 2013, 413–429; Emily Elizabeth Turner, Mission Infrastructure Development in the Canadian North, c. 1850–1920, University of Edinburgh, 2018.

7 Ellis, Infrastructure, 94.

8 See summary of approaches in: Kirby, Religious Infrastructure, 97–98.

realisable, specifically in the study of religion. What makes infrastructure religious, is, crucially, not an inherent nature or essence of religion that is part of *religious infrastructure*, but precisely the effect of infrastructure as such: it is religious, is experienced as religious, is read as religious, when the (material) structure and the relationship between actors with that (material) structure connect a (historically sedimented) reading of religion with a present-day experience of religion through the movement of bodies and information/knowledge within that infrastructure. Thus, history is crucial.

3. Space and Lefebvre

But before dealing specifically with the question of history, I want to engage with the concept of space. While this term typically invokes the material opposite to time, the use of space, thus, the spatial turn in social sciences has been centring the social aspects of space from the beginning.[9] In my reading, these understandings of infrastructure have been highly influenced by a specific understanding of space that works at the connection between the social and the material. That understanding was particularly shaped by Henri Lefebvre. As one of the most influential theorists of space in the twentieth century, he also had an impact on theories about space in religious studies and postcolonial studies. The main reason why I find his thoughts useful, is because they enable us to think about space in precisely such ways that incorporates infrastructure, the social, and history. Lefebvre, while heavily influenced by Marxist materialism, thinks about space as a response to the discourse theory of Michel Foucault. Therefore, his combination of Foucault and Marx always already conceptualises space as a social phenomenon. For him, the relational aspects are key for understanding the world. However, any relationship (between subjects, between object and subject, etc.) has to be actualised in a specific situation. This situation, in turn, transforms its state

9 John Corrigan, Spatiality and Religion, in: Barney Warf/Santa Arias (eds.), The Spatial Turn. Interdisciplinary Perspectives, London/New York 2009, 157–172; Kim Knott, The Location of Religion. A Spatial Analysis, London 2005; Kim Knott, Spatial Theory and Method for the Study of Religion, in: Temenos – Nordic Journal for the Study of Religion 41 (2005), 153–184; Kim Knott, Spatial Theory and the Study of Religion, in: Religion Compass 2 (2008), 1102–1116.

through the relationship that is actualised and is, thus, made effective. This (material) underpinning of social relationships structures his perspective on space.[10]

Space itself is the context – though not the (sole) basis – of knowledge production.[11] Hence, space is embedded in (discursively constructed) ideology and is the concealment of that very ideology that makes space function as the context of knowledge production.[12] The main ideology Lefebvre is interested in is capitalism (in the West). But as scholars of various disciplines have shown, this perspective can be applied to various contexts and fruitfully bring together the question of ontology and epistemology.[13]

While space is in a way concrete and materialised, for Lefebvre, space is always physical, mental, and social.[14] In that way it is not a »reality on its own« but embedded in power structures that are produced in and through social relations. It is the body of social relationships.[15] Seen from that perspective, space is always particular (as opposed to universal) and, thus, challenges (popular) notions of history. History, then, is not graspable in ways that historians typically think it is – because space itself is actualised and constituted in the moment and not a *form* of *physical reality* that can be read into from the outside.[16] I would go further than that and argue that space itself produces history and is indistinguishable from it.

But then, how to analyse it? Lefebvre proposes a conceptual triad of (1) representations of space, (2) spatial practice, and (3) representational spaces. Representation of space is, effectively, the *conceived space* – how it was envisioned by planners, architects, artists, etc. It hence ties space to the »order which those relations impose, and hence to knowledge«.[17] Spatial practice, or: *perceived space*, is the moment of concomitant production and reproduction of space and society and their relationship. Lastly, *representational spaces*, or: lived space, is the passively

10 Henri Lefebvre, The Production of Space, trans. Donald Nicholson-Smith, Oxford 1991, 401.
11 Lefebvre, Space, 8.
12 Lefebvre, Space, 9.
13 Knott, Location; Stefan Kipfer et al., Henri Lefebvre. Debates and Controversies, in: Progress in Human Geography 37/1 (2013), 115–134; Stefan Kipfer/Kanishka Goonewardena, Urban Marxism and the Post-Colonial Question. Henri Lefebvre and ›Colonisation‹, in: Historical Materialism 21/2 (2013), 76–116.
14 Lefebvre, Space, 11.
15 Henri Lefebvre, The Production of Space (1981), in: Jen Jack Gieseking/William Mangold (eds.), The People, Place, and Space Reader, New York/London 2014, 289.
16 Lefebvre, Production (1981), 289.
17 Lefebvre, Production (1981), 290.

experienced and, therefore, dominant space. It links (cultural) symbols and meanings through space with the inhabitants of that space.[18] So, while space is *there*, including things, smells, movements and such, space is always produced. Crucially, the three elements described above that produce space are interconnected in a way that the individual moves within a space and between spaces »without confusion« – without implying that it is a »coherent whole«.[19]

Depending on the perspective, infrastructure is a part, an underlying structure or a result of space. What is most important for my reading here, is that infrastructure is what *enables connections*. To put it on a more basic and less materialistic level, infrastructure is what »facilitates movement«[20] and is, thus, a way to expand Lefebvre's conception of space in terms of transformation. That is not to say that this is missing in Lefebvre – who clearly speaks about agency – but that transformation is itself connected to the material possibility of movement (infrastructure).

History is movement. It is transformation. However, history only exists within the present and is a reading of the past read through the perspective of the present. That means that it is transformed in every reading. That reading, though, is always part of (a) space and, thus, relying on infrastructure. Let me now come to the case study to illustrate my argument. I want to examine the Chapel of the Hope of the World from these perspectives. How does it produce a religious space and how does that space relate to the school as a space? But also, what is it that makes this space function *as a religious space* – or not? Lastly, how does that relate to history and identity?

4. The Chapel of the Hope of the World and Anglican History in Sri Lanka

The *Chapel of the Hope of the World* as it is called, is one of the only explicit markers of Christianity at Ladies' College. While there are only 1.6 million Chris-

18 Lefebvre, Production (1981), 290–291.
19 Lefebvre, Production (1981), 292.
20 Ellis, Infrastructure, 94.

tians (about 7.5 per cent of the population) in the country out of which roughly 50,000 are Anglican, about a third of the students at Ladies' College are Christian and the majority is Buddhist.[21] This is one reason why the school is considered to be Christian, the others being restrictions on principals, some teachers, prefects, etc. having to be Christian and, crucially, the role of the chapel in the daily school lives. Strikingly, it is the only religiously marked space in the school and the site of not only some extracurricular activities, such as the choir, but also the site of school events and the commemoration of founders and previous principals. In many ways, it is where (religious) identity is made, lived, and experienced at Ladies' College.

Anglicanism was introduced to Sri Lanka – then Ceylon – in 1799, when the Church of England became the ecclesiastical arm of the British colonial state, beginning with a colonial chaplain assigned to the garrison in Colombo and to serve British officials. The Diocese of Colombo was formally established in 1845, becoming the institutional centre of Anglican presence on the island. It was disestablished in 1885, giving way to more synodical governance, and by 1930, the Church of Ceylon was formally constituted as a distinct entity within the Anglican Communion. A second diocese, Kurunegala, was created in 1950 to serve the central and north-western regions. Following the dissolution of the Church of India, Pakistan, Burma, and Ceylon in 1970, attempts to form a united church in Sri Lanka were hindered by legal challenges. As a result, the two dioceses remained outside any provincial structure, retaining their status as extra-provincial and continuing under the direct metropolitan authority of the Archbishop of Canterbury. In 2007, the Church of Ceylon was incorporated by an act of the Sri Lankan Parliament, along with the adoption of a national constitution for the Church. This established a distinctive model of ecclesial jurisdiction – neither a province nor a typical extra-provincial diocese – though it has not yet been formally recognised by the wider Anglican Communion.[22] Even though the numbers are quite small, the influence of the Church of Ceylon is high in another regard: through educational institutions. Notably, four of the most elite schools (all semi-private) in the

21 Country Policy and Information Note. Minority Religious Groups, Sri Lanka, February 2025, GOV.UK, 4 March 2025, https://www.gov.uk/government/publications/sri-lanka-country-policy-and-information-notes/country-policy-and-information-note-minority-religious-groups-sri-lanka-february-2025-accessible.

22 Marc Billimoria, Sri Lanka, in: Mark D. Chapman et al. (eds.), The Oxford Handbook of Anglican Studies, Oxford 2016, 219–220.

country belong to the Church of Ceylon: St. Thomas' College, Mount Lavinia, Trinity College, Kandy – two boys' schools – and Bishop's College and Ladies College – both girls' schools in Colombo. Students at these schools mainly come from upper middle-class background with culturally, economically, and politically influential families. The ties made through Past Pupil Associations are some of the underlying cultural and political networks of the country and abroad.

The missionary activities in Ceylon, and many other places that the Anglican church was involved in, specifically activities concerned with education were mainly conducted by the Church Missionary Society (CMS) which was founded in the same year that Anglicanism was imported to the island, 1799. A hundred years later, in 1899, Lilian Nixon and Elizabeth Whitney were sent to Colombo to open an English language girls' school. Whitney became the manager and Nixon the school's first principal.[23] However, it was the next principal, Gwen Opie (1917–1944), who expanded the school with various buildings in the 1920s and 1930s, completing the Chapel of the Hope of the World in 1933. What is now the centre of the school, was one of the first buildings to be added onto the existing classrooms. However, it was in the last thirty years that the chapel was altered in ways that *made* history: into most of the building's walls, memorial plaques were inserted by the Old Girls' Association (OGA) to commemorate principals and other supporters of the school. In February 2025, Founder's Day and the 125 years anniversary of the school were celebrated, as typical for such celebrations, through a commemorative *Service of Thanksgiving* at the chapel, organised by the OGA, in addition to a Brunch and a Sports Day.[24] About 500 members of the OGA were present during the service, »a deeply moving tribute to God's blessings over the years«,[25] with only 120 more coming to the Brunch. The service was, evidently, essential for the celebration and the remembrance on that day.

23 For more information on the early history of the school and the relationship between the British educational system and Ladies' College, specifically the role of Cheltenham Ladies' College, see: Jessica A. Albrecht, The Coloniality of Girls' Education in Sri Lanka. Agency, Transformation and Adaptation, in: Entremons: UPF Journal of World History (2022), 4–30; Jessica A. Albrecht, Producing Religion, Gender and National Identity in Sri Lankan Elite Girls' Schools. Histories, Myths, Resistances, London forthcoming.

24 Ladies' College OGA, Facebook, 30 December 2024, https://www.facebook.com/photo.php?fbid=1174001031392251&id=100063470955937&set=a.516894487102912.

25 LCOGA. Thank You, Instagram, 23 March 2025, https://www.instagram.com/p/DEM7dPTIwIo/.

5. Space and the Chapel

In the following, I structure my analysis of the chapel according to Henri Lefebvre's spatial triad – representation/conceived, spatial/perceived, and representational/lived – each corresponding to a subchapter that examines the representations of history, the social practices of space, and the symbolic perceptions that produce and sustain a gendered Christian identity at Ladies' College.

5.1 Representations of History/Conceived Space

The first, and presumably easiest way to engage with history and a specific space is looking at the history of that space – in this case the Chapel of the Hope of the World. In 1915, Gwen Opie (principal from 1917 to 1944) came from New Zealand and as the school biographies written about her maintain, she was a devout Christian, who placed the missionary aspect of Ladies' College at the centre of her work. This was felt by students of the time who said that the chapel was to be a »constant reminder of the Christian foundation of the school.«[26]

In fact, space, in a more literal understanding, had to be made for building the chapel. In 1928, the school had already expanded to its extend and needed to acquire new room. The *Hanover Villa* next door had just come on the market, and it was bought »preparing for the fulfilment of a noble dream, the building of a Chapel which was to be the really great achievement of that period.«[27] The architect R. G. Booth and the CMS missionary and artist L. J. Gaster (who later built the *Gaster House* for the boarders) were trusted with this project. Hanover Villa was seen as the only suitable site in light of any future developments on the property. In other words: the centre of an envisioned future campus. The money for the project was raised by »those who shared her [Opie's] dream.«[28]

On Founder's Day 1933, the Bishop of Colombo laid the foundation stone, and the building was consecrated on 11th August that year. The building itself was finished quickly, and prayers were started to be held there in September.

26 Ranjini Obeyesekere (ed.), Ladies' College. A Centennial Narrative 1900–2000, Colombo 2000, 137.
27 Olive Hitchcock (ed.), A History of C.M.S. Ladies' College. 1900–1955, Colombo 1957, 69.
28 Hitchcock, History, 85.

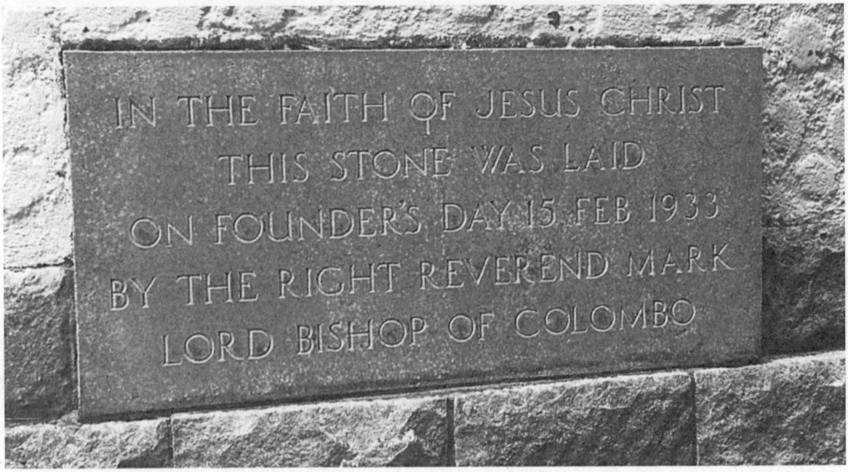

Figure 3: Foundation Stone, picture taken by author in 2021

Foundation stones mark the *official* beginning of a building, when it is put into place through a figure of power – in this case the Bishop of Colombo. Other bishops will lay more stones in the chapel, that will become important in the last subchapter. However, it is important to stress that his religious authority was needed to mark the chapel as a legitimate part of the Church of Ceylon. Thus, it is not only *L'cites* who visit the chapel, but for example also female university students since the 1970s on the weekends.[29]

When local Ceylonese newspapers reported on the new chapel, their main focus was on architecture. One reason for that was that while »the chapel has been designed on orthodox Basilican lines,« the »character of the detail and finish« differed »from the usual class of building commonly met with in Ceylon.«[30] It is unclear what this »usual class of building« meant: churches in general or Anglican churches? If they referred to the main Anglican church on the island, then there was a significant difference. In 1853, the Christ Church Galle Face was built in Colombo in a distinct gothic style. In the nineteenth century, the Gothic Revival played a key role in shaping the architecture of the Church of England, both within Britain and across its growing empire. Especially in colo-

29 Obeyesekere, Centennial Narrative, 68.
30 Hitchcock, History, 85.

nial contexts, neo-Gothic church buildings became powerful symbols of faith and cultural identity during the latter half of the century. Architecturally, the style not only created a visual connection to Britain but also embodied the authority and character of the Church of England and broader ideas of Englishness. Missionary organizations such as the Society for the Propagation of the Gospel (SPG) and the CMS deliberately promoted this medieval-inspired style throughout the Empire, using it as part of broader efforts to establish missions and expand colonial infrastructure.[31] That changed in the mid-nineteenth century and by the 1920s, specifically in Ceylon, the churches were designed to become »unique Sinhalese Chapels« on »indigenous lines.«[32] The reason for this was to limit the fear amongst new converts that when becoming Christian, they would be »less native.«[33] A »house of worship« that responded »to their culture and environment« changed the character of Englishness of the Anglican mission – shifting the focus to conversion and away from Anglicising.[34]

This was specifically the case with the school chapels of St. Thomas' College, Trinity College, Bishops College and Ladies' College. The boys' school chapels were built in the 1920s – which might have been another reason of Opie to also include one in her girls' school – and before that all the Colombo schools visited Christ Church Galle Face for their services on the weekends and holidays. Trinity College, based in the Kandyan tropical forest, is the most striking example of »Indigenisation«. Called the »Chapel without walls«, Trinity Chapel is built on granite pillars with a rood of wooden and rock carvings that are supposed to represent Kandyan architecture.[35] As I have shown elsewhere,[36] Kandy was and is crucial to the Ceylonese imagination of a pre-colonial past. Even though the Kingdom of Kandy did not reach to the coastal areas, in architectural style, at least, it was seen as a cultural symbol that was used for St. Thomas' Chapel of Transfiguration and Ladies' Chapel of the Hope of the World. This planned form of indigenisation is, therefore, based on a specific image of the Ceylonese

31 Emily Turner, The Church Missionary Society and Architecture in the Mission Field. Evangelical Anglican Perspectives on Church Building Abroad, c. 1850–1900, in: Architectural History 58 (2015), 197–228.

32 Billimoria, Sri Lanka, 223–224.

33 Turner, Church Missionary Society, 200.

34 Turner, Church Missionary Society, 200.

35 Chapel | Trinity College Kandy, Sri Lanka, 20 September 2016, https://trinitycollege.lk/chapel/.

36 Albrecht, Producing.

past that is used to conceive the space that was constructed by the architects and planners of these buildings.

Another effect of this representation of space is that it is also a representation of history. As with the Kandyan art, the Chapel of the Hope of the World itself is marked as a witness of the past, connecting the present with the missionary zeal of Opie and the founders. However, the whole school premises and buildings changed significantly throughout the twentieth century, as did the chapel. One significant change occurred in 1991 as a result of the JOC bombing, a suicide car bomb, carried out by the Tamil separationists (LTTE) during the civil war (1983–2009) on 21 June 1991. The attack was aimed for the Joint Operations Command (JOC) of the Sri Lankan Armed Forces which had been erected in the same street as Ladies' College only a short while before. Mrs Gunawardana, then principal, had been aware of the danger and had made appeals to the authorities, also speaking for many other schools in the area. She had also prepared the students and staff for such a possibility and, thus, possibly minimised the danger. However, many buildings were damaged. But it only took the school a week to be functioning again. The chapel was the first building »to be fully restored.« It was re-dedicated in 1992, and the description of a former student clearly shows the connection between history and Christian identity:

> »[It] was a moving event, symbolising the faith and trust that had created the school and its vision. It revived the sense of hope and faith that had bonded generations. The organisation of the event itself was meticulous, combining efficiency with sentiment. Since the inception of the school, the Chapel had been a symbol for the students of Ladies' College.«[37]

Evidently, representational space (symbols that are experienced when in a space) cannot be differentiated from representations of space (how the space is conceived), but the argument I want to make here is that one crucial aspect of the conception of that space was the creation of history and, thus, Christian identity through the chapel as a conceived space.

37 Obeyesekere, Centennial Narrative, 81.

5.2 Spatial History/Perceived Space

Lefebvre was quite clear in arguing that space is a practice. This already shined through the extracts of the previous subchapter, for instance when the Bishop of Colombo placed the foundation stone. It becomes even more apparent in the memories of students and alumnae of the school. The chapel was central not only to my interviews undertaken in 2021, but also to school magazines and celebratory history books produced by the OGA. These illustrate that even the building of the chapel itself was a spatial practice as they planted grass »all round it as the lovely structure came up and [the] boarders were encouraged to water the grass in the evenings, before study hour.«[38] Furthermore, money was saved for the construction by foregoing the prizes the year before, which was happily accepted by most of the students.[39]

The notion of the chapel as a particularly beautiful place is notably present in the sources. Before I even visited the school, I spoke to the member of the OGA, Aashini,[40] who later got me access. When being asked about her main memories of being at the school, she replied, »the chapel is one thing. Have you seen the chapel? (…) Chapel is quite a beautiful place. It's actually quite breath-taking. I remember going for morning prayers, hymns and all that.«[41] What Aashini remembered was perceived space (»breath-taking«), see below, as well as spatial practice. The daily routine of the school-life, mostly, though not only, for Christian students,[42] was and continues to be centred around and takes place within the chapel. In other words: the spatial practice within the chapel, producing that space, also produces the infrastructure of daily school life.

Other alumnae also remember »the prayers in our beautiful Chapel.«[43] As mentioned, before the chapel was built, specifically the boarders of the school went to Christ Church Galle Face. As Anne Abayasekara reminisced, they »had

38 Ladies' College. A Century of Excellence 1900–2000, Colombo 2000.

39 Ladies College Old Girls' Association, One Family Unbroken. Celebrating a Hundred Years 1909–2009, Colombo, 2009, 44.

40 All names of interviewees are pseudonymised.

41 Aashini, 43, Ladies' College, 16 September 2021.

42 Until 1939, all children, irrespective of their religion attended chapel prayers as part of the routine of a Christian school. Then, the government required a written permission from parents for non-Christian students to attend. Hitchcock, History, 86. That was when other school buildings and rooms became places for religious rituals, such as *bhakti gee* for Buddhists, in the great hall, or the prayers for Muslim students, in a classroom.

43 Hitchcock, History, 87.

to wear white dresses and straw-hats that had a red-and-white band with the LC crest at the front.« Thus, the churchgoing was linked to establishing a school identity through clothes. However, for many students this routine was more than a religious event. They »enjoyed the outing in a bus that was requisitioned regularly to take us,« and it also created differentiations between the students as »the older girls had to go to church again in the evenings, but we younger ones and non-Christians were always taken for a walk to the beautifully-kept Racecourse.«[44]

Since 1933, it is the Chapel of the Hope of the World that structures the school-lives. Particularly »morning devotion« has been practiced throughout; and on the first Monday of the month, the Chaplain conducts a service of Holy Communion. Furthermore, new children admitted to grade one »are blessed by the Bishop of Colombo and the Valedictory service is held for school leavers in July.«[45] In addition, Founders' Day celebrations (see also below) take place in February and all other Christian holidays are celebrated in the chapel as well. This information is given on the school's website under the rubric: *worship*. This worship, however, is clearly a connection between a religious practice and the school practice, as they are enmeshed together on instances such as Founders' Day, admission, and valediction.

This combination is also visible when looking at one of the main activities in the chapel: the Chapel choir. As I have heard from an alumna from another elite Christian school, the chapel choir was one of the main extracurricular activities. Crucially, it heavily depended on the current principal whether only Christian students or all students were allowed. This meant that for some periods, Buddhists and Muslims »sang on Easter and Christmas and all, [singing] a lot of hymns and stuff«.[46] (At least) during the time of Miss Simon (principal 1946–1963), the church choir was almost synonymous with musical education. They regularly sang Bach cantatas for the daily Chapel service – as part of musical education as well – and the speakers in the chapel were connected to the Music Room so that once a week each class »sat through a session of sacred music – it was not to everyone's liking.«[47] But the chapel choir expanded its repertoire:

44 Century of Excellence.
45 *Worship*, Ladies' College, 8 May 2025, https://dev.ladiescollege.lk/index.php/worship/.
46 Sabiya, 25, Hillwood College, 23 September 2021.
47 Obeyesekere, Centennial Narrative, 98.

> »Singing took the form of Solo Singing Contests as well. (...) Singing contests within the School provided opportunities to strive for excellence, while the standards reached could be measured by the numerous trophies and prizes the school won year after year at Junior, Intermediate and Senior Choral Festivals and Concerts. (...) It is important to note that the choirs practised regularly throughout the year, not sporadically only for special events. (...) As Colombo's musical repertoire became more sophisticated, talented students became members of the Junior and Symphony Orchestras. One of them while still in school reached the level of a solo performance with the Symphony Orchestra. Carol Services of yesteryear graduated into Cantatas, Christmas Oratorios, Ancient and Modern Carols, the last of which came over the air, and even included a rock performance in the Chapel.«[48]

Evidently, the type of music and the relationship between the chapel choir and extra-school choirs and competitions cannot be clearly distinguished along religious or non-religious lines. This shows that the spatial practice of the chapel challenges the idea that a space is either religious or it is not, or that the practice within a religious space is automatically religious. Even more, it illustrates how history is produced socially within and through space: celebrations that take place, memories that are forged, morning prayers and choir practices that structure the school routines as well as the school's identity; they are all social productions of space.

5.3 Representational History/Lived Space

The notion of excellence, seen in the quote on the singing competitions, is one main image of the woman that Ladies' College sets itself out to produce. In general, the ideal student is heavily gendered and based on religious (Christian) ideals by the founders, principals and the bishop that includes a notion of class, superiority, and female empowerment. Specifically, the latter has been a significant marker of schools like Ladies' College since their inception. However, the meaning of female empowerment and therefore its spatial practices changed through the twentieth century. Thus, I propose to think of the idealisation of a specific Christian womanhood as perceived space and representational history.

Coming back to when the chapel was built, Hanover Villa was not fully demolished, but what remained was the kitchen. This was adapted for Domestic

48 Obeyesekere, Centennial Narrative, 56.

Figure 4: Memorial Tablet Nixon and Whitney, picture taken by author in 2021

Science teaching. This subject was core to girls' schools curricular until the second half of the twentieth century. It included child-welfare, first aid, cookery, hygiene and child psychology.[49] Later, this subject was transformed into (natural) sciences and the kitchens became school laboratories. This change also marks a shift between concepts of *empowered* womanhood. While the founders such as Nixon and the early missionary principals saw their goal in missionizing and creating an environment in which the students could become perfect (Christian)

49 Hitchcock, History, 90.

mothers, teachers, and wives, Christian womanhood has shifted to refer to a wide range of possibilities of womanhood(s) that (Christian) women can become.[50]

The idealisation of specific Christian women – the founders and early principals of the school – is markedly linked with the Chapel of the Hope of the World. As early as 1950, for the 50th anniversary celebrations, two memorial tables were put into the chapel, dedicated to the founders and Gwen Opie by the Bishop of Colombo.[51] In 2009, another two were installed to honour Miss Simon and Mrs. Gunawardena,[52] followed by one for Hitchcock in 2020. Notably, they all feature distinct aspects that were to be remembered.

This plate for the co-founders specifically mentions the CMS background of Nixon and Whitney and remembers them with »a tribute of love« and »grateful remembrance.« Opie's plate, however, which was put in at the same event, was much more elaborate and illustratively linked the chapel with Opie's work:

Her Christian identity is even more central to the way in which she is remembered than in the case of the co-founders. Moreover, it is the chapel itself that »stands as the embodiment of her faith and hopes and aspirations.« Considering that this large plate (about the height of a student), like the others, is clearly visible from most places in the chapel and therefore part of every interaction and perception of the space, it is precisely what Lefebvre described as the representational space: when symbols (in this case religious and gendered) passively produce a space that is perceived by the actors within it. As said above, this is the aspect of space that holds the most power, as this perception is passive and often invisible. The gendered and religious ideals of »a great teacher, a true friend, a wise counsellor, a devout Christian« are the representational aspects of the chapel as a space, and, thus, history: the connection between the past and the present is constantly invoked by this (and other) memorial tablets. It is within the production of that space (in the present, in every practice and perception of that conceived space) that history is produced.

This becomes even more apparent when looking at the memorial tablet of Mabel Simon:

50 For a debate on girls' Education in late colonial Ceylon, see: Legislative Council Papers XIX 1912. Education Committee, 1911–1912 n. d. For a discussion on the change of *Christian womanhood* in Christian schools in Sri Lanka, see: Albrecht, Producing.

51 Obeyesekere, Centennial Narrative, 32.

52 Ladies College Old Girls' Association, Family, 22.

Figure 5: Memorial Tablet Gwen Opie, picture taken by author in 2021

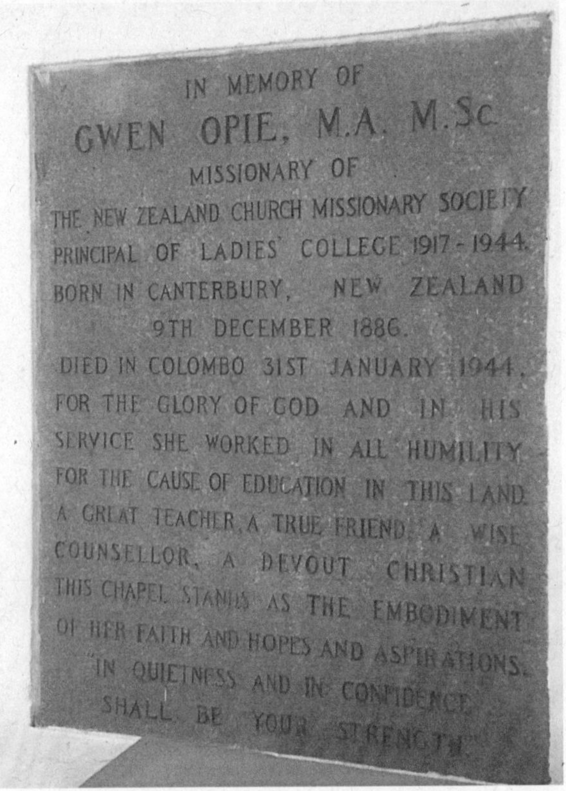

The moulding of »women of integrity, high ideals and tolerance, fostering in them the spirit of love, understanding and service« even more explicitly links ideal womanhood to the schools' conception of Christian identity and practice.

Notably, all of these memorial tablets were gifted by the OGA. This is not a surprise, considering that most of the money collected by various OGAs around the world have been put into the chapel, much more than into other buildings. As early as the 1930s, the OGA gifted various things to the chapel, for instance the altar and rails. The latter was specifically given as a memorial to Miss Whitney, one of the founders of the school.[53] Furthermore, in 1981, the UK branch gifted new curtains for the chapel,[54] in 1983, the local OGA provided an electric organ

53 Hitchcock, History, 85.
54 Ladies College Old Girls' Association, Family, 39.

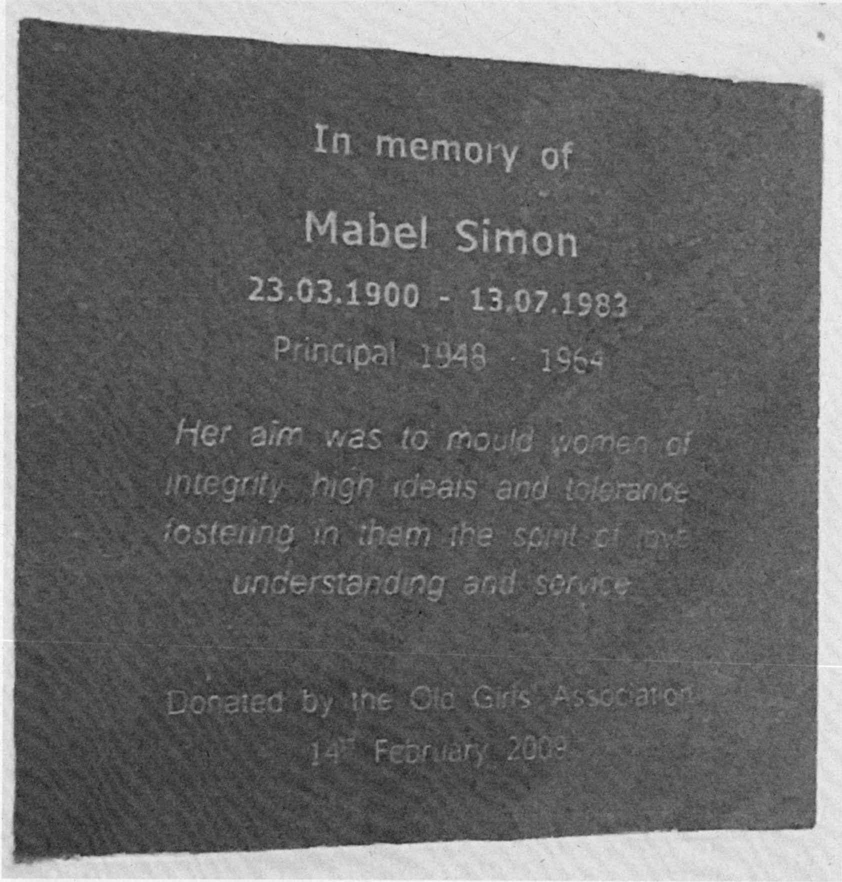

Figure 6: Memorial Tablet Mabel Simon, picture taken by author in 2021

for the Chapel,[55] and in 1991, the USA OGA gave money for the restoration of the chapel after the bomb blast.[56] These social practices producing the space show that the Lefebvre's triad cannot be separated, which he never proposed, though it helps to understand the different layers and complexities of space. However, specifically the gifting of the memorial tablets shows that this was not a repre-

55 Obeyesekere, Centennial Narrative, 64.
56 Ladies College Old Girls' Association, Family, 39.

sentational space / spatial practice / representation of space that was created *top down*. The image of Christianity and womanhood was taken on by these *Old Girls* and used to create that history within the chapel that was to be lived and be perceived and thus transformed by the future students.

6. Conclusion

»The chapel is our corner stone which enshrines our faith.«[57]

»Except the Lord build the house, they labour in vain that build it.«
Psalm 127:1[58]

These quotes are written as headings for the respective pages on the website of Ladies' College, Colombo that engage with the Chapel of the Hope of the World. Written in this virtual space, they specifically use the language of material space to mark the relation between the chapel and the school's Christian identity and practices. The »corner stone« that »enshrines our faith« is a materially marked name for the conception of that particular space. As noted, space is not to be seen as solely material. It is the product of the entanglement between physical and social components and, thus, ontological and epistemological possibilities and boundaries. This is even put forward in the second quote, Psalm 127:1. In relation to a building (the chapel), the psalm suggests that constructing a (religious) space is never done by human effort alone, but dependent on the Lord (assuming his blessing of that space). This is another instance in which representational space becomes apparent.

In the reminiscences of alumnae in the centennial celebration book, there is one narration that quite illustratively brings the various strands of this article together and shows how interconnected space, infrastructure and history are:

> »The building that was perhaps the most inspirational is the College Chapel. Built on the faith of a previous generation this enchanting building demystified religion for us through our own participation. We sang familiar hymns,

57 Worship.
58 *Chapel Life*, Ladies' College, 8 May 2025, https://dev.ladiescollege.lk/index.php/chapel-life/.

> watched the versatility of the choir mistress' face, and found comfort in the warmth and simplicity of the chapel built for children. We learned not the fear of God but the solidarity of our own little community that was bound by a simple morning ritual. We anticipated promotion from the tiny pews to large chairs at the back while our dog eared hymn books filled with interesting cards and pictures provided silent entertainment during lengthy sermons. We trod the pathway to and from the chapel each morning with that extra special effort at silence. I can almost feel the stucco of those pinkish colour walls and see above us shapes of suspended angels.«[59]

The quote highlights the embodied, affective experience of the chapel, how ritual (practice), memory (perceived) and architecture (conceived) come together to form a shared lived religious and student identity, especially through practices that might seem mundane but are embedded in the production of this religious and educational space. However, history is ever present, particularly in the differentiation between different forms of faith in the changing generations of principals and students. This might also refer to the changes between missionary and local principals. Nevertheless, the positive remembrance of the foreign principals through their connection to this space enabled the construction of a history that does not need to challenge the colonial and missionary period.

This shows that the chapel is not just a site within history but a site that produces history: it spatially produces a particular kind of Christian identity tied to gender, class, and memory in postcolonial Sri Lanka. Approaching the chapel through Lefebvre's spatial triad reveals how space is not simply a container but a producer of meaning – through its conception (planning and architecture), practice (ritual and memory), and symbolic perception (memorials, music, gender ideals). By incorporating infrastructure studies, we can see how the chapel *enables* and *structures* both religious and educational life, making visible the ways Christianity is maintained through routine, movement, and material form. This case pushes scholars of global Christianity to take the material and spatial turn seriously – not just to study beliefs or institutions, but to understand how Christian identities are entangled with buildings, rituals, and affective infrastructures.[60] A spatial and infrastructural study of the Chapel of the Hope of the World demonstrates how colonial and missionary legacies continue to shape

59 Obeyesekere, Centennial Narrative, 142.

60 For a conception of affect in relation to girls' schools and religion in Sri Lanka, for which there is no place here, see: Jessica A. Albrecht, Girls' Schools in Sri Lanka. Affect and Intersectionality in Religious and Gendered Identities, in: Implicit Religion 26 (2023), 225–244.

elite religious and gendered life in Sri Lanka today, not through imposition but through local appropriation and transformation – especially by girls and women in Christian schools.

(Dr. Jessica A. Albrecht is a postdoctoral research fellow at the Center for Advanced Studies, Erlangen [Alternative Rationalities and Esoteric Practices from a Global Perspective].)

ABSTRACT

Die *Chapel of the Hope of the World* am Ladies' College Colombo, einer 1900 von der Church Missionary Society gegründeten Eliteschule für Mädchen, ist mehr als ein religiöser Bau: Sie fungiert als räumliches und soziales Zentrum der Schule und ist zentral für die Produktion christlich geprägter Geschichte und Identität. Der Beitrag untersucht, wie räumliche Praxis, materielle Infrastruktur und symbolische Ordnung in der Kapelle miteinander verschränkt sind und zur Ausbildung einer spezifisch sri-lankisch-anglikanischen Frauenidentität beitragen. Anhand ethnographischer und archivarischer Forschung zeigt der Artikel, wie sich der *spatial turn* und Infrastrukturstudien für die Analyse des globalen Christentums fruchtbar machen lassen – insbesondere dort, wo Geschichte, Religion und Alltag räumlich erfahrbar und sozial produziert werden.

Die Nestorianische Stele im Spannungsfeld von Materie, Diskurs und Rezeption

Eine diskursanalytische Perspektive auf ein transkulturelles Artefakt

Tianji Ma

1. Einleitung

Objekte sind nie einfach nur Dinge – sie sind Knotenpunkte sozialer Bedeutungen, materielle Archive vergangener und gegenwärtiger Diskurse. Die sogenannte Nestorianische Stele (*Daqin jingjiao liuxing Zhongguobei* 大秦景教流行中國碑),[1] errichtet im Jahr 781 in der Tang-Hauptstadt Chang'an und seit ihrer Wiederentdeckung um das Jahr 1625 Gegenstand intensiver Debatten, stellt ein außergewöhnliches Artefakt dar, das in seiner materiellen Präsenz wie auch in

1 In diesem Artikel werden aus Gründen der Einheitlichkeit durchgehend traditionelle chinesische Schriftzeichen verwendet. Bei der Umschrift ins Lateinische – etwa bei Schlüsselbegriffen bzw. Namen – wird in der Regel das Hanyu-Pinyin-System angewendet. Name und Vorname von Autor*in bzw. Herausgeber*in werden erst in latinisierter Form, dann in der chinesischen Schrift angegeben. Bei chinesischen Namen in chinesischen Angaben ist die Reihenfolge des chinesischen Namens zuerst Familienname, dann Vorname; bei englischen oder deutschen Angaben eines*r chinesischen Autor*in wird der Name nach westlicher Reihenfolge dargestellt. – *Daqin* 大秦 bezeichnet in chinesischen Quellen ursprünglich das Römische Reich bzw. den weiteren Westen; in der Stele steht der Begriff stellvertretend für die Herkunftsregion der syrisch-nestorianischen Christ*innen.

seiner kulturellen Semantik zwischen den Koordinaten von Religion, Politik und Wissenschaft vermittelt. Als eines der frühesten physischen Zeugnisse christlicher Präsenz in China, nimmt sie eine Schlüsselstellung interkultureller Transferprozesse ein – und war dabei nie nur historisches Dokument, sondern stets auch symbolische Projektionsfläche konkurrierender Interessen und Identitätsentwürfe.

Die wissenschaftliche Auseinandersetzung mit der Nestorianischen Stele begann in der frühen Neuzeit durch Jesuiten wie Semedo, Trigault und insbesondere Kircher, dessen *China Illustrata* (1667) die europäische Wahrnehmung prägte, und wird heute in neuer Perspektive weitergeführt und kontrovers diskutiert.[2] Der vorliegende Beitrag interpretiert die Stele als »sprechendes Objekt« im Sinne des *material turn*[3] und analysiert ihre Rezeptionsgeschichte aus synchroner und diachroner Perspektive unter diskursanalytischen Prämissen. Dieser fragt, wie sich die Bedeutungen, die der Nestorianischen Stele zugeschrieben wurden, im

2 Hinsichtlich eines Forschungsüberblicks können hier aufgrund des beschränkten Umfangs nur einige zentrale Autor*innen genannt werden. Klassische sinologische Arbeiten, etwa von Alexander Wylie, Arthur C. Moule, P. Y. Saeki und Paul Pelliot, konzentrierten sich auf die Übersetzung und philologische Analyse der syrisch-chinesischen Inschrift sowie auf die historische Einordnung des Jingjiao (»Leuchtende Lehre«) in der Tang-Zeit. Besonders Pelliots postum veröffentlichte Studie (1984) gilt bis heute als grundlegendes Referenzwerk. Neuere Forschungsansätze legen verstärkt den Schwerpunkt auf Rezeptionsgeschichte und interkulturelle Kontextualisierung. Michael Keevak untersuchte die westliche Wahrnehmung der Stele vom 17. bis zum 20. Jahrhundert und zeigte auf, wie deren Interpretation im Spannungsfeld kolonialer und missionarischer Interessen variierte. Max Deeg bietet eine innovative Lesart, indem er die Steleninschrift als rhetorisch-politisches Dokument interpretiert, das christliche Inhalte bewusst im kulturellen Idiom der Tang-Zeit vermittelt. Damit verschiebt sich der Fokus von der Stele als bloßem Zeugnis christlicher Mission hin zu einem dynamischen interreligiösen und gesellschaftspolitischen Artefakt. Siehe dazu folgende Quellen: Paul Pelliot, Recherches sur les chrétiens d'Asie centrale et d'Extrême-Orient. Band II/1: La stèle de Si-ngan-fou, Paris 1984; Michael Keevak, The Story of a Stele. China's Nestorian Monument and its Reception in the West, 1625–1916, Hong Kong 2008; Max Deeg, Die Strahlende Lehre. Die Stele von Xi'an, Wien 2018; Qianzhi Zhu 朱謙之, *Zhongguo jingjiao* 中國景教 [Nestorianismus in China], Beijing 2014.

3 Diese theoretische Neuorientierung stellt die Materialität und die Handlungsmacht (»agency«) von Objekten verstärkt in den Vordergrund. Zentrale Autoren wie Bruno Latour, Arjun Appadurai und Alfred Gell betonen, dass materielle Dinge nicht bloß passive Bedeutungsträger oder Symbole sind, sondern als aktive Mitgestalter sozialer und kultureller Prozesse agieren. Dabei unterstreicht der *material turn*, dass Artefakte in Netzwerken mit menschlichen Akteur*innen interagieren und eigenständige Wirkungen in gesellschaftlichen Prozessen entfalten. Somit geraten auch die materielle Präsenz solcher Artefakte und ihre »Objektbiographien« verstärkt ins Blickfeld der Analyse: vgl. z. B. Bruno Latour, We Have Never Been Modern, Cambridge 1993; Arjun Appadurai (Hg.), The Social Life of Things. Commodities in Cultural Perspective, Cambridge 1986; Alfred Gell, Art and Agency. An Anthropological Theory, Oxford 1998.

Wechselspiel politischer, religiöser und wissenschaftlicher Diskurse vom 8. bis ins 21. Jahrhundert transformiert haben.

Im Zentrum steht die Stele als epistemisches Objekt, das nicht bloß Wissen vermittelt, sondern selbst an dessen Hervorbringung beteiligt ist – sei es als Beleg frühchristlicher Präsenz, als Symbol kolonialer Aneignungspraktiken oder als museales Replikationsobjekt. Ausgangshypothese ist, dass die Stele als Kristallisationspunkt transkultureller Wissensordnungen fungiert, deren Dynamik nur im Zusammenspiel von Text, Materialität und Rezeption analytisch erfasst werden kann. Sie wird nicht als statisches Artefakt, sondern als relationaler »Akteur« kultureller Aushandlungsprozesse verstanden. Ein diskursanalytischer Zugriff ermöglicht es, ein komplexes Bild der Stele als hybridem Artefakt an der Schnittstelle von Theologie, Historiographie, Museologie und Globalgeschichte zu rekonstruieren.

2. Die Nestorianische Stele im historischen und theologischen Kontext

Die Nestorianische Stele wurde vermutlich zwischen 1621 und 1625[4] bei Ausgrabungen in der Nähe des Chongren-Tempels, unweit von Xi'an, entdeckt und hat seither die Aufmerksamkeit von Historiker*innen, Religionswissenschaftler*innen und Kulturforscher*innen weltweit auf sich gezogen. Errichtet im Jahr 781 n. Chr., dokumentiert sie eine rund eineinhalb Jahrhunderte umfassende Phase christlicher Aktivität im China der Tang-Dynastie[5] und gilt heute als eines der bedeutendsten materiellen Zeugnisse frühmittelalterlicher interkultureller Kontakte.[6]

4 Die genaue Ausgrabungszeit der Stele ist in der Forschung umstritten. Die meisten Forscher*innen datieren das Ereignis auf die Zeit zwischen 1621 und 1625, jeweils gestützt auf unterschiedliche Analysen der Quellenlage: Hu Chen 陳虎, *Daqin jingjiao liuxing zhongguobei de qianshi jinsheng* 「大秦景教流行中國碑」的前世今生 [Die Vergangenheit und Gegenwart der Nestorischen Stele], in: *Gongjiao shenxue pinglun* [Katholische Theologische Zeitschrift] 4 (2023), 224–288, hier: 228; Glen L. Thompson, Jingjiao. The Earliest Christian Church in China, Chicago 2024, 28.

5 Vgl. Philip Jenkins, The Lost History of Christianity. The Thousand-Year Golden Age of the Church in the Middle East, Africa, and Asia – and How it Died, New York 2009, 64–65.

6 Vgl. hier die Argumentation in Zhijun Nie 聶志軍, *Tangdai jingjiao wenxian wenxian ciyu yanjiu* 唐代景教文獻詞語研究 [Untersuchung der Terminologie in den Dokumenten der Nestorianischen Kirche in der Tang-Dynastie], Guangzhou 2009, 14–15.

Der Begriff *Nestorianismus* bezeichnet die christologische Lehre des Patriarchen Nestorius (um 386–451), die im Zentrum des Konzils von Ephesus (431) stand und als häretisch verurteilt wurde. Nestorius lehrte eine klare Unterscheidung zwischen der göttlichen und der menschlichen Natur Christi und widersetzte sich der Bezeichnung Marias als »Gottesgebärerin« (*Theotokos*). Seine Anhänger*innen, aus der oströmischen Kirche verstoßen, fanden Schutz im Sassanidenreich und entwickelten dort die eigenständige *Kirche des Ostens* (auch »Assyrische Kirche des Ostens«), die sich später entlang der Handelsrouten bis nach Indien, Zentralasien und China ausbreitete.[7] In China wurde der Nestorianismus unter der Bezeichnung *Jingjiao* (景教, »Lehre des Lichts«) bekannt. Frühere chinesische Gelehrte seit der frühen Qing-Dynastie verwechselten die Jingjiao zunächst mit dem Zoroastrismus oder dem Manichäismus, nicht zuletzt aufgrund ähnlicher Lichtmetaphorik und der Verwendung syro-persischer Schriftzeichen.[8] Erst durch philologische und theologiegeschichtliche Studien – etwa durch die Arbeiten von Paul Pelliot und Saeki Yoshiro – konnte die Identifikation als syrisch-nestorianische Tradition gesichert werden.

Die Stele selbst ist ein imposanter Kalksteinblock von etwa 279 cm Höhe, 99 cm Breite und 27 cm Tiefe. Ihre Inschrift umfasst rund 1800 chinesische Zeichen sowie mehrere Zeilen in syrischer Estrangelo-Schrift. An der Spitze der Stele ist ein Kreuz eingraviert, das symbolisch die Verbindung zwischen östlicher und westlicher Sakralikonographie herstellt.[9] Errichtet wurde sie in einer Zeit kultureller Blüte: Die Tang-Dynastie (618–907) war geprägt von einer außergewöhnlichen Offenheit gegenüber ausländischen Religionen, Ideen und Praktiken. Chang'an, die damalige Hauptstadt, war ein kosmopolitisches Zentrum, durch das die großen Handelsrouten der Seidenstraße führten und das als Knotenpunkt zwischen Ost und West einen intensiven Austausch von Waren, Ideen und Religionen ermöglichte.[10] Der Tang-Hof unter Kaiser Taizong hatte Alopen (chin. *Aluoben* 阿羅本), den ersten bekannten christlichen Missionar, offiziell

7 Vgl. Erica C. D. Hunter, The Holy Apostolic Catholic Assyrian Church of the East, in: Lucian N. Leustean (Hg.), Eastern Christianity and Politics in the Twenty-First Century, New York 2014, 54, 601–620.

8 Vgl. Zhu, Nestorianismus, 6–7.

9 Vgl. R. Todd Godwin, Persian Christians at the Chinese Court. The Xi'an Stele and the Early Medieval Church of the East, London 2019, 8–10.

10 Eine ausführliche Darstellung zum historisch-kulturellen Kontext findet sich in: Ding Wang, Remnants of Christianity from Chinese Central Asia in Medieval Ages, in: Roman Malek/Peter Hofrichter (Hg.), Jingjiao. The Church of the East in China and Central Asia, Sankt Augustin 2006, 149–162.

empfangen und ihm gestattet, im *Yi Ning*-Viertel (*Yiningfang* 義寧坊) in Chang'an eine Kirche, das sogenannte »Daqin-Kloster«, zu errichten.[11]

Die Nestorianischen Missionar*innen in China bedienten sich einer ausgeklügelten Strategie kultureller Übersetzung, um die christliche Botschaft in der neuen Umgebung zu etablieren. Die Terminologie der Stele greift bewusst auf buddhistische und daoistische Begriffe zurück: Gott wird als »Wahre Majestät« (*Zhenzhu* 真主) bezeichnet, zentrale Begriffe wie *Dao* (道) oder *Zhen* (真) verweisen auf Begrifflichkeiten, die tief im chinesischen Denken verankert waren.[12] Dieser adaptative Ansatz kann als früher Ausdruck dessen verstanden werden, was heute als *Inkulturation* bezeichnet wird: nicht eine bloße Übertragung fremder Inhalte, sondern eine kreative Neudeutung christlicher Vorstellungen im Horizont der chinesischen Kultur. In dieser Hinsicht stehen die frühen nestorianischen Missionar*innen der späteren Jesuitenmission um Matteo Ricci (1552–1610) methodisch nahe.

Die Inschrift der Stele entfaltet eine erstaunlich komplexe Theologie: Sie preist die Schöpfung durch den einen wahren Gott, schildert den Sündenfall durch den *suodan* 娑殫 (Satan) und verkündet die Menschwerdung Christi durch die Jungfrau. Besonders auffällig ist, dass die Leidensgeschichte Christi (Passion und Auferstehung) kaum eine Rolle spielt – stattdessen dominiert eine kosmologische Erzählung von Licht und Erlösung. Die christologische Sprache bleibt eng an klassischen syrischen Vorlagen orientiert, wird jedoch durch Begriffe der chinesischen Philosophie subtil moduliert.[13] Die Liste der erwähnten Priester und Mönche am Rand der Stele unterstreicht die institutionelle Etablierung des Jingjiao in China: Die Kirche verfügte offenbar über ein gut organisiertes Netzwerk, das sowohl syro-persische als auch chinesische Mitglieder umfasste.

Im Horizont des *material turn* darf die Nestorianische Stele nicht als isoliertes Artefakt betrachtet werden, sondern als dynamischer Akteur in einem komplexen Geflecht sozialer, politischer und religiöser Prozesse. Sie ist zunächst Ausdruck und Medium der frühmittelalterlichen Präsenz der Kirche des Ostens im China der Tang-Dynastie und bezeugt den Versuch, eine interkulturelle christ-

11 Vgl. Jenkins, History, 65–66.

12 Siehe insbesondere Longfei Xu, Die nestorianische Stele in Xi'an. Begegnung von Christentum und chinesischer Kultur, Zugl.: Bonn, Univ., Diss., 2003, Bonn 2004, 95–103; Scott Fitzgerald Johnson, Silk Road Christians and the Translation of Culture in Tang China, in: Studies in Church History 53 (2017), 15–38.

13 Vgl. Xu, Stele, 108–166.

liche Identität in die rituelle, politische und literarische Ordnung des chinesischen Reiches einzuschreiben. Ihre Errichtung im Jahr 781 stellt einen Akt monumentaler Selbstvergewisserung dar, in dem theologische Selbstauslegung und diplomatische Anlehnung an die kaiserliche Autorität ineinandergreifen. Die Inschrift verwebt christologische Motive mit konfuzianischer Ethik und kosmischer Metaphorik und reflektiert so die Strategien kultureller Übersetzung und religiöser Inkulturation, die den Erfolg des Jingjiao im Tang-China ermöglichten.

3. Mythologisierung, Unsichtbarkeit und die diskursive Produktivität der Nestorianischen Stele

Die Stele ist ein Artefakt der »ersten Stunde« christlicher Präsenz in China – und doch ist ihr Ursprung in vielerlei Hinsicht von Unsicherheiten und Leerstellen geprägt. Ihre Entstehungsumstände sind bis heute Gegenstand intensiver, aber widersprüchlicher Deutungen: War sie Grabmal, Ehrenmonument oder ein liturgisches Zeichen kollektiver Identität? Der Forschungsstand ist uneinheitlich. Während renommierte chinesische Gelehrte wie Chengjun Feng 馮承鈞 sie als Grabstein für den Priester Yazedbuzid (chin. *Yisi* 伊斯) deuteten,[14] argumentieren andere – etwa Xinglang Zhang 張星烺 –, dass der Geehrte bei Errichtung der Stele noch lebte, womit die Funktion als Grabmal ausgeschlossen wäre.[15] Auch die syrischen Inschriften auf der Stele, in denen Yazedbuzid als Vater des Mönchs und Gelehrten Adam (Chin. *Jingjing* 景淨) bezeichnet wird, legen eine komplexere Memorialstruktur nahe, die offensichtlich über ein rein individuelles Grabgedenken hinausweist. Pelliot hat darauf hingewiesen, dass die Inschrift selbst sowohl Elemente eines Memorials als auch eines Ehrenmals enthält, ohne jedoch eine klare Funktionszuschreibung zu ermöglichen.[16] In ähnlicher Weise betont auch die Forschung um Saeki Yoshiro, dass die formale Vielschichtigkeit der Stele Ausdruck einer bewussten Strategie kollektiver Selbstvergewis-

14 Vgl. Chengjun Feng 馮承鈞, *Jingjiaobei kao* 景教碑考 [Die Forschung der Nestorianischen Stele], Shanghai 1931, 5.

15 Vgl. Xinglang Zhang 張星烺, *Zhongxi jiaotongshi huibian* 中西交通史料彙編 [Sammlung historischer Materialien zum Verkehr zwischen China und dem Westen]. Bd. 1, Beijing 1977, 108.

16 Vgl. Pelliot, Recherches, 58.

serung einer Minderheit im fremdkulturellen Umfeld sei.[17] So bleibt die Stele eine Projektionsfläche, auf der spätere Deutungen sedimentierten, ohne dass ein ursprünglicher, eindeutiger Funktionskontext je abschließend gesichert wäre.

Gerade die *Mythologisierung* des Artefakts – seine Herkunft im Ungewissen – befeuert seine diskursive Produktivität. Im Sinne des *material turn* zeigt sich hier, dass materielle Objekte nicht nur passive Träger von Bedeutungen sind, sondern selbst Lücken und Ambivalenzen erzeugen, die zur aktiven Produktion neuer Diskurse einladen. Diese Unbestimmtheit erweist sich nicht als Mangel, sondern als Motor kultureller Bedeutungsproduktion. Die offene Frage nach Ort, Zweck und Auftraggeber der Stele entwickelte sich zum semantischen Ankerpunkt vielfältiger historischer, nationaler und theologischer Narrative.

Der mythische Ursprung des Steins – seine schwer greifbare Provenienz – macht ihn zu einem *offenen Textkörper*, der immer neue Sinnangebote provoziert. Jede Rekonstruktion seiner Entstehung ist damit selbst Teil eines sich perpetuierenden Diskurses. Diese offene Textur verweist auf ein grundsätzliches Phänomen religiöser Materialität:[18] dass die Identität eines Artefakts ebenso sehr aus seinem materiellen Vorhandensein wie aus den imaginativen und diskursiven Operationen hervorgeht, die es über die Zeiten hinweg überformen. Der *material turn* sensibilisiert hier für die Einsicht, dass es die Unbestimmtheit der Stele selbst ist, die ihre diskursive Dynamik konstituiert – eine Dynamik, die sich weniger aus faktischer Evidenz speist als aus narrativer Verfügbarkeit.

Nicht nur die Herkunft der Stele bleibt von Unsicherheiten durchzogen – auch ihre jahrhundertelange physische *Abwesenheit* ist ein konstitutives Moment ihrer Wirkungsgeschichte. Nach dem Ende der offiziellen Anerkennung des Jingjiao unter Kaiser *Wuzong* (武宗) im Jahr 845, als Teil der sogenannten *Huichang-Verfolgung des Buddhismus* (*Huichang miefo* 會昌滅佛), verschwand die Stele

17 Vgl. Yoshiro Saeki, Keikyo hibun kenkyu [Die Studien zum Nestorianischen Monument], Tokyo 1911, 1–5.

18 Bezüglich des *material turn* in der Religionswissenschaft siehe dazu: Peter J. Bräunlein, Thinking Religion Through Things. Reflections on the Material Turn in the Scientific Study of Religion\s, in: Method & Theory in the Study of Religion 28/4/5 (2016), 365–399; David Morgan, Introduction. The Matter of Belief, in: Ders. (Hg.), Religion and Material Culture. The Matter of Belief, London/New York 2010, 1–18; Birgit Meyer/Dick Houtman, Introduction. Material Religion – How Things Matter, in: Dies. (Hg.), Things. Religion and the Question of Materiality, New York 2012, 1–24. Diese grundlegenden Werke zeigen, dass Glaube wesentlich in materiellen Artefakten und Praktiken verankert ist und heilige Dinge – von Reliquien bis zu Stelen – als zentrale Medien religiöser Erfahrung verstanden werden müssen.

aus dem öffentlichen Raum.[19] Ihre Vergrabung – sei es aus Angst vor politischer Verfolgung oder aus strategischer Selbsterhaltung – entzieht sich ebenfalls eindeutiger historischer Verortung. Zur Erklärung der Vergrabung der Nestorianischen Stele existieren unterschiedliche Hypothesen, die auf voneinander abweichende historische Kontexte verweisen. Während einige Forscher*innen – etwa Saeki Yoshiro – einen Zusammenhang mit dem Usurpationsversuch des Prinzen Ci Zhu 朱泚 vermuten, der sich zum »Daqin-Kaiser« ausrief und möglicherweise eine politische Vereinnahmung der Stele befürchten ließ,[20] führen andere die Ereignisse auf die umfassenden religiösen Säuberungen unter Kaiser Wuzong zurück.[21] Letztere richteten sich nicht nur gegen den Buddhismus, sondern trafen auch die ausländisch geprägten christlichen Gemeinden, was nach Ansicht vieler jüngerer chinesischer Historiker*innen die plausiblere Erklärung darstellt.

Doch unabhängig vom konkreten historischen Anlass verweist die lange Unsichtbarkeit der Stele auf ein entscheidendes Moment im Zusammenhang mit dem *material turn*: Auch das *Nicht-Sein*, die *Absenz* eines Objektes, wirkt kulturell und diskursiv. Wie Derrida in seiner Theorie der *Spur* formuliert, produziert das Verschwinden eines Zeichens eine *negative Präsenz*, eine Wirksamkeit im Modus des Fehlens.[22] Abwesenheit wird damit nicht als bloße Lücke verstanden, sondern als aktive Konstitution neuer Bedeutungsfelder. Wie in den folgenden Abschnitten noch gezeigt werden wird, erzeugte die jahrhundertelange Unsichtbarkeit der Stele jene spezifische Form eines *»sprechenden Schweigens«*: Ihre physische Abwesenheit war nicht bloß Verlust, sondern konstituierte einen Raum für Erinnerung, Verlustnarrative und imaginierte Vergangenheiten. So wuchs im kulturellen Gedächtnis der Wunsch nach Wiederentdeckung, die Idee eines ver-

19 Vgl. Zhu, Nestorianismus, 81–82; Edwin O. Reischauer, Ennin's Travels in Tang China, New York 1955, 221–270.

20 Vgl. Zhengxiang Zhou 周幀詳, *Guanyu jingjiaobei chutu wenti de zhengyi* 關於景教碑出土問題的爭議 [Die Kontroverse um die Ausgrabung der Nestorianischen Stele], in: *Wenbo* 5 (1994), 42–50, hier: 47.

21 Vgl. Nie, Terminologie, 4.

22 Jacques Derrida entwickelt in seinem Werk »De la grammatologie« (1967) das Konzept der »Spur« (trace), das besagt, dass Bedeutung nicht aus unmittelbarer Präsenz entsteht, sondern immer durch Abwesenheit, Verschiebung und Differenz konstituiert wird. Zeichen tragen Spuren dessen, was ihnen vorausging, und sind nie vollständig anwesend. Diese Theorie eröffnet die Einsicht, dass auch das Verschwinden oder Fehlen eines Artefakts – wie im Fall der Nestorianischen Stele – produktiv Bedeutung erzeugen kann: siehe Jacques Derrida, Grammatologie, Frankfurt am Main 1983, 35–37.

borgenen Schatzes, der vermeintliche »Wahrheiten« über Chinas Vergangenheit neu zu beleuchten versprach.

Als das Artefakt im 17. Jahrhundert unter der Erde gefunden wurde, bedeutete seine Wiederkehr nicht einfach die Restaurierung eines verlorenen Textes, sondern die Emergenz eines neuen Diskurses – jener einer verlorenen, wiederentdeckten und umkämpften christlichen Spur in China. Die »zweite Geburt« der Stele unter jesuitischer Vermittlung lebt weniger von materieller Kontinuität als von narrativer Neukonstitution. Es wird deutlich, dass materielle Kultur nicht nur durch Präsenz, sondern gerade auch durch Abwesenheit bedeutungsproduktiv ist. Die Stele »sprach« nicht trotz, sondern wegen ihrer Unsichtbarkeit – sie strukturierte kulturelle Erwartungen, schuf Leerräume und provozierte Rekonstruktionsphantasien, die ihre wissenschaftliche und theologische Rezeption prägen. Ihre Wirksamkeit oszilliert dabei zwischen Fakt und Fiktion, Geschichte und Imagination – und macht sie so zu einem paradigmatischen Objekt transkultureller Diskursgeschichte.

4. Die Stele im Westen: Projektionsfläche im Spannungsfeld religiöser, kolonialer und eurozentrischer Diskurse

Die Wiederentdeckung, die »materielle Wiederkehr« der Nestorianischen Stele fiel in eine Zeit, in der Europa intensiv damit beschäftigt war, sein Verhältnis zur nicht-europäischen Welt neu zu definieren. Wie Michael Keevak in seiner grundlegenden Studie *The Story of a Stele* zeigt, wurde die Stele im westlichen Diskurs von Anfang an weniger als historisches Zeugnis Chinas gelesen, sondern vielmehr als *Projektionsfläche* eigener Wünsche, Ängste und Selbstvergewisserungen:[23]

23 Vgl. Keevak, Story, 8–9. Deeg spricht dagegen von einem »Hyperorientalismus«, einer spezifischen Steigerungsform des von Edward Said beschriebenen Orientalismus: siehe Deeg, Lehre, 17–24. Im kolonial-missionarischen Kontext diente die »Entdeckung« vermeintlicher Spuren biblisch-christlicher Religionen in nicht-europäischen Kulturen dazu, die eigene missionarische Tätigkeit historisch zu legitimieren und moralisch zu rechtfertigen. Indem Missionar*innen behaupteten, einen ehemals vorhandenen, später jedoch verschütteten oder »degenerierten« christlichen Glauben wiederzubeleben, überschritten sie die Grenzen des klassischen Orientalismus: Sie eigneten sich fremde Vergangenheit nicht nur interpretativ an, sondern konstruierten sie aktiv neu, häufig auf äußerst dünner Quellenbasis. Dieses rekonstruierende Moment, das weit über die bloße exotisierende Wahrnehmung hinausgeht, bezeichnet Deeg als Hyperorientalismus. Er bleibt weiterhin der kolonialen Logik von Machtbeanspruchung und kultureller Überlegenheit verpflich-

Sie diente den unterschiedlichsten Parteien – katholischen Missionar*innen, protestantischen Polemiker*innen, aufklärerischen Philosoph*innen und kolonialen Strateg*innen – als Vehikel, um jeweils eigene Vorstellungen über Religion, Kultur und Macht zu artikulieren. Im Horizont des *material turn* zeigt sich die Stele als materieller Akteur in den westlichen Diskursen: Ihr bloßes Sein, ihre steinerne Faktizität, zwang zur kulturellen und theologischen Reaktion und eröffnete neue Felder hermeneutischer und politischer Aushandlung.

Die ersten westlichen Deutungen der Stele wurden maßgeblich von den Jesuiten geprägt, die im 17. Jahrhundert in China tätig waren und ein doppeltes Ziel verfolgten: die Etablierung des Christentums im Reich der Mitte und die Verteidigung der Legitimität ihrer Missionsstrategie gegenüber skeptischen europäischen Beobachter*innen.[24] Die materielle Evidenz der Stele wurde strategisch funktionalisiert, um die eigene missionarische Agenda diskursiv zu legitimieren: Sie dokumentierte nicht nur die frühe Ankunft des Christentums in China, sondern auch die offizielle Anerkennung durch die Tang-Dynastie.

Jesuitische Missionare wie Álvaro Semedo und Nicolas Trigault verbreiteten Übersetzungen und Interpretationen der Inschrift, die explizit darauf abzielten, das Christentum als eine uralte, ursprünglich akzeptierte Religion in China zu präsentieren.[25] Diese Strategie sollte sowohl chinesische als auch europäische Vorbehalte gegenüber der Missionstätigkeit entschärfen. Athanasius Kircher, der in seinem Werk *China Illustrata* (1667)[26] eine besonders einflussreiche Interpretation der Stele vorlegte, verband diese apologetische Zielsetzung mit einem universalistischen Weltbild, in dem China als Teil eines göttlichen Plans erscheint, der über Ägypten und das frühe Christentum zur globalen Ausbreitung gelangen sollte. Kirchers Darstellung blendete die spezifisch nestorianische Prägung der

tet, da die postulierte historische Präsenz des Christentums im außereuropäischen Raum die Rechtmäßigkeit und den Anspruch der missionarischen Expansion nachträglich absichern sollte.

24 Chen kommentiert treffend dazu: »Da die Jesuiten bei ihrer Ankunft in China unter schwierigen Bedingungen wirkten, hätte der Nachweis, dass bereits vor dem Katholizismus christliche Aktivitäten in China stattgefunden hatten, ihrer Missionsarbeit erheblichen Auftrieb verliehen. Aus diesem Grund widmeten chinesische wie europäische Jesuiten der Nestorianischen Stele seit ihrer Wiederentdeckung große Aufmerksamkeit und berichteten ausführlich darüber.« Siehe Chen, Vergangenheit, 254 [Übersetzung Tianji Ma].

25 Vgl. David E. Mungello, Curious Land. Jesuit Accommodation and the Origins of Sinology, Honolulu 1989, 165–168.

26 Der erste Abschnitt (1–45) trägt den Titel Pars I. Monumenti Syro-Sinici interpretatio und ist vollständig der Nestorianischen Stele gewidmet; eine Faksimile-Wiedergabe des Steins findet sich auf einer ausklappbaren Tafel nach S. 12. Siehe auch die Darstellung in Feng, Forschung, 12–13.

Stele weitgehend aus und integrierte sie stattdessen in ein katholisch-eschatologisches Narrativ. In diesem Sinne wird die Stele von den Jesuiten nicht einfach als historische Quelle verstanden, sondern als *missionarische Ressource*, deren Bedeutung selektiv akzentuiert und auf die eigene Strategie hin instrumentalisiert wurde.[27]

Dem jesuitischen Narrativ stand von Anfang an eine protestantische, antikatholische Polemik gegenüber, die der Stele mit erheblicher Skepsis begegnete. Gelehrte wie Georg Horn und Gottlieb Spitzel sahen in der Stele keinen glaubwürdigen Beleg für eine christliche Vergangenheit Chinas, sondern vermuteten vielmehr eine jesuitische Fälschung oder zumindest eine gezielte Manipulation.[28] Besonders Voltaire griff diese Perspektive auf und verwandelte sie in ein Mittel aufklärerischer Kritik an religiöser Überheblichkeit.[29] Für Voltaire war China ein Idealbild rationaler, ethischer Kultur ohne die »abergläubischen Exzesse« des europäischen Christentums. Die Vorstellung, dass China frühzeitig vom Christentum beeinflusst worden sei, widersprach seinem philosophischen Projekt, weshalb er die Echtheit der Stele entschieden in Frage stellte. In Voltaires Denken wird die Stele damit zum Symbol einer unzulässigen Überlagerung europäischer Dogmen über eine ansonsten bewahrte asiatische Vernunftkultur.

Hier zeigt sich ein erstes divergentes Muster: Während die Jesuiten die Stele als Beleg für universale Wahrheit inszenierten, verweigerten aufklärerische Autor*innen ihre Anerkennung, um die kulturelle Autonomie Chinas zu verteidigen – wenn auch nicht selten aus einer paternalistischen, eurozentrischen Perspektive heraus.

Im 19. Jahrhundert verschob sich die Funktion der Stele erneut, diesmal im Kontext imperialer Weltaneignung. Charles William Wall etwa sah die Stele im Licht kolonialer Deutungsmuster.[30] In seiner Argumentation dominieren Vorstellungen kultureller Stagnation und der Notwendigkeit westlicher Intervention: Da China seine eigene Geschichte angeblich nicht angemessen bewahren oder verstehen könne – etwa aufgrund der nicht-phonemischen Natur der chinesischen Schrift –, sei westliches Wissen und Kontrolle erforderlich, um Chinas kulturelle Vergangenheit überhaupt zu rekonstruieren. Diese Position steht exemplarisch

27 Für eine ausführliche Darstellung siehe Keevak, Story, 25–27.
28 Vgl. Mungello, Land, 170–171; Chen, Vergangenheit, 253–268.
29 Keevak, Story, 65–73.
30 Keevak, Story, 82–88; Mungello, Land, 169. Eine ausführliche Argumentation von Wall findet sich in Zhu, Nestorianismus, 78–80.

für eine kolonial bestimmte Hermeneutik, die nicht nur auf Skepsis gegenüber der Authentizität der Stele gründete, sondern auch auf der Überzeugung, dass China und dessen Historiographie fundamental defizitär seien und daher europäischer »Rettung« bedürfen würden. Während die Jesuiten China noch als potentiellen Partner im globalen Heilsplan sahen, betrachteten Wall und andere Kolonialstrategen es zunehmend als Objekt westlicher Überformung.

Eine differenzierte Analyse zeigt, dass die westlichen Zugriffe auf die Stele vielfältig und keineswegs monolithisch waren. Vielmehr bildeten die westlichen Lesarten der Stele ein Spannungsfeld konkurrierender Interessen und Perspektiven, das sich historisch verschob und immer neu differenzierte. Trotz dieser divergierenden Zugriffe bleibt eine grundlegende Gemeinsamkeit: Alle westlichen Lesarten der Stele sind Akte der Interpretation, geprägt von spezifischen kulturellen, theologischen und politischen Vorannahmen. Derridas Konzept der *différance* sowie Gadamers hermeneutischer Zirkel[31] legen nahe, dass jede Interpretation von einem bestimmten historischen und kulturellen Ort ausgeht, der die Wahrnehmung und Deutung steuert. Der westliche Diskurs über die Stele verkörpert exemplarisch diese Bedingtheit: Er schwankt zwischen religiöser Intoleranz (antiprotestantische Polemik der Jesuiten), kolonialer Ambition (Wall) und kulturellem Eurozentrismus (Voltaire).

Die Nestorianische Stele fungiert im westlichen Diskurs nicht primär als »Fenster« nach China, sondern als *Spiegel* westlicher Selbstbilder. Ob als Bestätigung der katholischen Weltkirche, als Argument gegen religiöse Dogmatik oder als Beleg kolonialer Überlegenheit – stets ging es darum, das Eigene am Anderen zu profilieren. Gerade in ihrer materiellen Präsenz – als schwerer, unwiderlegbarer Stein – bot die Stele eine Projektions- und Angriffsfläche, die über den reinen Text hinausging und Interpretation herausforderte: Sie verkörperte im Sinne des *material turn* die diskursiven Verschiebungen zwischen religiöser Legitimation, kultureller Selbstvergewisserung und imperialer Überformung. Diese Funktion der Stele verweist auf die grundsätzliche hermeneutische Bedingtheit aller interkulturellen Deutungen: Was als China erschien, war immer schon ein Europa über Umwege. In der kritischen Reflexion dieses Sachverhalts liegt nicht nur ein besseres Verständnis der historischen Diskurse, sondern auch

31 Vgl. Jacques Derrida, Die différance, in: Peter Engelmann (Hg.), Postmoderne und Dekonstruktion. Texte französischer Philosophen der Gegenwart, Stuttgart 1990, 76–111; Hans-Georg Gadamer, Wahrheit und Methode. Grundzüge einer philosophischen Hermeneutik, Tübingen ^{4}1975.

die Herausforderung, heutige globale Kulturkontakte bewusster, reflektierter und dialogischer zu gestalten.

5. Raub, Rettung und Replik: Die Nestorianische Stele als umkämpftes Kulturerbe

Lange Zeit blieb der westliche Blick auf die Stele von einem Aneignungsimpuls geprägt. 1907 inszenierte der dänische Abenteurer Frits Holm einen Akt kolonialer Objektrekonstruktion, indem er versuchte, die Nestorianische Stele aus China zu exportieren.[32] Zwar verhinderten die chinesischen Behörden den physischen Abtransport, doch Holm ließ eigenmächtig eine maßstabsgetreue Kopie anfertigen, die er zunächst in New York ausstellte und später als Geschenk an den Papst nach Rom transferieren ließ. Repliken dieser Holm'schen Kopie befinden sich heute unter anderem an der Georgetown University in Washington D. C., in Paris, Berlin, Rom, Tokio und Guangzhou.[33] Holms Vorhaben steht paradigmatisch für eine epistemische Praxis des Kolonialzeitalters: Kulturobjekte werden extrahiert, repliziert und in neue Wissensregime eingebettet, um als Zeugen eigener zivilisatorischer Projektionen zu fungieren. Holms Handeln kann daher als symptomatisch für ein koloniales Begehren angesehen werden, das in der Stele eine verlorene Spur europäischen Einflusses identifizieren wollte.

Holms Eingriff war nicht nur ein kolonialer Aneignungsversuch, sondern eine performative Umkodierung des Objekts: Die materielle Kopie wurde zum Vehikel epistemischer Machtverschiebung – nicht nur ein Duplikat, sondern ein diskursiv aufgeladenes Artefakt westlicher Weltdeutung. Indem Holm die Stele nicht einfach reproduzierte, sondern sie gezielt kopierte, transportierte, ausstellte und symbolisch neu rahmte, verwandelte er eine konkrete materielle Handlung in ein diskursives Ereignis. Die Replik selbst wurde dabei zum Träger einer Narration, die westliche Interpretationshoheit behauptete – ein exemplarischer Ausdruck dessen, was als Diskursmacht durch Materialität bezeichnet werden kann: die Fähigkeit, über physische Reproduktion symbolische Ordnungen zu erzeugen und kulturelle Bedeutungen zu verschieben.

32 Vgl. Keevak, Story, 117–121; Chen, Nestorianismus, 257–268.
33 Vgl. Chen, Nestorianismus, 286–287.

Dieser koloniale Zugriff auf ein chinesisches Kulturgut, auf die Nestorianische Stele, rief die chinesischen Behörden unmittelbar auf den Plan: Sie verhinderten die Ausfuhr des Originals und überführten es in den Beilin- Stelenwald in Xi'an, wo es bis heute in Halle 2 als erstes Exponat auf der linken Seite zu sehen ist. 2003 wurde die Stele in die offizielle Liste der besonders schützenswerten Kulturgüter aufgenommen, die das Land nicht verlassen dürfen.[34]

Während die Stele in Europa für Furore sorgte, blieb sie in China in der Tat zunächst lange unbeachtet – bis Holms öffentliches Vorgehen ein breiteres nationales Bewusstsein für den Wert dieses Kulturguts weckte. In der frühen Republikzeit wurde die Rettung der Stele zunehmend als Akt kultureller Selbstbehauptung interpretiert. Schon der Gründungsvater der Republik, Sun Yat-sen, verwies nach der Revolution von 1911 explizit auf die Stele als Beleg für Chinas historische Offenheit. In Suns republikanischer Rhetorik wurde die Stele zur Allegorie einer zukunftsoffenen, weltoffenen Nation: Sie legitimierte ein modernes China durch Rückgriff auf ein idealisiertes Bild vergangener religiöser Toleranz – ein Diskurs, der das Artefakt als Kristallisationspunkt nationaler Identitätsbildung instrumentalisierte.[35] Die Stele wurde so in ein chinesisch-nationales Narrativ integriert, das Chinas kulturelle *Inklusivität* und die Fähigkeit zur selektiven Aufnahme fremder Elemente unter Wahrung kultureller Eigenständigkeit betonte.

Gleichzeitig entfaltete sich im 20. Jahrhundert ein kritischer Diskurs, der sich dezidiert gegen die westliche Deutungshoheit über die Stele richtete. In den 1920er bis 1940er Jahren behaupteten einzelne Intellektuelle – etwa Juxian Wei 衛聚賢 – die Stele sei eine jesuitische Fälschung aus dem 17. Jahrhundert, möglicherweise unter Mitwirkung chinesischer Konvertit*innen wie Zheng Wang 王徵. Besonders die Verwendung des Begriffs »Zhongguo« 中國 [»China«] im Titel galt ihnen als Indiz für eine nachträgliche Konstruktion. Diese nationalistisch motivierte Lesart – eine symbolische Zurück-Aneignung durch Leugnung – blieb in der akademischen Forschung marginal, wurde aber in populären Veröffentli-

34 Vgl. Chen, Nestorianismus, 286–287.

35 Es ist bemerkenswert, dass Sun Yat-sen in seinem ersten offiziellen republikanischen Manifest, das er am 5. Januar 1912 – nur vier Tage nach seiner Amtsübernahme – verkündete, bewusst auf eine idealisierte Frühgeschichte Chinas zurückgriff, um sich vom Erbe der Qing-Dynastie abzugrenzen: Er beschwor ein Zeitalter, in dem China offen für den Austausch mit dem Ausland gewesen sei und religiöse Toleranz geherrscht habe – belegt, so Sun, sowohl durch die Berichte Marco Polos als auch durch die Inschrift der Nestorianischen Stele.

chungen, etwa im Tencent-Portal 2021, erneut propagiert.[36] In ausführlichen Erwiderungen wurden die Argumente der sogenannten »Pseudo-Geschichts-Schule« jedoch von chinesischen Fachhistoriker*innen systematisch widerlegt.[37] Sie verwiesen auf den Stil der Inschrift, die paläographische Konsistenz, die Steinbearbeitung und unabhängige zeitgenössische Aufzeichnungen, die klar für einen Ursprung in der Tang-Zeit sprechen. Bereits in den 1930er Jahren hatten Historiker*innen wie Yuan Chen 陳垣 und später Qianzhi Zhu 朱謙之 die Texte der Jingjiao-Gemeinde quellenkritisch analysiert und die Authentizität bestätigt.

In den letzten Jahrzehnten ist das akademische Interesse an der Stele in China stark gewachsen – auch unter nicht-christlichen Historiker*innen. Zahlreiche Studien und Veröffentlichungen belegen die zunehmende Relevanz der Jingjiao als Teil der eigenen chinesischen Religionsgeschichte. In offiziellen Museumstexten erscheint die Stele heute nicht als Triumph christlicher Mission, sondern als Zeugnis des kulturellen Austauschs entlang der Seidenstraße. Sie steht für ein historisches China, das fremde Einflüsse zeitweise integrierte, ohne sich ihnen zu unterwerfen – und wird so zu einem Symbol nationaler kultureller Selbstdefinition.

Im 21. Jahrhundert riss das westliche Interesse an der Nestorianischen Stele keineswegs ab. Populärwissenschaftliche Werke wie Martin Palmers *Die Jesus-Sutras* (2001) stilisierten sie zu einem Zeugnis eines harmonischen, spirituellen Ost-West-Dialogs. Palmer betonte enthusiastisch die Synthese daoistischer, buddhistischer und christlicher Elemente, die in den Texten der Jingjiao-Gemeinschaft zutage träten. Zugleich bemühten sich moderatere Stimmen des globalen Diskurses um eine Entschärfung der Polemik zwischen romantisierender Aneignung und nationalkultureller Reserviertheit. In neueren transkulturellen Forschungsansätzen wird zunehmend hervorgehoben, dass die Stele sich in einem interkulturellen Zwischenraum bewegt, einem hybriden Bedeutungsraum, der durch syrisch-persische Christ*innen auf chinesischem Boden geschaffen wurde

36 Vgl. Qing He河清, *Xixi/Xian beilin tangbei jingjiaobei he kaifeng youtaibei xi chuanjiaoshi weizao* 翕兮|西安碑林唐碑 »景教碑« 和開封 »猶太碑« 系傳教士偽造 [Die Tang-Stele »Jingjiao-Stele« im Steinwald von Xi'an und die »Jüdische Stele« in Kaifeng sind Fälschungen von Missionar*innen], https://news.qq.com/rain/a/20211127A02XN600#:~:text=%E7%BF%95%E5%85%AE%EF%BD%9C%E8%A5%BF%E5%AE%89%E7%A2%91%E6%9E%97%E5%94%90%E7%A2%91%E2%80%9C%E6%99%AF%E6%95%99%E7%A2%91%E2%80%9D%E5%92%8C%E5%BC%80%E5%B0%81%E2%80%9C%E7%8A%B9%E5%A4%AA%E7%A2%91%E2%80%9D%E7%B3%BB%E4%BC%A0%E6%95%99%E5%A3%AB%E4%BC%AA%E9%80%A0/ (27.5.2025).

37 Vgl. Chen, Nestorianismus, 253–256.

– verfasst in chinesischer Sprache, unter Rückgriff auf buddhistische und daoistische Begriffe zur Artikulation christlicher Konzepte.

Diese hybride Natur macht die Stele in aktuellen Diskursen zu einer möglichen Brücke zwischen Kulturen und Konfessionen – sie könnte ein Symbol sein für das Potenzial theologischer Übersetzbarkeit und kultureller Durchlässigkeit und gleichzeitig ein Symbol der *Unübersetzbarkeit*. Die Auseinandersetzungen um ihre Deutung bleiben kontrovers: postkoloniale, konfessionelle und nationalistische Perspektiven können weiterhin aufeinanderprallen. Dies zeigt exemplarisch, dass Artefakte wie die Nestorianische Stele nicht nur historische Objekte, sondern bis heute lebendige Projektionsflächen gegenwärtiger Weltbilder, Deutungshoheiten und Machtansprüche sind.

Im Zuge ihrer musealen Kanonisierung wurde die Nestorianische Stele nicht nur konserviert, sondern auch global repliziert. Frits Holms maßstabsgetreue Kopie von 1907 markierte den Beginn einer multiplen westlichen Präsenz. Diese formal als Duplikate verstandenen Objekte haben sich diskursiv verselbständigt: Ihre »Aura«[38] beruht nicht auf materieller Einzigartigkeit, sondern auf symbolischer Aufladung. Die Kopie wird hier nicht mehr als minderwertige Reproduktion gelesen, sondern als produktives Artefakt im eigenen Recht – als *materialisierter Diskurs*, der eine zweite Geschichte des Objekts entfaltet: nicht mehr lokal gebunden, sondern global anschlussfähig.

Sie sind zu Trägern globaler Aufmerksamkeit geworden, eingebettet in nationalkulturelle und wissenschaftliche Narrative, die zwischen Universalismus und geopolitischer Aneignung oszillieren. Im Sinne des *material turn* wird deutlich: Die Replikation der Stele erzeugt keine bloße Kopie, sondern neue kulturelle Wirklichkeit. Die Stele ist nicht mehr ein singuläres Artefakt mit lokaler Verankerung, sondern ein transnationaler Akteur, dessen materielle Vervielfältigung immer neue diskursive Kontexte hervorbringt. Ihre »Aura« transformiert sich von einem ästhetischen in einen epistemischen Begriff – sie wirkt als Index glo-

38 Walter Benjamin beschreibt die »Aura« als die Einzigartigkeit eines Kunstwerks, die aus seiner materiellen Unverfügbarkeit, historischen Verankerung und räumlich-zeitlichen Einmaligkeit resultiert – und die im Zeitalter der technischen Reproduzierbarkeit unwiederbringlich verloren geht. Vgl. Walter Benjamin, Das Kunstwerk im Zeitalter seiner technischen Reproduzierbarkeit, in: Siegfried Unseld/Walter Benjamin (Hg.), Illuminationen. Ausgewählte Werke, Frankfurt a. M. 1977, 136–169.

baler religiöser Verflechtungen,[39] als Marker kollektiven Erinnerns und als Bezugspunkt akademischer wie populärer Aneignungen.

In dieser Perspektive wird die Stele nicht nur musealisiert, sondern globalisiert. Sie fungiert als *Knotenpunkt globaler Christentumsgeschichte* (Walls, Sanneh)[40] ebenso wie als »sprechendes Objekt« im digitalen Zeitalter: in Online-Datenbanken, Podcast-Formaten, theologischen Bildungsplattformen und öffentlich zugänglichen Repositorien. Ihr Wert bemisst sich nicht mehr allein an ihrer physischen Originalität, sondern an ihrer diskursiven Anschlussfähigkeit – an ihrer Fähigkeit, weltweit religiöse Identität, historische Tiefenschichten und kulturelle Zugehörigkeit neu zu verhandeln.

6. Schlussgedanken

Die Nestorianische Stele erweist sich in ihrer materiellen Persistenz und diskursiven Wandelbarkeit als paradigmatisches Objekt einer transkulturell sensiblen Religionsgeschichte. Als *palimpsestisches Diskursobjekt* trägt sie nicht nur Zeichen vergangener Theologien, Rituale und politischer Narrative, sondern bleibt bis in die Gegenwart hinein ein Ort symbolischer Aushandlung. Im Sinne des *material turn* lässt sich ihre Wirkung nicht auf ihre Textualität reduzieren: Die Stele *wirkt*, weil sie *ist* – ein physischer Akteur kultureller Bedeutungsproduktion, dessen Replikationen, Rahmungen und museale Inszenierungen neue Lesarten ermöglichen und erzwingen. Ihre hybride Semantik, entstanden im *third space* religiöser Kreolisierung, fordert eine Hermeneutik, die Ambiguität nicht als Störung, sondern als Konstitutionsprinzip erkennt.

Im Zusammenspiel von kultureller Integration, theologischer Hybridisierung und diskursiver Mobilität eröffnet die Stele neue Perspektiven für eine postkolonial reflektierte Globalgeschichte. Sie ist nicht nur Objekt historischer Analyse, sondern methodische Provokation: ein sprechendes Artefakt, das bestehende Deutungshoheiten herausfordert und die religionswissenschaftliche Forschung

39 Vgl. Thompson, Jingjiao, 51, 62.

40 Vgl. z. B. Andrew F. Walls, The Missionary Movement in Christian History. Studies in the Transmission of Faith, Maryknoll, NY ^{13}2009; sowie Lamin O. Sanneh, Translating the Message. The Missionary Impact on Culture, Maryknoll, NY ^{2}2009.

auffordert, Differenz, Mehrdeutigkeit und materiale Präsenz nicht als Ausnahme, sondern als Erkenntnisform zu begreifen.

Aus der Perspektive des *material turn* und diskursanalytischer Hermeneutik erscheint die Nestorianische Stele somit nicht als stummer Zeuge, sondern als aktiver Produzent historischer Sinnordnungen – ein Objekt, das durch seine materielle Persistenz ebenso wie durch seine narrative Vielstimmigkeit die Auseinandersetzungen um Religion, Kultur und Identität bis in die Gegenwart hinein prägt.

(Tianji Ma ist wissenschaftlicher Mitarbeiter der Forschungsstiftung für Kultur und Religion in Gießen, Gastdozent am Chinese Lutheran Seminary in Taiwan und Promotionsstudent an der Kirchlichen Hochschule Wuppertal.)

ABSTRACT

The Nestorian Stele represents one of the most significant material testimonies of early medieval transculturation. This article interprets the stele within the horizon of the material turn, viewing it as a dynamic agent of religious, political, and cultural discourses from the 8th century to the present. The analysis traces how its material presence – and periods of physical invisibility – enabled discursive productivity: from theological self-affirmation to colonial appropriation, national self-assertion, and global musealization and digital reception. Applying discourse-analytical approaches, the stele is read as a palimpsestic object of discourse – one that not only conveys meaning but actively generates it. Replications and symbolic framings – especially by Western missionaries, colonial actors, and transcultural scholars – highlight the discursive power inherent in materiality. Today, the stele functions as a hybrid medium of global religious history and intercultural theology, continually raising questions about hybridity, cultural translation, and postcolonial interpretive authority.

Spaltungen der *Einen Welt*

Zur Materialität von *Vergeschlechtlichungen* in der deutschen evangelischen Entwicklungsarbeit

Doris Günther-Kriegel

1. Was und warum? Klärende Ausgangsfragen

1.1 Was Bildungsbroschüren zum Thema Fairer Handel mit Materialität verbindet

In einigen kulturwissenschaftlichen Disziplinen ist ein besonderes Interesse an der Erforschung von Körpern, Räumen oder Praktiken auszumachen, das als *material turn* thematisiert wird.[1] Dabei wird Materiales im Gegensatz zu sprachlich Fixiertem untersucht. Dieser *turn* hat mit Ansätzen, die unter dem Namen *New Materialism* firmieren, in den letzten zwei bis drei Jahrzehnten wiederum weitere Wendungen genommen.[2] Die entsprechenden Ansätze sind nicht zu generalisieren, stellen jedoch »a priori oppositions between subjects and objects«[3] infrage, die auf anthropozentrische Sichtweisen zurückgehen. Ist also vom *material turn* die Rede, werden auch ontologische Fragestellungen zu Materialisie-

1 Vgl. Sonia Hazard, The Material Turn in the Study of Religion, in: Religion and Society. Advances in Research 4/1 (2013), 58–78, hier: 58.

2 Vgl. Katharina Hoppe/Thomas Lemke, Neue Materialismen zur Einführung, Hamburg 2021, 9f. Die Kennzeichnung *New Materialism* wurde Mitte der 1990er Jahre sowohl von Manuel DeLanda als auch von Rosi Braidotti unabhängig voneinander ins Spiel gebracht. Vgl. Hazard, Material Turn, 64.

3 Hazard, Material Turn, 59.

rung und Materialität aufgerufen: Wie kommen die Dinge – hier nicht als Objekte im Gegensatz zu Subjekten gedacht – ins Sein? Wie nehmen sie Gestalt an? Auf welche Weise werden sie in Kraft gesetzt? Was grenzt ein Ding von anderen Dingen ab? Was wird wodurch material?

Dieser Fragenkomplex, der aus den Perspektiven des *New Materialism* hervorgeht,[4] markiert den Ausgangspunkt für den hier vorliegenden Aufsatz. Er soll zur Auseinandersetzung mit dem *material turn* in der Erforschung des Globalen Christentums beitragen. Dabei wird allerdings von einer Bezugnahme auf bestimmte Entwürfe des erwähnten *New Materialism* abgesehen.[5] Ebenso wenig soll auf entsprechende religionswissenschaftliche und interkulturell-theologische Fachdebatten referenziert werden.[6] Was folgt ist eine in diesem Sinne *klassische* Betrachtung von Sprache in Texten. Daran soll gezeigt werden, dass Mechanismen von Materialisierung nachgegangen werden kann, auch ohne Raumrelationen oder Körperpraktiken zu untersuchen. Der Beitrag nimmt seinen Ausgang bei der Annahme, dass es Sprache ist, die materialisiert.[7]

Diese Grundannahme lässt sich an einem Textkorpus zum Thema Fairer Handel entfalten. Die Texte gehen auf das Feld der deutschsprachigen evangelischen Entwicklungsarbeit zurück, das wiederum ein lokales Terrain auf dem globalen Atlas des Christentums markiert. Betrachtet werden aktuelle Publikationen, die bis ins Jahr 2002 zurückreichen. Im November desselben Jahres fasste die Synode der Evangelischen Kirche in Deutschland (EKD) das erste Mal einen Beschluss zum Fairen Handel. Darin forderte sie ihre Kirchen und Gemeinden dazu auf, »den Fairen Handel weiterhin und verstärkt zu fördern als Zeichen der Solidarität und als Beitrag zu einer nachhaltigen Entwicklung«[8]. Die synodale Empfehlung lässt sich damit in globale Debatten des sogenannten Rio-Folgeprozesses zu nachhaltiger Entwicklung einzeichnen. Daraufhin konnten sich die Evangelischen Kirchen in Deutschland als Motor nachhaltiger Entwicklung in-

4 Vgl. Hazard, Material Turn, 67–69.

5 Vgl. beispielsweise Donna Harraway, Manifesto for Cyborgs. Science, Technology, and Socialist Feminism in the 1980's, in: Socialist Review 80 (1985), 65–108 und Karen Barad, Diffracting Diffraction. Cutting Together Apart, in: Parallax 20/3 (2014), 206–223.

6 Vgl. Claudia Jahnel, »Pentecostal Body-Logics«. Pentekostale Körperpraktiken und Körperwissen als Anfrage an Körper- und Religionsdispositive der Moderne – Eine Annäherung, in: Klaus Hock (Hg.), Wissen um Religion. Erkenntnis – Interesse. Epistemologie und Episteme in Religionswissenschaft und Interkultureller Theologie (VWGTh 64), Leipzig 2020, 189–213.

7 Vgl. Judith Butler, Körper von Gewicht. Die diskursiven Grenzen des Geschlechts, Frankfurt a. M. 1997, 51–87.

8 Kirchenamt der EKD (Hg.), Amtsblatt der Evangelischen Kirche in Deutschland 56/12 (2002), 380f.

nerhalb der deutschen Institutionenlandschaft behaupten. Kirchen in Deutschland zeigten sich damit global wie lokal gesellschaftlich relevant.

Um besagtem Beschluss im Einzelnen umsetzen zu können, war und ist es erforderlich, Gemeinden für das Thema Fairer Handel zu sensibilisieren. Dementsprechend werden beispielsweise von *Brot für die Welt*, dem Evangelischen Werk für Diakonie und Entwicklung e. V., Informationsbroschüren, Kampagnenblätter, Unterrichtsbausteine, Gottesdienstentwürfe und Zeitschriftenartikel (mit-)herausgegeben, die Auskunft über weltwirtschaftliche Zusammenhänge geben. Durch diese Art von Bewusstseinsbildung sollen Kirchen, Gemeinden und Christ:innen zum Kauf fair gehandelter Produkte angehalten werden. Deshalb lassen sich derartige Texte unter dem Stichwort *Bildungsmaterial* zusammenfassen.[9] Die Texte in dieser Hinsicht zu vereinheitlichen, geht aber noch auf eine weitere entscheidende Gemeinsamkeit zurück. Sie repräsentieren diejenigen, die die Fair-Handels-Produkte herstellen. Das erklärt, weshalb Fairer Handel hier ausschließlich in dieser einen Funktionsweise perspektiviert wird. Er kommt weder als Soziale Bewegung noch als Wirtschaftskonzept in den Blick, sondern als »Repräsentant der Produzenten«[10], wie ihn der Historiker Ruben Quaas in seiner global-lokalen Geschichte des fair gehandelten Kaffees in den Diskurs eingetragen hat.

Diese Bildungsmaterialien umfassen demzufolge die hier untersuchten Quellen. Die Perspektive des Beitrages richtet sich also nicht auf reale, fiktive oder verborgene Diskriminierungen als solche, sondern auf eher unerwartete Bedingungen ihrer Entstehung und Verfestigung, die auf beste Absichten zurückgehen. Dabei wird von der These ausgegangen, dass besagte Texte in mindestens einer Weise materialisieren.[11] Sie basieren auf Repräsentationen, die einen bestimmen Typus von Fair-Handels-Produzentin als materialisierten Effekt hervorbringen.

9 Zur Funktionsweise dieses Bildungsmaterials vgl. Doris Günther-Kriegel, Women Empowerment als Gradmesser von Entwicklung? Grundlegung und Kategorienkritik am Beispiel Fairer Handel, in: BThZ 42 (2025).

10 Ruben Quaas, Fair Trade. Eine global-lokale Geschichte am Beispiel des Kaffees, Köln 2015, 344.

11 Der Diskurs zum Fairen Handel materialisiert noch in einer weiteren Hinsicht. Denn das Terrain der evangelischen Entwicklungsarbeit inklusive *fairer Kirchen* wird erst herausbildet. Darüber hinaus ist zu erwähnen, dass Fairer Handel konzeptionell als Leerer Signifikant erschlossen werden kann. Als solcher benennt er eine Äquivalenzkette aus differenten Gliedern, die sich nur in der antagonistischen Gegenüberstellung mit einem so bezeichneten konventionellen Handel vereinheitlichen lassen. Beides wird in meiner im Entstehen begriffenen Dissertation (Universität Halle) elaboriert unter dem Arbeitstitel »Fairer Handel und globale Ordnung. Eine religionswissenschaftliche Kategorienkritik«.

Das Erkenntnisinteresse besteht demzufolge darin, dieser Annahme anhand der Sichtbarmachung konkreter Repräsentationspraktiken nachzugehen. Dazu gilt es, die regelhaften Mechanismen ihrer Funktionsweise herauszuarbeiten. Dabei wird ersichtlich, auf welche Weise sie ordnen, was auf dem Feld evangelischer Entwicklungsarbeit als wahr und als nicht wahr akzeptiert werden kann. Anhand solcher, sich wiederholender Ein- und Ausschlusspraktiken lässt sich zeigen, dass der Spalt zwischen dem sogenannten globalen Süden und dem sogenannten globalen Norden kontinuierlich verfestigt wird. Diese Prozesse der Materialisierung vollziehen sich – so die These – anhand von intersektional miteinander verwobenen *Vergeschlechtlichungen*. Ebenjene stellen einen vermeintlich selbstbestimmten *nördlichen* Teil von Frauen einem *südlichen* Teil vermeintlich mehrfach abhängiger Fair-Handels-Produzentinnen kategorial gegenüber, die hier als *Viktigene* eingeführt werden.

1.2 Warum die Betrachtung von Fair-Handels-Bildungsmaterialien ein verhärtetes Forschungsnarrativ aufbricht

Die Ausgangsthese gibt Aufschluss darüber, weshalb wissenschaftliche Studien zu Repräsentationen in Bildungsmaterialien zum Thema Fairer Handel bisher ausbleiben – sowohl in der theologischen und (religions-)historischen als auch in der sozialwissenschaftlichen Forschung.[12] Fairer Handel wird in verschiedenen wissenschaftlichen Disziplinen als Erfolgsgeschichte – nicht zuletzt von Kirchen im deutschsprachigen Raum – erzählt. Wissenschaftliche Beiträge, gleich welcher Fachrichtung, geben einen linearen Plot von der Ausdehnung der Vermarktung fairer Produkte im zeitlichen Verlauf wieder. Mit jeder Veröffentlichung wird der Eintritt in den sogenannten kommerziellen Massenmarkt respektive ins Discounterregal erneut aufgegriffen. Dadurch verfestigt sich ein Narrativ, das die steigende Verfügbarkeit fairer Produkte als Erfolgsmoment in die vermeintlich geradlinige Geschichte einzeichnet, die vom Dritte-Welt-Handel über den Alternativen Handel zum Fairen Handel führt. Je nach Fachdisziplin und Fragestellung variieren lediglich die Kategorien, anhand derer der besagte Erfolg taxiert wird. Die Bestimmung, *dass* Fairer Handel durch einen steigenden

12 Vgl. Günther-Kriegel, Fairer Handel.

Absatz als Erfolg geltend gemacht wird, verhärtet sich zum voraussetzungslosen, selbstevidenten Faktum.

Daraus folgt wiederum, dass Untersuchungen, die Mechanismen perspektivieren, mit denen Erzeuger:innen im entsprechenden Bildungsmaterial festgeschrieben werden, von der wissenschaftlichen Auseinandersetzung mit dem Thema Fairer Handel bislang ausgeschlossen werden. Der Grund dafür lässt sich im erfolgsbestimmten Bezugsrahmen des transdisziplinären Forschungsdiskurses finden. Der bietet nämlich keinen Anknüpfungspunkt für eine Problematisierung derjenigen Texte, die einer breiten (Kirchen-)Öffentlichkeit vorführen, warum es selbstverständlich sei, fair gehandelte Produkte zu erwerben. Das heißt nicht, dass Repräsentationen gar keine Erwähnung im entsprechenden Diskurs fänden. Ganz im Gegenteil weisen Forscher:innen wiederholt auf die Relevanz ebenjener Darstellungen für den Erfolg von Fairem Handel hin: »Fair Traders need to frame workers as impoverished, exotic, and needy to compel customers to support their cause.«[13] Dass genauere Untersuchungen solcher Beobachtungen bislang jedoch fehlen, zeigt, dass sie durch das Erfolgsnarrativ vom Diskurs als nicht sagbar ausgeschlossen werden. In dieser Hinsicht erkennt beispielsweise Ruben Quaas die Tragweite von Repräsentationen für den ökonomischen Erfolg des Fairen Handels an und schreibt deren Auftreten in dessen vermeintliche Erfolgsgeschichte ein.[14] Er macht auf die »Vereinheitlichung und Vereinfachung«[15] in den Darstellungen der Erzeuger:innen aufmerksam, die dazu beigetragen hätten, den Konsum fair gehandelter Waren zu steigern. Zwar führt er weiter aus, dass die entsprechenden Darstellungen zu diesem Zweck »dichotome Muster

13 Keith Brown zitiert nach Debarati Sen, Everyday Sustainability. Gender Justice and Fair Trade Tea in Darjeeling, Albany 2017, 26.

14 Auch Historiker:innen wie Andrea Franc, Benjamin Möckel, Konrad Kuhn und Peter van Dam beziehen sich auf die in entsprechenden Bildungsmaterialien enthaltenen Repräsentationen, ohne sie jedoch auf ihre Wirkungen hin zu betrachten. Vgl. Andrea Franc, Von der Makroökonomie zum Kleinbauern. Die Wandlung der Idee eines gerechten Nord-Süd-Handels in der schweizerischen Dritte-Welt-Bewegung (1964–1984), Oldenburg 2020; Konrad Kuhn, Fairer Handel und Kalter Krieg. Selbstwahrnehmung und Positionierung der Fair-Trade-Bewegung in der Schweiz 1973–1990, Rubingen 2005; Benjamin Möckel, Dilemmas of Moral Markets. Conflicting Narratives in the West German Fair Trade Movement, in: Stefan Berger/Alexandra Przyrembel (Hg.), Moralizing Capitalism. Palgrave Studies in the History of Social Movements, London 2019, 267–292; Peter van Dam, The Limits of a Success Story. Fair Trade and the History of Postcolonial Globalization, in: Comparativ: Zeitschrift für Globalgeschichte und vergleichende Gesellschaftsforschung 25/1 (2015), 62–77.

15 Quaas, Fair Trade, 334.

wie Arm, Hilflos und Unterdrückt gegenüber Reich und Mächtig«[16] bedienten, lässt jedoch derartige Dichotomisierungen ungeklärt liegen. Er unterlässt die Klärung, obwohl er den Repräsentationen der Erzeuger:innen für die Etablierung der Bewegung nicht mehr Bedeutung hätte beimessen können: »Die Glaubwürdigkeit des Fairen Handels hing schließlich davon ab, dass ihm die Position als Repräsentant der Produzenten zugeschrieben wurde.«[17] Dieses verhärtete Forschungsnarrativ, das gegen jegliche Infragestellung immunisiert scheint, dürfte demnach auch erklären, weshalb keine mir bekannte Arbeit die Frage danach stellt, auf welche Weise insbesondere weibliche Produzierende in den entsprechenden Bildungsmaterialien dargestellt werden. Bislang fehlt eine Betrachtung der materialisierten Effekte der Repräsentationen von Produzent:innen.

Die sich anschließende Problematisierung zielt demzufolge darauf ab, dieses erstarrte Erfolgsnarrativ aufzubrechen, indem konkrete Materialisierungen besagter Repräsentationen in den Blick genommen werden. Dazu ist in drei Schritten vorzugehen. Zuerst wird anhand der zugrundeliegenden Quellen herausgearbeitet, wie sich die wiederholenden *vergeschlechtlichen* Bezeichnungspraktiken sichtbar machen lassen. Daran schließt sich die Darstellung der sich daraus resultierenden, materialisierten Wirkungen an, die die sogenannte *Eine Welt* spalten. Abschließend wird der Bezug zum *material turn* wieder aufgegriffen und nach dem ontologischen Status dieser epistemischen Welt-Spaltung gefragt.

2. *Viktigenisierungen* – Intersektional verwobene *Vergeschlechtlichungspraktiken* in Texten zum Fairen Handel

Im Folgenden gilt es, die inhaltlichen Festschreibungen herauszukristallisieren, die auf Repräsentationen in den untersuchten Textquellen zurückzuführen sind. Dazu werden die auftretenden Repräsentationsmuster theoretisch reflektiert und auf eine analytische Ebene übertragen. In den untersuchten Texten werden die Menschen, die Rohstoffe oder Waren für den Fairen Handel herstellen, als Frauen

16 Quaas, Fair Trade, 334.
17 Quaas, Fair Trade, 334.

und Männer in »Kakao-Kooperativen«[18] oder in »Textilfabriken«[19] gekennzeichnet. Repräsentation funktioniert demzufolge über Darstellungen von vermeintlich typisch Weiblichem im Gegensatz zu vermeintlich typisch Männlichem. Solche Repräsentationspraktiken, die auf diese Weise permanent die Geschlechterdifferenz bekräftigen, lassen sich als *Vergeschlechtlichungen* beschreiben.[20] Selbige machen sich in den untersuchten Bildungsmaterialien allerdings nicht an beiden dargestellten Geschlechtern gleichermaßen fest. Nicht der »Bananenbauer«[21], sondern die »Arbeiterin auf einer Blumenplantage«[22] wird vermehrt charakterisiert – und zwar als multiple *vergeschlechtliche* Figur. Das heißt, dass die Geschlechterdifferenz zum Mann – sprich: Die Differenzkategorie Geschlecht – mit weiteren Kategorien wie Ethnie, Klasse und Sexualität verflochten auftritt.[23] Diese lassen sich als Differenzkategorien erfassen, insofern sie jeweils Unterscheidungen markieren. Ethnie bezieht sich hier auf kulturell-ethnisierte Gegenüberstellungen wie indigen und modern. Klasse erfasst Kontrastierungen von arm und reich. Sexualität markiert Dichotomisierungen zwischen heteronorm und nicht-heteronorm. Diese Differenzkategorien treten aber nicht als eine bloße Addition auf, sondern sind intersektional verwoben. Sie verdichten sich in ihrem Schnittpunkt, der als Kategorienkomplex charakterisiert werden kann.

Diese, in theoretischer Hinsicht miteinander verwobenen Kategorien lassen sich auf der analytischen Ebene als Bezeichnungsverfahren erkennbar machen, die die Repräsentierten auf verschiedene Weise *vergeschlechtlichten*. Die Funktionsweise dieser Bezeichnungspraktiken beruht auf Wiederholung, auf Re-Ite-

18 Brot für die Welt (Hg.), Eine süße Alternative. Faire Preise und transparente Lieferketten bei Kakao können Bauernfamilien aus der Armut befreien, in: Aktuell 32 (2014), 2.

19 Brot für die Welt (Hg.), Gerecht wirtschaften, in: Brot für die Welt. Global Lernen (2021), 6.

20 Die theoretische Herleitung lässt sich nachlesen in Günther-Kriegel, Fairer Handel.

21 Brot für die Welt (Hg.), Gemeinsam aus der Armut, in: Projektinformation. Bio-Bananen für den Fairen Handel (2019), 4–7, hier: 7.

22 Gertrud Falk, Vom Luxus eines Firmenbusses. Was die Zertifizierung für Arbeiter einer kenianischen Blumenfarm bringt, in: Verein zur Förderung der entwicklungspolitischen Publizistik e.V. (VFEP) (Hg.), Flower Power. Blumen aus fairem Handel. Ein Dossier von VFEP in Zusammenarbeit mit der Redaktion eins. Zeitschrift Entwicklungspolitik 18–19/9 (2006), V–VI, hier: V.

23 Die hier betrachteten Dimensionen Geschlecht, Ethnie, Klasse und Sexualität werden nicht als feststehende Identitätsgrößen verstanden. Sie entsprechen multiplen, vorläufig einzunehmenden Positionierungen, die sich überlappen und ineinander verwoben sind. Vgl. Günther-Kriegel, Fairer Handel.

ration.[24] Ziel der Analyse ist es folglich, das zu rekonstruieren, was als (gewissermaßen stereotype) »Zitathaftigkeit«[25] von *Vergeschlechtlichungen* bezeichnet werden könnte. Infolgedessen gilt es, zu zeigen, in welcher Weise auf die vier miteinander verwobenen Differenzkategorien Geschlecht, Ethnie, Klasse und Sexualität zurückgegriffen wird. Diese wiederkehrenden Rückgriffe geben Aufschluss darüber, wie durch bloße Iteration bestimmter Bezeichnungsmechanismen respektive *Vergeschlechtlichungen* die typische Fair-Handels-Produzentin hervorgebracht wird.

In dieser Hinsicht lässt sich zuerst feststellen, dass die Fair-Handels-Produzentin durch ein sich wiederholendes Grundmuster festgeschrieben wird, in welchem die Bezeichnungspraktiken operieren. Dieses Grundmuster kann besonders gut an folgendem Textabschnitt offengelegt werden. Er ist einem Artikel mit der Überschrift »Gemeinsames Wirtschaften als Chance« aus einem Dossier von Welt-Sichten – Magazin für globale Entwicklung und ökumenische Zusammenarbeit entnommen, das im Jahr 2011 publiziert wurde.

> »Neben dem Export von Kaffee und Biohonig betreibt Chajul auch eine Weberei, in der 70 Frauen hochwertige Textilien herstellen, mit traditionellen Mustern oder nach den Vorgaben ausländischer Auftraggeber gewebt. Außerdem unterhält Chajul eine Radiostation, die in Ixil sendet, und eine einfache Herberge für Touristen. Insbesondere für die Frauen aus der Gegend ist der Verband [Chajul] ein wichtiger Arbeitgeber. Neben der Arbeit in der Weberei bietet Chajul während der Erntezeit weiteren 150 Frauen einen Arbeitsplatz. Sie übernehmen die Qualitätssicherung der Kaffeebohnen in Handarbeit. Maschinen werden nur bei der Verarbeitung von Bohnen zweiter Wahl eingesetzt, auch wenn es billiger wäre, diesen Produktionsschritt komplett maschinell zu machen. ›Wir wollen den Frauen nicht den Arbeitsplatz wegnehmen‹, erklärt Chajul-Mitarbeiter Miguel Tsoy. ›Hier in den Bergen gibt es sonst keine Arbeit. Die Qualitätssicherung per Hand sehen wir als soziale Kosten, die die Organisation gerne trägt.‹ Cadech und Chajul, [zwei Zusammenschlüsse aus bäuerlichen Genossenschaften], bieten Kleinbauern und ihren Familien die Möglichkeit, ihre Entwicklung in die eigenen Hände zu nehmen. Gerade im abgelegenen Hochland Guatemalas ist das

24 Mit Jacques Derrida gehe ich davon aus, dass Bezeichnung als Re-Iteration funktioniert. Vgl. Jacques Derrida, Signatur, Ereignis, Kontext, in: Peter Engelmann (Hg.), Limited Inc, Wien 2001, 15–45, hier: 40.

25 Derrida, Signatur, 40.

gemeinsame Wirtschaften für viele Menschen die einzige Chance, dem Teufelskreis von Armut, Landflucht und Perspektivlosigkeit zu entkommen.«[26]

In der Bestimmung von bäuerlichen Familien und dem besonderen Fokus »auf die Frauen aus der Gegend« zeigen sich zwei miteinander verzahnte Bezeichnungsmuster, die ich als Indigen-Machung[27] und Viktimisierung charakterisiere.

Indigen-Machung beschreibt artikulatorische Prozesse vielfältiger Peripherisierungen. Die »Frauen aus der Gegend« werden erstens geographisch verortet, beispielsweise in eine »Gegend« Guatemalas, die als »abgelegene[s] Hochland« spezifiziert wird. Diese signifikatorischen An-den-Rand-Stellungen beschränken sich dabei nicht nur auf kartographische Parameter. Produzentinnen fair gehandelter Produkte werden darüber hinaus regelmäßig ins geographische Off gestellt, ins bereits erwähnte »abgelegene [...] Hochland Guatemalas«[28], in die Landschaft eines »abgeschiedenen Dorfs«[29], »an den Rand des Amazonas«[30], »in abgelegene[...], ländliche[...] Regionen«[31] oder in die »Wüstengegend«[32]. Danach lebten Produzentinnen fernab von selbstbestimmten Arbeits- und Lebensgestaltungen sowie von (städtischer) Infrastruktur. Derartige Projektionen stellen Erzeugerinnen außerhalb sogenannter zivilisatorischer Verhältnisse, indem wiederholt auf kulturelle Eigenheiten zurückgegriffen wird. In dieser Hinsicht flankieren die »traditionellen Muster«[33] im zitierten Beispieltext das »abgelegene [...] Hochland Guatemalas«[34]. Vermeintlich traditionelle Alltagsgestaltungen, Einstellungen oder Erzeugnisse, wie die der Chajul-Weberei, werden als konkrete kulturelle Ausprägungen extra hervorgehoben. Das führt vor Augen, dass auf

26 Eva Bahner/Ulrike Lohr, Gemeinsames Wirtschaften als Chance. Genossenschaften in Guatemala, in: Oikocredit Deutschland (Hg.), Gemeinsam für eine bessere Welt. Genossenschaften gestalten Entwicklung. Ein Dossier von Oikocredit Deutschland in Zusammenarbeit mit der Redaktion Welt-Sichten 4/10 (2011), 17–19, hier: 19.

27 »Indigene«/»indigen« soll im Beitrag nicht als kulturelle Festschreibung verstanden werden, sondern als eine konkrete Praktik von Ethnisierung, die sich nicht nur auf rurale Gebiete beschränkt. Sie soll jedoch, der besseren Lesbarkeit wegen, typographisch nicht hervorgehoben werden. Mehr dazu in Günther-Kriegel, Fairer Handel.

28 Bahner/Lohr, Gemeinsames Wirtschaften, 17.

29 Johannes Süßmann, Edelbitter am Äquator, in: Welt-Sichten 9/9 (2016), 48–49, hier: 49.

30 Süßmann, Edelbitter, 49.

31 Brot für die Welt (Hg.), Klimawandel. Herausforderung für den Fairen Handel, in: Aktuell 63 (2018), 2.

32 Brot für die Welt (Hg.), Harte Arbeit, fairer Lohn, in: Projektinformation. Bio-Bananen für den Fairen Handel (2019), 10–12, hier: 10.

33 Bahner/Lohr, Gemeinsames Wirtschaften, 19.

34 Bahner/Lohr, Gemeinsames Wirtschaften, 19.

Kultur in den entsprechenden Texten überhaupt nur dann Bezug genommen wird, wenn eine irgendwie *anders geartete* Kultur hervorgehoben wird. Der dagegenstehende kulturelle Maßstab wird unerwähnt vorausgesetzt. Letzterer wird durch dessen imaginierte Abgrenzung von der erwähnenswerten und damit als besonders herausgestellten *anderen* Kultur erst als Maßstab erzeugt. Das vollzieht sich hier mit der expliziten Benennung »der traditionellen Muster« und geht damit über eine bloß räumliche Festschreibung hinaus. Die Produzentin wird in ein kulturell-topographisches Abseits platziert. Topographische Abseitigkeit wird mit indigener Kultur gleichgesetzt und indigene Kultur in topographische Abseitigkeit eingeschrieben.

Besonders deutlich wird diese Praktik in Texten, in denen Artikulationen wie »traditionelle[…] Gesellschaften«[35] und »von Männern dominierte[…] Dörfer[…]«[36] in einem Zusammenhang stehen. Diese Verknüpfung von Kultur und Geschlechterverhältnissen wird in den hier untersuchten Quellen repetitiv verfestigt. Dabei werden im Kontext von Fair-Handels-Produktion bestimmte Verhältnisbestimmungen zwischen benachteiligten Frauen und dominanten Männern auf kulturelle Parameter zurückgeführt. Bekräftigungen von kulturbedingten patriarchalen Geschlechterverhältnissen ereignen sich in Texten beispielsweise durch die »traditionellen bzw. kulturellen Praktiken, die Frauen immer wieder in den Hintergrund drängen«[37]. Das heißt im Umkehrschluss, dass nicht-patriarchale Konstellationen unter den Geschlechtern zur Norm avancieren und überall zu verorten sind, wo nicht das Gegenteil herausgestellt wird. Daran zeigt sich: Etwas als indigen respektive kulturell bedingt zu bezeichnen, kommt einem wirkmächtigen Akt der diskursiven Hervorbringung eines normativ Universalen gleich.[38] Dessen Gegenüber, das, der oder die Indigene, wird zum Besonderen, Partikularen. Indigen-Machung steht in diesem Beitrag folglich für ein übergreifendes Bezeichnungsmuster, das *effektiv* zweierlei hervorbringt: eine kulturell-topographische Peripherie als Abweichung von einem Zentrum, das die Norm verkörpert.

35 Nishant Pandey, Fairer Handel verschafft Frauen einen Platz am internationalen Markt. Das Beispiel SHARE in Tamil Nadu, Indien, in: Welt & Handel 7/5 (2003), 3–6, hier: 3.
36 Pandey, Fairer Handel, 3.
37 Victoria Abankwa, Fairer Handel und Gender. Der Fall von Kuapa Kooko, in: Welt & Handel 6/12–13 (2002), 2–3, hier: 2.
38 Vgl. Namsoon Kang, Whose/Which World in World Christianity? Toward World Christianity as Christianity of Wordly-Responsibility, in: Akintunde E. Akinade (Hg.), A New Day. Essays on World Christianity in Honor of Lamin Sanneh, New York 2010, 31–48.

Der zweite Mechanismus von Bezeichnung lässt sich als Viktimisierung herausstellen. In dieser Hinsicht lassen sich insbesondere Frauen in den »Teufelskreis von Armut, Landflucht und Perspektivlosigkeit« einzeichnen, wie die oben herangezogene Quelle zeigt. Denn sie seien es, denen der Arbeitsplatz nicht weggenommen werden soll. Produzentinnen werden in den entsprechenden Texten als Opfer festgeschrieben, die beispielsweise »unendliches Leid, schwerste Krankheiten«[39] oder »Ausbeutung und Hungerlöhne«[40] ertragen müssten. Oder wie es in der Informationsbroschüre »Mehr Gleichberechtigung durch Fairen Handel« heißt: »Überstunden, Löhne unterhalb des Existenzminimums, mangelnder Gesundheitsschutz, Diskriminierung, sexuelle Belästigungen und Übergriffe sowie Gefahren durch mangelnden Brandschutz sind Beispiele für die Bedingungen, unter denen Frauen in der Stadt arbeiten.«[41] Ihnen blieben »häufig nur der Haushalt, Kochen und die Kinderbetreuung als gesellschaftliche Aufgaben«[42].

Diese zwei Bezeichnungsmechanismen stehen, wie die hier zitierten Quellen veranschaulichen, nicht isoliert nebeneinander. Sie treten als aufeinander bezogene *Vergeschlechtlichungspraktiken* auf. Denn sie konzentrieren sich auf die Frauen unter den Produzierenden und bekräftigen damit permanent die Differenz unter den Geschlechtern. Das sich wiederholende Muster der Verflochtenheit von Indigen-Machung und Viktimisierung lässt sich infolgedessen als *Viktigenisierung* apostrophieren. Diesen Neologismus trage ich hier in den Diskurs ein, weil es bislang an einer analytischen Kategorie mangelt, die auf den Punkt brächte, in welchen spezifischen Hinsichten die Bezeichnungspraktiken beim Thema Fairer Handel operieren und die entsprechenden Produzentinnen harmonisieren. Damit kann vor Augen geführt werden, dass den Indigen-Gemachten im Fair-Handels-Material *per se* ein Opferstatus zugeschrieben wird.

39 Frank Kürschner-Pelkmann, »Blumen sind keine Ware, sondern eine Vision«. Interview mit Marlies Olberz, Aktivistin einer Blumenkampagne, in: Verein zur Förderung der entwicklungspolitischen Publizistik e.V. (VFEP) (Hg.), Flower Power. Blumen aus Fairem Handel. Ein Dossier von VFEP in Zusammenarbeit mit der Redaktion eins. Zeitschrift Entwicklungspolitik 18–19/9 (2006), XI–XII, hier: XII.

40 Susanne Reiff, Sensible Produkte. Worauf Einkauf und Beschaffung achten müssen, in: Engagement Global gGmbH (Hg.), Für menschenwürdige Arbeitsbedingungen. Kommunen setzen auf fairen Handel und faire Beschaffung. Ein Dossier von Engagement Global in Zusammenarbeit mit der Redaktion Welt-Sichten 14/11 (2021), 8.

41 Brot für die Welt (Hg.), Mehr Gleichberechtigung durch Fairen Handel? Wie der Faire Handel Frauenrechte stärken kann, in: Aktuell 44 (2015), 6f.

42 Brot für die Welt (Hg.), Mehr Gleichberechtigung, 4.

Trotz ihrer quasi natürlichen Verwobenheit als Grundmuster handelt es sich hierbei um zwei Bezeichnungsweisen. Diese Einsicht lässt sich auf das Verhältnis zwischen der analytischen und der theoretischen Ebene zurückführen, das im hier vorliegenden Beitrag nur ansatzweise skizziert werden kann.[43] Indigen-Machen und Viktimisierung sind Bezeichnungsverfahren, die dazu beitragen, Prozesse der Materialisierung im Fair-Handels-Material zu erfassen. Demzufolge befinden sie sich als konkrete artikulatorische Praktiken auf der analytischen Ebene. Zugleich lassen sie sich auf die theoretische Ebene übertragen, geben sie doch den entsprechenden intersektionalen Differenzkategorien Geschlecht, Sexualität, Klasse und Ethnie Gestalt. So werden Inhalte, die Geschlecht, Sexualität und Klasse artikulieren, im Material als Viktimisierungen wiederholt, als patriarchale, heteronormative und ökonomische Abhängigkeiten, unter denen Frauen – im Unterschied zu Männern – zu leiden hätten. Wohingegen die theoretische Kategorie der Ethnie im Bezeichnungsmuster der Indigen-Machung, also der kulturell-topographischen Partikularisierung weiblicher Produzierender, eine konkrete Ausprägung findet. Auf den Punkt gebracht, lässt sich also festhalten, dass *Viktigenisierungen* Bezeichnungsmuster im Bildungsmaterial zum Fairen Handel darstellen, die als intersektional verwobene *Vergeschlechtlichungspraktiken* auftreten. Sie platzieren Produzentinnen kontinuierlich an kulturell-topographische Ränder, die verschiedene Opferzusammenhänge nach sich ziehen. In diesem Sinne lassen sich verschiedene *Viktigenisierungsarten* festmachen. Produzentinnen erscheinen als finanziell Abhängige, die »in bitterer Armut leben«[44] würden, als von Schulbildung Ausgeschlossene, denen »Wissen […] fehle«[45] oder als Mütter, die »allein im Kampf um das Überleben der Kinder und ihr eigenes Überleben«[46] blieben.[47] Nach dieser Veranschaulichung der sich wiederholenden Bezeichnungsmuster als *Viktigenisierungen*, folgt die Herausstellung ihrer materialisierenden Wirkungen.

43 Vgl. Günther-Kriegel, Fairer Handel.

44 Brot für die Welt (Hg.), Fairer Handel im Norden – Chance oder Fehler?, in: Es geht auch fair! Erfolge. Herausforderungen. 50 Jahre Fairer Handel (2020), 22–23, hier: 23.

45 Brot für die Welt (Hg.), »Traditionelle Machtstrukturen werden aufgebrochen«. Interview mit Yerlly Gúmez Montalván, in: Projektinformation. Bio-Bananen für den Fairen Handel (2019), 8–9, hier: 8.

46 Aktion 3. Welt Saar & Ökumenisches Netz (Hg.), Fairer Handel – Ist eine bessere Welt käuflich?, in: Flugschrift der A3WS (2015/2016), 3.

47 Eine ausführliche Herausstellung von sieben verschiedenen *Viktigenisieurngsarten* aus den untersuchten Quellen lässt sich nachvollziehen in Günther-Kriegel, Fairer Handel.

3. Zur Materialität der Effekte der Repräsentationen in den Bildungsmaterialien zum Fairen Handel

3.1 Zur *Viktigenen* als Machteffekt

Aus den sich wiederholenden Darstellungen von Produzentinnen in den Bildungsmaterialien zum Thema Fairer Handel geht eine Wirkung hervor, die sich nicht in einem linguistischen Phänomen erschöpft. Die im vorliegenden Aufsatz als *Viktigenisierungen* eingeführten Bezeichnungspraktiken ziehen einen materialisierten Machteffekt nach sich. Dieser verkörpert sich als ein Typus von Produzentin, den ich – den Bezeichnungsmechanismen entsprechend – als *Viktigene* attribuiere. Mithilfe dieser Vokabel lässt sich auf den Punkt bringen, in welchen Hinsichten die vielfältig miteinander verflochtenen *Vergeschlechtlichungspraktiken* im Diskurs zum Fairen Handel wirken. Die *Viktigene* streicht das signifikatorische Grundmuster der Repräsentationen heraus, mit denen die verschiedenartig betitelten Produzentinnen fair gehandelter Waren typisiert werden. Sie gibt den Charakterisierungen als »Blumenarbeiterinnen«[48], »Frauen in der Weberei«[49], »Teepflückerinnen«[50], »Frauen auf dem Feld«[51] oder »Näherinnen«[52] einen übergreifenden Ausdruck.

Die *Viktigene* ist damit nichts weiter als die analytische Präzisierung des spezifischen Effektes, der auf Iterationen in den Bezeichnungspraktiken zurückgeht. Diese sind komplex miteinander verflochten und liegen demzufolge nicht unmittelbar offen. Deren Effekt ist folglich ebenso komplex. Damit erklärt sich, weshalb ein gängiger Ausdruck dafür fehlt, würde er doch immer nur einen Aspekt des Effekts benennen. Anders formuliert dechiffriert die Bestimmung als *Viktigene* die in dieser Hinsicht vereinheitlichten Produzentinnen als materialisierten Effekt eines bestimmten intersektional verfahrenden, »regelgebundenen Diskurses«[53], der Fairer Handel genannt wird. Daran wird deutlich, weshalb die

48 Brot für die Welt (Hg.), Rosige Aussichten. Fairtrade-Blumen verhelfen zu einem menschenwürdigem Leben, in: Aktuell 24 (2013), 1.

49 Bahner/Lohr, Gemeinsames Wirtschaften, 19.

50 Tillman Elliesen, »Supermarkt oder Weltladen ist für uns kein Gegensatz«, in: Welt-Sichten 16/6 (2023), 8.

51 Süßmann, Edelbitter, 49.

52 Reiff, Sensible Produkte, 8.

53 Judith Butler, Das Unbehagen der Geschlechter, Frankfurt am Main 1991, 212.

Viktigene keine vermeintlich dahinterliegende *reale* Sache nur auf den *symbolischen* Begriff bringt.

Diese These, dass sprachliche Repräsentationen keine *a priori* gegebene Identität lediglich in Worte fassen, lässt sich am theoretischen Ansatz von Judith Butler konkretisieren. In diesem Sinne verstehe ich die *Viktigene* als Machteffekt,[54] der sich aus sedimentierten signifikatorischen Wiederholungen materialisiert. Die *Viktigene* geht deshalb nicht in einem linguistischen Verständnis auf, weil sie das Wissen sichtbar macht, das – nicht nur aber auch – auf dem Feld der evangelischen Entwicklungsarbeit über Frauen *herrscht*, die Baumwolle anbauen, Teeblätter sammeln oder Turnschuhe nähen. Das durch wiederholte Bezeichnung hervorgerufene Wissen ist weder zufällig noch notwendig und alles andere als folgenlos. Es ist material vorhanden.[55] Es existiert in der Welt und wird in Sprache eingeschrieben. Das geschieht allerdings im hier untersuchten Feld nicht anhand einer singulären Vokabel, sondern als ein Komplex aus vielfältigen Vorstellungen, die den erschlossenen *Viktigenisierungen* entsprechen. Das, was über die Produzentin gewusst wird, ist inhaltlich (vorübergehend) genauso festgelegt, wie das, was die Produzentin alles *nicht* darstellt. Denn sie geht auf artikulatorische Einschluss- genauso wie auf Ausschlusspraktiken zurück, durch die sie iterativ verfestigt wird. In diesem Sinne umfasst der Ausdruck der *Viktigenen* die gesamte *Realität* der Produzentin. Die Produzentin *ist* die *Viktigene*. Anders als indigen-gemachte Opfer sind »Kakaobäuerinnen«[56], »Produzentinnen […] von Kunsthandwerk«[57] und »Plantagenarbeiterinnen«[58] kaum vorstellbar. In genau diesem Sinne ist die *Viktigene* als Materialität aufzufassen. Sie ist etwas zur Materie Gewordenes, fällt sozusagen ins Gewicht. Denn Gewicht zu haben, materiell zu sein, heißt nichts anderes, als dass etwas etwas und nichts anderes bedeutet. So gesehen ist das Erzeugen von Bedeutung durch *viktigenisierende* Bezeichnungspraktiken eine konkrete Ausprägung von Verfahren der Materialisierung.

54 Vgl. Butler, Unbehagen, 211–213.
55 Vgl. Butler, Körper, 56.
56 Brot für die Welt (Hg.), Süße Alternative, 3.
57 Katrin Frank, Solidarisch durch die Krise. Die Covid-19-Pandemie macht dem fairen Handel schwer zu schaffen, in: Engagement Global gGmbH (Hg.), Für menschenwürdige Arbeitsbedingungen. Kommunen setzen auf fairen Handel und faire Beschaffung. Ein Dossier von Engagement Global in Zusammenarbeit mit der Redaktion Welt-Sichten 14/11 (2021), 20–21, hier: 20.
58 Gundis Jansen-Garz, Eine gute Kombination. ÖKO-TEST bewertet GEPA Bio Cashewnüsse mit »Sehr gut« – Fair und Bio zahlt sich aus, in: Welt & Handel 18/8 (2014), 4.

In dieser Material-Werdung, der Wissensgenese darüber, dass die Produzentin *Viktigene* ist, zeigt sich die Wirkung von Macht, die diesen Mechanismen nichts Äußerliches ist. Die Bezeichnungspraktiken der *Viktigenisierung* sind Machtpraktiken, weil »Macht […] sich darin [zeigt], dass etwas zum ›diskursiven Ereignis‹ und damit zum Gegenstand des Wissens wird«[59]. In diesem Sinne kann Butler von der »Macht des Diskurses [als dem], was er benennt«[60], sprechen. Die *Viktigene* ist also das komplexe, bisher unbenannte, weil unsichtbare, Destillat miteinander verwobener Komponenten einer sich »ständig wiederholende[n] und zitierende[n] Praxis, durch die der Diskurs die Wirkung erzeugt, die er benennt.«[61] Infolgedessen lassen sich *Viktigenisierungen* als signifiaktorische Machtpraktiken auffassen, die sich aus verflochtenen Machtachsen zusammensetzen, und die *Viktigene* als deren geronnenes, materialisiertes Ereignis hervorrufen. Dadurch werden die Bezeichnungsverfahren wiederum selbst stabilisiert. Daran zeigt sich, dass sich Effekt und Verfahren einer diskursiven Ordnung nicht getrennt voneinander erfassen lassen, werden doch auch die Verfahren selbst wieder durch ihre Effekte verfestigt. Das lässt sich auch anders ausdrücken: Wenn Materialität die Wirkung von Macht ist, ist iterative Signifikation, die sich in den *Viktigenisierungen* zeigt, gleichbedeutend mit Materialisierung.

Der analytische Ausdruck der *Viktigenen* ist demzufolge ein epistemischer, als er auf eine Analyse zurückgeht, die die Wirkung von Wiederholungen bestimmter Bezeichnungsmuster auf konkrete Vorstellungen sichtbar machen konnte: Es sind signifikatorische *Vergeschlechtlichungspraktiken* von Indigen-Machung und Viktimisierung, die sich in der Repräsentation der Produzentin in den Bildungsmedien zum Thema Fairer Handel verknoten, womit bestimmtes Wissen reproduziert wird. Der daraus hervorgehende Knoten, die *Viktigene*, ist, von einem anderen Blickwinkel aus betrachtet, nichts anderes als ein Komplex aus miteinander verwobenen und sich dadurch machtvoll potenzierenden Partikularitäten: das kulturell-topographisch abseitige Opfer Nicht-Mann. Diese Feststellung führt zu der Frage nach dem vermeintlich universalen Bezugspunkt, an dem die in diesem Sinne partikularisierte *Viktigene* taxiert wird, um Gestalt anzunehmen.

59 Hannelore Bublitz u. a., Diskursanalyse – (k)eine Methode? Eine Einleitung, in: Dies. et al. (Hg.), Das Wuchern der Diskurse. Perspektiven der Diskursanalyse Foucaults, Frankfurt/New York 1999, 10–21, hier: 11.
60 Butler, Körper, 309.
61 Butler, Körper, 22.

3.2 Zur Ko-Konstitution der *emanzipierten Europäerin*

Der artikulatorische Effekt der *Viktigenen* zieht eine entsprechende Ko-Konstitution nach sich. Diesem, im Diskurs gewissermaßen mit konstruierten *Nebeneffekt* der *Viktigenen* mangelt es ebenfalls an einem übergreifenden Ausdruck. Da sich besagte Ko-Konstitution aber nicht so scharf konturieren lässt wie die *Viktigene* selbst, werde ich sie als *emanzipierte Europäerin* kennzeichnen. Was mit dieser Umschreibung zum Ausdruck gebracht werden soll, ist das vermeintlich Universelle, das die *Viktigene* gerade nicht verkörpert. Die Universalitäts-Behauptung könnte in verschiedenen Hinsichten näher bestimmt werden. Den in dieser Untersuchung entschlüsselten kartographischen Grenzziehungsprozessen entsprechend, attribuiere ich die behauptete Zentralität mit Europa. Dabei sei jedoch mit Dipesh Chakrabarty daran erinnert, dass europazentrierte Narrative, die eine behauptete europäische Universalität bekräftigen, nicht auf europäische, sondern auf global verflochtene Diskurse zurückzuführen sind.[62]

Das heißt, dass die emanzipierte Europäerin lediglich als Bezugspunkt der *Viktigenen*, nicht als eigener Kristallisationspunkt des Diskurses Gestalt annimmt. In dieser Hinsicht greife ich zur Herausstellung ebenjener Ko-Konstitution entsprechende *Viktigenisierungspraktiken* auf, die Produzentinnen festschreiben und die im oben genannten Sinne als eurozentrisch geltend gemacht werden können. Wie beschrieben, wird die Produzentin als Opfer in die Peripherie von »abgelegenen, ländlichen Regionen«[63] in »von Männern dominierten Dörfern«[64] eingezeichnet. Damit verbunden ist die Verortung in die Gemeinschaft, die als genuine Lebensform der Produzentinnen vorausgesetzt wird. Gemeinschaft gehöre insofern wesenhaft zur »kulturellen Kodierung vieler traditioneller Gesellschaften«[65] dazu, als sie dem »Wertesystem [...] des modernen Marktes«[66] und damit der vermeintlich individualisierten Kultur entgegenstehe. Die dazu vorgestellte Dorfgemeinschaft wird dabei wiederholt als Kollektiv aus »Kleinbauernfamilien vor Ort«[67] bekräftigt, in dem »man sich [kennt] und sich

62 Vgl. Dipesh Chakrabarty, Europa als Provinz. Perspektiven postkolonialer Geschichtsschreibung, Frankfurt a. M. 2010, 41–65.

63 Brot für die Welt (Hg.), Klimawandel, 2.

64 O. V., Faire Vielfalt. Erstes Kaffeeforum in Düsseldorf, in: Welt & Handel 7/5 (2003), 6.

65 Pandey, Fairer Handel, 3.

66 Pandey, Fairer Handel, 3.

67 Brot für die Welt (Hg.), Harte Arbeit, fairer Lohn, in: Es geht auch fair! Erfolge. Herausforderungen. 50 Jahre Fairer Handel (2020), 10–12, hier: 10.

als Teil einer Gemeinschaft [fühlt]«[68]. Solche Produktionsgemeinschaften, wie die exemplarisch zu nennende »Kichwa-Genossenschaft«[69], gelten wiederum als Instrument erfolgreichen Wirtschaftens, weshalb sie durch Zertifizierungsprozesse von Fair-Handels-Organisationen initiiert und speziell gefördert werden müssten. Die dadurch hervorgerufenen Herausforderungen verbalisiert die Bananenbäuerin Maria Magdalena Valladares im *Brot für die Welt*-Jubiläumsheft zum vermeintlich fünfzigjährigen Geburtstag des Fairen Handels wie folgt: »Wir wussten zwar, wie man Bananen anbaut, aber nicht, wie man als Gemeinschaft Entscheidungen trifft – es gab Streit.«[70] Damit wird die Vorstellung verfestigt, dass es für die Etablierung einer kleinbäuerlichen Genossenschaft vonnöten wäre, Wissenslücken zu beheben, die vor allem den Produzentinnen zugeschrieben werden, wie der nachstehenden Absatz deutlich macht:

> »Frauen benötigen eine gezielte Förderung und Qualifizierung, da meistens sie es sind, die Überschüsse aus dem Gemüseanbau auf lokalen Märkten verkaufen, während die lukrativen Cash Crops oft von Männern vermarktet werden. Da ihre Kontakte in vielen Ländern beschränkt sind, haben Kleinbäuerinnen Nachholbedarf bei der Vernetzung mit anderen Akteuren in der Wertschöpfungskette.«[71]

Produzentinnen werden mit Behauptungen über ihre vermeintlich mangelnde Qualifizierung nicht nur als ungebildet markiert. Zugleich erscheinen sie deshalb als provinziell, weil die Forderung nach »Nachholbedarf bei der Vernetzung mit anderen Akteuren« damit begründet wird, dass deren »Kontakte in vielen Ländern beschränkt« seien. Damit bekräftigen Bezeichnungspraktiken dieser Art ein Fortschrittsdenken, das partikulare, zumal kontingente Prozesse als universal durchzusetzende Errungenschaften präsentiert, deren Ursprung auf Europa projiziert und damit regionalisiert wird. Das führt zum imaginierten, ko-konstituierten Vergleichspunkt, dem gegenüber die *Viktigene* etwas nachzuholen habe. Den herausgestellten *viktigenisierenden* Bezeichnungspraktiken entsprechend

68 TransFair, Arbeit für Europas Schokohunger. Kakaobauern in der Elfenbeinküste wollen ihre Situation weiter verbessern, in: TransFair e. V. (Hg.), Fairtrade bewegt. Der Faire Handel als demokratische Bewegung in Süd und Nord. Ein Dossier von TransFair e. V. in Zusammenarbeit mit der Redaktion Welt-Sichten 7/6 (2014), 8–10, hier: 9.

69 Knut Henkel, Neue Märkte für die Kaffeekooperativen, in: Welt-Sichten 12/11 (2019), 45–47, hier: 46.

70 Brot für die Welt (Hg.), Harte Arbeit, 10.

71 Brot für die Welt (Hg.), Gemeinsam sind wir stärker. Wie Kleinbauernfamilien vom Fairen Handel profitieren, in: Aktuell 20 (2016), 4.

ließe sich diese Ko-Konstitution als wohlhabendes, unabhängiges, gleichberechtigtes, gebildetes, urbanes, weibliches Individuum attribuieren.[72] Das Schweigen über diesen Vergleichspunkt der *emanzipierten Europäerin* erzeugt denselben als Norm, an dem die *Viktigene* als erwähnenswerte Ableitung erscheint.

3.3 Zur globalen Spaltung der *Einen Welt*

Die effektive Imagination eines in diesem Sinne binär ausgeformten *Ko* geht jedoch weit über den Frau-Frau-Vergleich hinaus und verfestigt einen Spalt entlang einer kartographisch imaginierten Linie. In der Verhältnissetzung von *Viktigener* zu *emanzipierter Europäerin* wird die Welt in zwei Hälften geteilt. Die Zweiwelten-Imagination,[73] wie sie sich in den Bildungsmaterialien zum Thema Fairer Handel rekonstruieren lässt, untermauert damit die Erkenntnisse Judith Butlers. Mit ihr lässt sich die Zweiteilung der Welt auf die Prämisse zurückführen, nach der »unterschwellig die Geschlechter-Unterdrückung als symptomatisch für eine wesentlich nicht-westliche Barbarei erklärt«[74] wird. In diesem Sinne trennt die *Viktigene* mit ihrer Kartierung ins Abseits eines kulturell-topographischen Patriarchats die vermeintlich eine von der anderen Welthälfte ab. Die Sichtbar-Machung dieser wirkmächtigen Prozesse geht auf die Entschlüsselung von *Viktigenisierungen* als machtvollen Repräsentationspraktiken zurück. Dadurch konnte wiederum das Erfolgsnarrativ vom Fairen Handel in der so bezeichneten *Einen Welt* erschüttert werden.

Die freigelegte epistemische Spaltung wird nämlich von ebenjenem »Eine-Welt«[75]-Narrativ verdeckt, das im Diskurs zum Fairen Handel permanent abge-

72 Chandra Talpade Mohanty hat als eine der ersten Wissenschaftlerinnen zur Sprache gebracht, wie sich eurozentrische Prämissen in Entwicklungsdiskursen auf die Repräsentation von sogenannten nicht-westlichen Frauen auswirken. Vgl. Chandra Talpade Mohanty, Aus westlicher Sicht. Feministische Theorie und koloniale Diskurse, in: Beiträge zur feministischen Theorie und Praxis 11/23 (1988), 149–162.

73 Die Verfestigung imaginärer Geographien hat vor allem Edward Said für den Orientalismus-Diskurs westlicher (Orient-)Wissenschaftler:innen im 18. Jahrhundert herausgestellt. Vgl. Edward W. Said, Orientalism, London 2003.

74 Butler, Unbehagen, 19.

75 Stefan Kreutzberger, Faire Kaffeebohnen vom kommunalen Partner. 40 deutsche Kommunen haben sich 2009 am Wettbewerb um die »Hauptstadt des Fairen Handels« beteiligt, in: Servicestelle Kommunen in der Einen Welt/InWEnt. Internationale Weiterbildung und Entwicklung gGmbH (Hg.), Globalisierung lokal gestalten. Die Rolle von Kommunen in der Entwicklungszusammen-

lagert wird. In dieser Hinsicht wird auch die entsprechende Bewusstseinsbildung und deren Textmaterial ebendieser »Eine-Welt-Arbeit« zugerechnet. Darauf macht Markus Raschke in seiner Dissertationsschrift zum Fairen Handel aufmerksam: »Dass […] auf unterschiedlichen Organisationsebenen die Idee des Fairen Handels aufgegriffen wird, ist in der kirchlichen Eine-Welt-Arbeit gewissermaßen zur Selbstverständlichkeit geworden.«[76] Was mit solchen Bezugnahmen auf die sogenannte *Eine Welt* unsichtbar gemacht wird, ist die Produktivität von *Viktigenisierungen* hinsichtlich kartographischer An-Ordnungen. Diese bekräftigen eine Grenzlinie, die zwischen Europa und Nicht-Europa, globalem Norden und globalem Süden, Zentrum und Peripherie verläuft. An diesem Spalt stehen sich Wohlstand und Armut, Individualismus und Gemeinschaft, Emanzipation und Paternalismus, Bildung und Unwissenheit, Stärke und Schwäche sowie Stadt und Land gegenüber. Zwischenräume, Übergänge, Grenzbereiche, Zweite Welten kommen hier nicht vor. Der Diskurs zum Fairen Handel zementiert damit sehr konkret die *Eine Welt* als *Ein-geteilt-e* Welt.

In dieser Hinsicht können die konkreten *Vergeschlechtlichungspraktiken* als *global* apostrophiert werden. *Global* ist demzufolge die Produktivität der *Viktigenisierungen*, indem sie Wissen erzeugen, auf das hin die Erdkugel als zweiteilig erscheint. Im Bezugsrahmen geographisch-kultureller Differenzierungen werden Weltgegenden bestimmte Attribute zuteil. Das eurozentrische Produkt aus der deutschsprachigen evangelischen Entwicklungsarbeit nimmt erst in Ableitung von und in Abgrenzung zu ihrem Gegenüber auf *dem anderen* Teil des Globus Gestalt an. Dieses emanzipierte, europäisch ko-konstituierte Gegenüber tritt wiederum nur als Negation zur *Viktigenen* in Erscheinung. Die Veranschaulichung dieser komplexen signifikatorischen Bezugnahmen macht sichtbar, dass hier intersektional verflochtene *Vergeschlechtlichungen* vorliegen. Eben jene verfestigen Vorstellungen darüber, wo auf der Welt welche Art von Frauen – als Nicht-Männer – zu finden seien. Damit wird Wissen von der sogenannten *Einen Welt* verfestigt – sprich: ihre epistemisch-globale Spaltung zementiert.

arbeit. Ein Dossier von der Servicestelle Kommunen in der einen Welt/InWEnt gGmbH in Zusammenarbeit mit der Redaktion Welt-Sichten 3/10 (2010), 8–9, hier: 8.

76 Markus Raschke, Fairer Handel. Engagement für eine gerechte Weltwirtschaft, Ostfildern 2009, 202.

4. Zum ontologischen Status der epistemischen Zweiteilung der Welt

Die globale Spaltung der sogenannten *Einen Welt* ließ sich anhand der Betrachtung von Bildungsmaterial zum Thema Fairer Handel aus der deutschen evangelischen Entwicklungsarbeit sichtbar machen. Damit wurde ein bestimmtes lokales Terrain auf der Landkarte des Globalen Christentums betrachtet. Es konnte herausgestellt werden, dass die entsprechenden Texte auf *vergeschlechtlichte* Repräsentationen von Produzentinnen zurückgreifen. Diese ziehen materialisierte Effekte nach sich, aus denen eine epistemisch-globale Spaltung resultiert. Diese Erkenntnis kann auf den *material turn* und insbesondere auf das Anliegen der Neuen Materialismen zurückgebunden werden. Das geschieht mithilfe der Frage nach dem ontologischen Status der besagten epistemischen Welt-Teilung: Auf welche Weise existiert dieser Spalt? Geht dessen Sein im erzeugten Wissen um ebenjene Spaltung auf?

Die Antwort richtet sich an der Auffassung davon aus, was unter Ontologischem zu verstehen ist. Das Anliegen des *material turn* gibt darauf eine Antwort. Das besteht darin, nicht sprachlich Fixiertes, sondern Praktiken zu erforschen und beruht damit auf der Prämisse, dass es einen konstitutiven Unterschied zwischen Sprache und Verkörpertem gäbe, dass Objekte ohne signifikatorische Praktiken Bedeutung tragen würden. Der daraus zu ziehende Schluss lautet, dass Sprache nicht materialisieren würde, Epistemisches – kurz: sprachlich erzeugtes Wissen – keine ontische Materialität besäße.

Die hier präsentierten Befunde zu den materialisierten Effekten von textlichen Repräsentationspraktiken in Fair-Handels-Bildungsmaterialien brechen diese stabilisierte Vorannahme auf und decken sich in diesem Sinne mit dem Erkenntnisinteresse von Vertreter:innen der Neuen Materialismen: »Sie problematisieren das cartesianisch-newtonsche Verständnis von Ontologie, um Handlungsfähigkeit jenseits des menschlichen Subjekts zu begreifen.«[77] Das lässt darauf schließen, dass die Grenze zwischen subjektivem Wissen und objektiver Materialität, zwischen Repräsentation und Realität – sprich: zwischen Epistemischem und Ontischem – selbst als Effekt bestimmter, sedimentierter Diskurse aufzufassen ist.[78] Die Starrheit solcher Grenzziehungen kommt mit den hier dargelegten Er-

77 Hoppe/Lempke Neue Materialismen, 15.
78 Vgl. Butler, Körper, 53–57.

gebnissen jedoch ins Bröckeln. Die Trennlinie wird durchlässig, verschiebbar. Gleiches gilt für die Grenze, die durch die wiederholte Inanspruchnahme vom *material turn* in Abgrenzung zum *linguistic turn* gezogen wird.

Diese grundsätzlichen theoretischen Schlussfolgerungen können aus der konkreten Untersuchung von Texten aus der kirchlichen Entwicklungsarbeit gezogen werden. Anhand der globalen Ordnungskategorie der *Viktigenen* ließ sich offenlegen, dass Dinge in Relation zu anderen Dingen ins Sein kommen, insofern sie erst durch Different-Setzungen Kontur annehmen, sprachlich fixiert werden, material werden und sich damit erkennen lassen. Das hat die Sichtbarmachung der gegenseitigen relationalen Ableitung von *Viktigener* und *emanzipierter Europäerin* vor Augen geführt, deren So-und-nicht-anders-Sein – ihr ontologischer Status – durch sprachlich wiederholte *Vergeschlechtlichungspraktiken* verfestigt werden. In dieser Hinsicht konnte hervorgehoben werden, dass derartige epistemisch-ontische Relationierungen nicht erst mit dem Aufkommen des *New Materialism* im Erkenntnisinteresse bestimmter Betrachtungsweisen stehen. Denn es wurde gezeigt, dass Seiendes durch Verhältnissetzungen hervortritt und in diesem Sinne weder fest fixiert noch abseits sprachlicher Praktiken von anderem Seienden abgrenzbar ist.[79] Materialitäten werden nur in Bezug zueinander zementiert, wie es die Praktiken der epistemischen Welt-Spaltung zeigen, die mithilfe des diskurstheoretischen Ansatzes von Judith Butler entschlüsselt werden konnten.

(Dr. des. Doris Günther-Kriegel ist Wissenschaftliche Mitarbeiterin am Seminar für Religionswissenschaft und Interkulturelle Theologie an der Theologischen Fakultät der Martin-Luther-Universität Halle-Wittenberg.)

79 Vgl. Karen Barad, Diffraktionen. Differenzen, Kontingenzen und Verschränkungen von Gewicht, in: Corinna Bath u. a. (Hg), Geschlechter Interferenzen. Wissensformen – Subjektivierungsweisen – Materialisierungen, Münster 2013, 27–67, hier: 61.

ABSTRACT

Based on an investigation of educational material on the topic of fair trade, which traces back to the Development work of Protestant churches, it can be shown that the gap between the so-called Global South and the so-called Global North is continuously being reinforced. This takes place on the basis of powerful practices of representation that categorically contrast a *southern* part of supposedly multi-dependent female fair trade producers with a supposedly self-determined *northern* part of women. In line with the critical epistemological interest of the article, the representations of female producers in the corresponding sources are uncovered as entangled *genderizations*. The guiding question here is how material such permanently repeated *genderization practices* are, which shape both the commonly notions of women and of world regions.

herchurch als Palimpsest

Dimensionen feministisch-neopaganer Reinterpretation des *whitemalegod*

Thorsten Wettich

1. Eine lilafarbene Kirche in Twin Peaks

Ebenezer Lutheran Church oder *herchurch*[1] in San Franciscos Twin Peaks Distrikt ist kaum zu übersehen: Seit einigen Jahren erstrahlen der Glockenturm und das Sanktuarium von außen lila- bzw. magentafarben. Hauptpastorin Stacy Boorn erklärt in einem Interview, dass dies zum einen Ausdruck der Unterstützung ihrer Gemeinde für die Gleichstellung homosexueller Ehen im bürgerlichen Gesetz sei, dass die Farbe Lila ferner historisch von der Frauenbewegung genutzt worden und sie in der Religionsgeschichte Ausdruck des göttlichen weiblichen Prinzips gewesen sei.[2] Sinnbildlich ist damit schon die grundsätzliche Intention der speziellen Mischung aus christlicher Theologie, feministischer Kritik am patriarchalen christlichen Gottesbild und einer Mischung aus christlichen und paganen Formen in *herchurch* angesprochen: Anstelle von Jesus Christus wird »das

1 *herchurch* wird nach Aussage der hier tätigen Pastorinnen bewusst immer klein geschrieben, um nicht zu suggerieren, dass Gott dem Menschen überlegen sei. Vgl. Jennifer Mantle, Circling the Goddess. Reclaiming the Rosary in Her Name, Palo Alto 2010, 2.

2 Interview mit Duffy-Burke, https://www.youtube.com/watch?v=ehjk7A5cHSk, 8:32–8:46 (19.3. 2025).

göttliche Weibliche« (*the Divine Feminine*)[3] in unterschiedlichen Personifikationen (Weisheit *Sophia*, Mutter *Maria* oder weibliches Urprinzip *ah-she*) verehrt.

Der vorliegende Aufsatz untersucht die Gemeinde einerseits auf Basis ihrer inhaltlichen Grundlagen: Auf der Homepage wird erklärt, man lehne sich mit der Verehrung der als Frau verkörperten Weisheit (*Sophia*) an jüdische und hellenistische Traditionen an.[4] Das bedeutet aber nicht, dass sich *herchurch* gänzlich von seinen christlichen Traditionen losgesagt hätte. Die Gemeinde ist nach wie vor Mitglied der größten US-amerikanischen lutherischen Kirche *Evangelical Lutheran Church in America* (*ELCA*), auch wenn ihr Status gelegentlich von innen wie außen infrage gestellt wird. Andererseits sollen die konkreten materiellen Dimensionen in den Vordergrund gestellt werden: In *herchurch* nähert sich die Gemeinde der göttlichen Weiblichkeit unter anderem mithilfe von Ikonenmalerei, der »Anrufung der Großmutter«[5] im Rosenkranzgebet, Trommelkursen zu Vollmond und astrologischen Lesungen der fest angestellten Hexe (*resident witch*).

Wie ich zeigen möchte, lässt sich *herchurch* durch ihre theologischen Grundlagen und materiellen Ausdrucksformen als ein Palimpsest lesen, ein wiederbeschriebenes Manuskript, bei dem die redigierten Konturen jener früheren Schichten christlicher Theologie, Liturgie und Architektur nicht gänzlich unsichtbar werden. »Das Sinnbild des Palimpsests lädt dabei zu einer relationalen Lektüre« ein, in welcher die »zu verschiedenen Zeiten kreierten Textschichten stets in Bezug aufeinander zu begreifen« sind.[6] Traditionen und materielle Ausdrucksformen, die hierbei aufeinander Bezug nehmen, sind im Falle von *herchurch* christliche, feministische und christopagane Diskurse, die sich jeweils auch materiell ausdrücken: In *Ebenezer Lutheran Church* ist allmählich aus der Kritik am *white savior* Jesus Christus und im Speziellen an christlichen liturgischen Formen eine »göttinnen-inklusive« Anbetung entstanden, deren mit paganen Elementen gespickte künstlerische Ausdrucksformen bemerkenswert sind.

Diese in *herchurch* entwickelten göttinnen-inklusiven und christopaganen liturgischen Formen möchte ich im Sinne des Ansatzes der Religionswissenschaftlerin Birgit Meyer als *sensational forms* auffassen, also als sinnlich erfahrbare,

3 https://www.herchurch.org/ (19.3.2025).
4 https://www.herchurch.org/about/our-purpose (19.3.2025).
5 https://www.herchurch.org/events (19.3.2025).
6 Victoria Hegner, Hexen der Großstadt. Urbanität und neureligiöse Praxis in Berlin, Bielefeld 2019, 88.

medial vermittelte und emotional wirksame religiöse Praktiken,[7] die als »autorisierte Modi einen Zugang zum Transzendenten herzustellen und zu organisieren«[8] verstanden werden. Das Konzept der *sensational forms* ist deshalb aufschlussreich, weil es in *herchurch* darum geht, mit ästhetischen Formen Transzendenzerfahrungen zu ermöglichen, wobei hier die Mittel vergleichsweise ungewöhnlich sind und der Gegenstand der Transzendenz variabel gedacht wird. *Sensational forms* sind im weiteren Kontext des *material turn* zu verorten,[9] welcher den »Gebrauch von Medien und Objekten als Materialisierungen der Erfahrungsdimension von Religion« fokussiert[10]. Er stellt räumliche Anordnungen und deren Wirkung auf die Körper der religiösen Akteur_innen[11] ins Zentrum und beleuchtet ihre Erfahrungsdimensionen, Ästhetik und Performanz im religiösen Zusammenhang.

Um zu einem tieferen Verständnis des Göttinnen-Rosenkranzgebets zu gelangen, werde ich zunächst die grundsätzlichen inhaltlichen Schichten des Palimpsests von *herchurch* – die Kritik am *whitemalegod*, göttinnen-inklusive Liturgie und christopagane Ausdrucksformen – rekapitulieren. Die materiellen Dimensionen des Göttinnen-Rosenkranzgebets, an welchem ich im November 2024 teilnehmen konnte,[12] sollen danach beispielhaft im Sinne von Meyers *sensational forms* analysiert werden. Zum Ende werde ich unter dem Stichwort »Stein des Anstoßes« einige kritische Außenwahrnehmungen ausführen.

7 Birgit Meyer, Religious Sensations. Why Media, Aesthetics and Power Matter in the Study of Contemporary Religion, Amsterdam 2006.

8 Birgit Meyer, Aesthetics of Persuasion. Global Christianity and Pentecostalism's Sensational Forms, in: South Atlantic Quarterly 109/4 (2010), 741–763, hier: 752.

9 Bärbel Beinhauer-Köhler, Religionen greifbar machen? Der material turn in der Religionswissenschaft, in: Pastoraltheologie 104 (2015), 255–265. Ich betrachte alle jene *turns*, die auf den *linguistic turn* folgten, als dessen Folge und würde deren singuläre Tragweite im Sinne eines kuhnschen Paradigmenwechsels zugunsten eines Paradigmenwechsels als Summe aller *turns* inklusive des *linguistic turn* einschränken, vgl. Doris Bachmann-Medick, Cultural Turns. Neuorientierungen in den Kulturwissenschaften, Hamburg 2011, 7–13.

10 Inken Prohl, Materiale Religion, in: Michael Stausberg (Hg.), Religionswissenschaft, Berlin u. a. 2012, 379–392.

11 Jürgen Mohn, Religionsaisthetik. Religion(en) als Wahrnehmungsräume, in: Michael Stausberg (Hg.), Religionswissenschaft, Berlin u. a. 2012, 329–342.

12 Der Vor-Ort-Untersuchung von *herchurch* war eine Beschäftigung mit dem Gegenstand auf der Basis von Online-Recherche vorausgegangen, die ich an anderer Stelle publiziert habe: Thorsten Wettich, »HerChurch« – feministischer Christopaganismus in US-amerikanischer lutherischer Gemeinde, in: Zeitschrift für Religion und Weltanschauung 85/3 (2022), 194–196. Die Förderung der Forschungsreise erfolgte aus Mitteln der Zentralen Forschungsförderung der Universität Bremen.

2. *herchurch* als Palimpsest

Der Begriff des Palimpsests entstammt dem Typus der Schichttheorie. In seiner kulturwissenschaftlichen Verwendung verweist er darauf, dass »räumliche, zeitliche und semiotische Überlagerungen«[13] in einer Quelle vorliegen. Ich betrachte im Folgenden *herchurch* als Palimpsest, um einen Fokus »auf Momente der Mischung, der Disruption, der Zerstörung, des Verlusts, aber auch der Erneuerung«[14] der miteinander korrespondierenden Strömungen des lutherischen Christentums, der feministischen Kritik am patriarchalen Gottesbild, göttinnen-inklusiver Liturgie und christopaganen materiellen Ausdrucksformen zu legen.

Die Kulturanthropologin Victoria Hegner bevorzugt im Rahmen ihrer Studie über »Hexen der Großstadt« den Begriff des Palimpsests gegenüber jenem des Synkretismus, um dessen abwertender Konnotation zu entgehen. Wie sie möchte ich den Begriff nutzen, um die Zusammenhänge zwischen widerstreitenden Strömungen in ein und derselben Quelle aufzuzeigen. Hegner verweist jedoch auf eine Problematik der Metapher,

> »ist doch das Kennzeichen von (konkreten) Palimpsesten eigentlich und in erster Linie, dass versucht wird, alte Texte, soweit es geht, verschwinden zu lassen, um eine nahezu unbeschriebene Oberfläche wiederherzustellen und zu nutzen.«[15]

Gerade in der Spannung zwischen dem Versuch, frühere Schichten auszulöschen, und der Beobachtung, dass man die redigierten Schichten weiterhin erkennt – mit anderen Worten in der »Dialektik von Präsenz und Absenz«[16] –, liegt der Reiz der Metapher des Palimpsests. Im herkömmlichen Sinne, das heißt in jenem der Geschichtswissenschaft, wird der Begriff des Palimpsests verwendet, um »einen Kodex oder Teile davon zu bezeichnen, deren Beschreibstoff von einer vorherigen Beschriftung gereinigt und so für die Wiederbeschreibung nutzbar

13 Bernadette Malinowski u. a., Von der Schichtung zur Palimpsestierung. »Palimpsest« als kulturwissenschaftlicher Grundbegriff, in: Zeitschrift für Semiotik 43/1–2 (2021), 177–212.
14 Malinowski u. a., Palimpsestierung, 179.
15 Hegner, Hexen der Großstadt, 43.
16 Malinowski u. a., Palimpsestierung, 192.

gemacht wurde«[17]. Damit handelt es sich beim Palimpsest ursprünglich nicht um eine Form der Zensur, sondern des Recyclings.[18]

Nimmt man diesen Gedanken mit in die kulturwissenschaftliche Verwendung der Metapher hinein, so ist es interessant danach zu forschen, in welchen Fällen das Überschreiben tatsächlich die Absicht verfolgt, frühere Schichten verschwinden zu lassen, oder ob der neue Text diese mindestens teilweise weiterhin gelten lässt. Letzteres zeigt etwa die Aussage der Pastorin Boorn, dass allumfassende göttinnen-inklusive Theologie und die Gottes- und Menschenliebe Jesu letztlich kongruent seien.[19] Später werde ich weitere Beispiele der Kongruenz oder Harmonie zwischen unterschiedlichen Schichten anführen.

In vielerlei Hinsicht zielen die Kritik am *whitemalegod*, die göttinnen-inklusive Liturgie und die christopaganen *sensational forms* in *herchurch* jedoch durchaus auf eine Zensur früherer Schichten ab. Dies wird etwa deutlich im Werk der Theologin und Sozialpsychologin Christina Cleveland, deren Buch »God is a Black Woman«[20] umfangreich in *herchurch* rezipiert und deswegen im folgenden Kapitel besprochen wird. Cleveland wird nicht müde zu betonen, dass der *whitemalegod* nicht dazu in der Lage sei, allen Menschen als Vorbild und Bezugspunkt zu dienen und deswegen durch das Konzept von Gott als schwarzer Frau ersetzt werden müsse.

Die Literaturwissenschaftlerin Cecile Sandten spricht in diesem Zusammenhang auch von »toxischen Palimpsestdimensionen«[21], wenn sie interpretiert, dass postkoloniale Erzählungen subalterner Autor_innen koloniale – mithin toxische – Schichten zum Vorschein bringen, die im Bild des Manuskripts die abgeschabten Textteile darstellen. Andersherum kämen postkoloniale Erzählungen einem Empowerment gleich, insofern »die durch die koloniale Erfahrung unterdrückte, verschüttete oder überlagerte Vergangenheit freigelegt wird und die verborgenen Kontinuitäten ans Licht gebracht«[22] würden. Im Sinne einer Freilegung vermeintlich älterer Wahrheiten über die göttinnen-inklusive Liturgie argumentieren auch die beiden in *herchurch* angestellten Pastorinnen Stacy Boorn und Jennifer

17 Malinowski u. a., Palimpsestierung, 180.
18 Malinowski u. a., Palimpsestierung, 180.
19 Interview mit Duffy-Burke, 6:42–6:47 (19.3.2025).
20 Christina Cleveland, God is a Black Woman, New York 2022.
21 Cecile Sandten, Toxisches postkoloniales Palimpsest. Der Versuch einer Zusammenführung, in: Marian Nebelin u. a., Palimpsest und Raum. Über ein neues Konzept für die Kulturwissenschaften, Bielefeld 2024, 193–216.
22 Sandten, Toxisches Palimpsest, 198.

Mantle, wenn sie anführen, dass die patriarchalen liturgischen Formen des Christentums lediglich ältere, inklusivere Anbetungsformen überlagert hätten.

Es geht also um die Frage, welche Schichten des Palimpsests bis an die Oberfläche durchscheinen und in welchem Verhältnis diese zu den älteren und jüngeren Überschreibungen oder Eintragungen stehen. Mit meiner Klassifikation »christopaganer Ausdrucksformen« deute ich bereits an, dass sich dieses Verhältnis durchaus harmonisch gestalten kann. In diesem Fall wäre es angemessen, von einem Recycling statt von einer Zensur zu sprechen. In einem weiteren Fall, auf den ich später noch ausführlicher eingehen werde, wird die Frage relevant, ob feministische Formen neuer Spiritualität sich innerhalb der christlichen Tradition verorten lassen (*Christian feminist spirituality*) oder als »post-christlich« verstanden werden sollten.[23]

Im Folgenden sollen also drei Schichten des in *herchurch* vorfindlichen Palimpsests als solche analysiert werden: 1. Die Kritik am *whitemalegod*, 2. die göttinnen-inklusive Liturgie und 3. christopagane Ausdrucksformen. Sie alle bringen in Bezug auf den Umgang mit den von ihnen jeweils abgeschabten Gegenpositionen unterschiedliche Voraussetzungen mit sich, was sich letztlich auch in der Kritik vonseiten Dritter, die ich am Ende rekapitulieren werde, spiegelt.

3. Kritik am *whitemalegod*

Die spezielle Form der christlichen Verehrung mit neopaganem Einschlag, die sich in dieser außergewöhnlichen Gemeinde in San Francisco findet, ist einer Kritik am patriarchalen Gottesbild erwachsen, das nach dortiger Auffassung im Christentum (wie in anderen Religionen) verbreitet ist. In *herchurch* orientiert man sich mit der Kritik am *whitemalegod* an dem bereits zitierten Werk »God is a Black Woman«[24] von Christina Cleveland.

Cleveland argumentiert, dass die Vorstellung eines männlichen Gottes grundsätzlich mit dessen Transzendenz einhergehe und diese einerseits die physische Welt der Gläubigen und andererseits »die weibliche Idee Gottes intimer Präsenz

23 Linda Woodhead, Post-Christian Spiritualities, in: Religion 23 (1993), 167–181.
24 Cleveland, Black Woman.

in unserem Leben«[25] vernachlässigen würde. Wenn die feminine Seite Gottes zum Schweigen gebracht würde, entstünde die Vorstellung eines *fatherskygod*, eines von dieser Welt getrennten, exklusiv maskulinen Gottes, der gerade, wenn er am meisten gebraucht werde, unerreichbar sei.[26]

Die Verbreitung der Vorstellung des *fatherskygod* bringt Cleveland mit den indoeuropäischen »Streitaxtkulturen« der mesolithischen Periode (15 000–8000 vor unserer Zeitrechnung) in Verbindung. Seine Eigenschaften seien »ominös und bedrohlich«[27]. Die »Invasion und Kolonisation des globalen Südens«[28] durch die Indoeuropäer_innen um 2400 v. Chr. hätte jahrhundertealte Mutter-Gott-Vorstellungen dezimiert und das Verständnis des jüdisch-christlichen Gottes *YHWH* entscheidend geprägt. Da der *fatherskygod* und damit auch *YHWH* dafür einstünden, dass Männer heiliger seien als Nicht-Männer, schafften sie die Legitimation toxischen Verhaltens durch cis-Männer:

> »Male god is a patriarchal myth that attempts to declare that men are more sacred than women, non-binary, and gender-expansive people. Since male god was created to silence and control nonmen, male god's primary allegiance is with men and toxic masculinity.«[29]

Doch die toxische Allianz des *malegods* sei nach Cleveland nicht nur auf Geschlecht beschränkt, sie trage auch noch eine rassistische Komponente in sich: Während laut Cleveland antike Quellen darauf hinwiesen, dass Jesus ausgesehen haben müsse wie ein »Palästinenser afrikanischer Herkunft«, sei demgegenüber das Konzept des *white Christ* erfunden worden, des »Patrons der weißen Vorherrschaft«[30]. Im Konzept des *whitemalegods* komme es zur »fatalen Intersektion von weißer Vorherrschaft und toxischer Maskulinität«[31]. Der *whitemalegod* biete laut Cleveland keine Identifikationspunkte für nicht-weiße, nicht-männliche Gläubige an. Dagegen lade die »befreiende heilige schwarze Weiblichkeit«[32]

25 Cleveland, Black Woman, 27.
26 Cleveland, Black Woman, 27.
27 Cleveland, Black Woman, 28.
28 Cleveland, Black Woman, 28.
29 Cleveland, Black Woman, 33.
30 Cleveland, Black Woman, 37f.
31 Cleveland, Black Woman, 42; vgl. auch Nathalie Eleyth/Alena Höfer, Kritische Rassismusforschung und Interkulturelle Theologie, in: Franz Gmainer-Pranzl u. a. (Hg.), Handbuch Interkulturelle Theologie, Berlin/Heidelberg 2024, 1–8.
32 Cleveland, Black Woman, 43.

dazu ein, die bisher rezipierten Gottesbilder zu reflektieren und zu korrigieren. Sie sei eher dazu geeignet, alle Menschen, vor allem nicht-weiße nicht-cis-Männer, anzusprechen, und sei damit wesentlich inklusiver.

Wie ist also das Verhältnis des Konzepts der befreienden heiligen schwarzen Weiblichkeit zu jenem des *whitemalegods* zu interpretieren? Handelt es sich um Recycling oder Zensur? Wird die Schicht des *whitemalegods* im Palimpsest bewusst überdeckt und gänzlich abgeschabt oder scheint sie weiterhin durch?

Bei Cleveland und in *herchurch* wird davon ausgegangen, dass bereits die Schicht des *fatherskygod* im Palimpsest eine Zensur früherer, inklusiverer Anbetungsformen darstellte. Durch die gewaltsame Durchsetzung dieses Konzepts sei eine toxische Palimpsestschicht entstanden, die zum Wohle aller abgeschabt werden müsse. Schließlich würden dadurch im Sinne von Sandten die unterdrückte Vergangenheit freigelegt und verborgene Kontinuitäten ans Licht gebracht.[33] Die Überschreibung des *fatherskygod* durch *the Divine Feminine* im Palimpsest wird hiermit als historisch angemessene Wiederherstellung älterer Schichten legitimiert.[34]

Pastorin Boorn spricht in einem Interview davon, dass es sich bei *the Divine Feminine* gegenüber dem *whitemalegod* »nicht um denselben Gott«, »nicht um dasselbe Paradigma«, »nicht um dieselbe Ratio« handele.[35] Konkreter materieller Ausdruck dieser theologischen Annahmen ist etwa der Ersatz des Weihnachtsfestes in *herchurch* durch die Feier der »Wiederkehr der Göttin«, welche in der Adventszeit in den vier »antiken Inkarnationen« *Mother of us all*, *Our Lady of Guadalupe*, *The Black Madonna* und *Christ Sophia* begangen wird.[36] Laut Pastorin Mantle handelt es sich bei *the Divine Feminine* nicht nur um einen Ersatz des christlichen Gottes, sondern um »eine gänzlich andere Weltsicht«:

> »More than merely a female replacement of the Christian concept of God, the concept of Divine Feminine entails an entirely different world view that is deeply rooted in the experience of femaleness, particularly as it applies

33 Sandten, Toxisches Palimpsest, 198.

34 Dieser Gedanke ist im Übrigen nicht neu, sondern wird beispielsweise bereits 1979 von Merlin Stone in einem Aufsatz unter dem sprechenden Titel »When God was a Woman« behandelt. Dort heißt es: »In the beginning, people prayed to the Creatress of Life, the Mistress of Heaven. At the very dawn of religion, God was a woman. Do you remember?«; Merlin Stone, When God was a Woman, in: Carol P. Christ/Judith Plaskow (Hg.), Womanspirit Rising. A Feminist Reader in Religion, San Francisco 1979, 120–130, hier: 120.

35 Interview mit Duffy-Burke, 6:36–6:39 (19.3.2025).

36 Interview mit Duffy-Burke, 10:59–11:12 (19.3.2025).

to women's blood mysteries, a reverence for and connection to all living things, the earth and the moon and their cycles.«[37]

Letztlich muss aber festgehalten werden, dass die Kritik am *whitemalegod*, die in göttinnen-inklusiver Liturgie und christopaganen Ausdrucksformen mündet, nicht konsequent diametral zu christlichen Ausdrucksformen funktioniert. Dies trifft zu, weil der Gegenstand der Anbetung – das transzendente Gegenüber des *Divine Feminine* – eine veränderbare Gestalt hat. Das kann so weit gehen, dass *the Divine Feminine* gänzlich diffus wird, wenn Pastorin Boorn es mit dem Kosmos identifiziert, der sich jeden Tag ändern könne.[38] Eine dieser pluralen Ausdrucksformen kann ein biblischer Jesus oder auch die lutherische Befreiungstheologie sein: Pastorin Boorn äußert, dass »das simple Konzept der Befreiung« insofern Geltung habe, als es dazu aufrufe, alles, was »uns von der Verbindung mit dem Göttlichen abhält«, zu identifizieren und zu korrigieren.[39] Eine feministische Lesart der Befreiungstheologie könnte also darin liegen, bestehende patriarchale Machtverhältnisse zu reflektieren und zu einer Solidarisierung mit Unterdrückten aufzurufen.[40] In der Konsequenz folgten der lutherischen Theologie die Kritik am *whitemalegod*, eine göttinnen-inklusive Liturgie und christopagane Ausdrucksformen nach.

4. Göttinnen-inklusive Liturgie

Die göttinnen-inklusive Liturgie in *herchurch* ist eng mit der Hauptpastorin Boorn verbunden. Ihre Berufsbiographie gleicht einer Emanzipationsgeschichte von patriarchalen Zwängen des Christentums in den USA.[41] Stacy Boorn wurde in der *Lutheran Church Missouri Synod* (*LCMS*), der kleineren und konservativeren der beiden großen US-amerikanischen lutherischen Dachorganisationen, sozialisiert. Nach ihrer Konfirmation übernahm sie Lesungen im Sonntagsgot-

37 Mantle, Circling the Goddess, 7.
38 Interview mit Duffy-Burke, 02:50–03:05 (19.3.2025).
39 Interview mit Duffy-Burke, 03:58–04:20 (19.3.2025).
40 Für diesen Hinweis danke ich Tom Kleinwort. Dafür spricht, dass Pastorin Boorn feststellt, dass der Feminismus und das Evangelium letztlich identisch seien. Vgl. Jann Aldregde-Clanton, Changing Church. Stories of Liberating Ministers, Eugene 2011, hier: 21.
41 Aldregde-Clanton, Changing Church, 11–23.

tesdienst ihrer Gemeinde.[42] Als Theologiestudentin erhielt sie gegen anfänglichen Widerstand des Pastors die Erlaubnis, eine Predigt zu halten. Dies rief unter einigen anwesenden weiblichen Gemeindegliedern Protest hervor, der sich in deren Verlassen des Gottesdienstes äußerte.[43]

Da es unmöglich war und ist, als Frau in der *LCMS* ordiniert zu werden, wechselte Stacy Boorn zur liberaleren *Association of Evangelical Lutheran Churches* und wurde hier im Jahr 1987 ordiniert. Diese Dachorganisation ging wenig später in der *ELCA* auf, zu der auch *Ebenezer Lutheran Church* in San Francisco gehört, in welche Stacy Boorn später berufen wurde. Erst hier begann sie, sich mit feministischer Theologie auseinanderzusetzen.[44]

In einem Interview erklärt Boorn, dass sie sich in dieser Zeit die Frage stellte, »was es sei, das uns davon abhält, uns für uns selbst und mit anderen für göttliche Liebe zu engagieren«[45]. Dabei sei sie »vor Jahren hier in der Gemeinde« zu dem Ergebnis gekommen, dass es »die Sprache der Liturgie« sei, die »uns« davon abhalte.[46] Dies macht sie daran fest, dass die »liturgische Sprache der traditionellen Christenheit« voll von maskulinen Konzepten wie »Vater«, »Herr« und »Meister« sei.[47]

Als Konsequenz begann Pastorin Boorn »ein wenig Mutter Gott«[48] in die Liturgie aufzunehmen, indem sie etwa bei der Taufe von Gott sprach, »der_die uns ist wie eine Mutter und ein Vater«[49], und dies zu jenem Zeitpunkt für einen »großen Wurf«[50] hielt. Tatsächlich bekam sie erheblichen Gegenwind von einigen Mitgliedern ihrer Gemeinde, die sich an den Synodalbischof wandten, weil Pastorin Boorn in ihren Augen »nicht die angemessene Terminologie für Gott«[51] verwandte.

Die folgenden Veränderungen waren jedoch tiefgreifender. Die Eröffnungslitanei des regulären Sonntagsgottesdienstes etwa spricht heute von *Christ Sophia*, einer Kombination von Christus und der weiblichen Personifikation der

42 Aldregde-Clanton, Changing Church, 13.
43 Aldregde-Clanton, Changing Church, 14.
44 Aldregde-Clanton, Changing Church, 16.
45 Interview mit Duffy-Burke, 2:50–4:20 (19.3.2025).
46 Interview mit Duffy-Burke, 2:50–4:20 (19.3.2025).
47 Interview mit Duffy-Burke, 4:26–4:29 (19.3.2025).
48 Aldridge-Clanton, Changing Church, 16.
49 Interview mit Duffy-Burke (5:29–5:31).
50 Aldridge-Clanton, Changing Church, 16.
51 Aldridge-Clanton, Changing Church, 17.

Weisheit, die die Eigenschaften von Gnade, Befreiung und Hoffnung auf sich vereint.[52] Laut einem gedruckten Kommentar, der mir vor Ort ausgehändigt wurde, sei *Christ Sophia* »ein Symbol der Göttlichkeit, das Geschlechter, Rassen und Glaubenstraditionen verbindet und damit ein Vorbild ist für eine Gemeinschaft, in der alle in Partnerschaft leben«[53]. Mit Referenz zu 1 Kor 1,30 (»Christus Jesus, der für uns zur Weisheit wurde«)[54] und weiteren Quellen wird hier eine enge Verbindung zwischen beiden Konzepten nahegelegt, die Gleichberechtigung anstelle von Herrschaft symbolisiere.[55]

Die lutherische Agende des Sonntagsgottesdienstes lässt sich in ihren grundsätzlichen Formen erkennen. Also scheint auch hier eine ältere Palimpsestschicht durch, die offenbar weiterhin eine gewisse Nachfrage befriedigt. Sie ist jedoch im Sinne der göttinnen-inklusiven Theologie umfangreich ergänzt und verändert worden. Das *Vater Unser* etwa wurde in *herchurch* durch einen neuen Wortlaut ersetzt, der die »Mutter, die in uns wohnt« preist, die den Gläubigen alles gebe, was sie bräuchten, ihnen ihre Grenzen aufzeige, unterstütze, ein Zuhause schaffe, ermutige und zur Freude anrege.[56] Beispiele für materielle Ergänzungen sind die Salbung mit heilendem Öl, die Möglichkeit zu trommeln und Räucherwerk anzuzünden. Viele Lieder des regulären Sonntagsgottesdienstes stammen aus einem Liederbuch, das die als *Sister of Song* oder auch als *Priestess* firmierende Chorleiterin Katie Ketchum herausgebracht hat. Laut Verlagsangabe sollen durch das Besingen weiblicher Namen Gottes »die Wunden geheilt werden, die die patriarchale Unterdrückung und Gewalt«[57] hervorgerufen hätten.

In *herchurch* nimmt, wenn es um den (im weiteren Sinne liturgischen) Zugang zu *the Divine Feminine* geht, die Ikonenmalerei eine wichtige Rolle ein. Der größte der Räume, in denen diese Kunstwerke sowohl von den Angestellten der Gemeinde als auch ihren übrigen Mitgliedern angefertigt werden, wird als *art womb*, also als »Kunst-Mutterleib« bezeichnet. Hier werden Ausdrücke von *the*

52 Aldridge-Clanton, Changing Church, 13.
53 Jann Aldregde Clanton, Christ Sophia, graue Literatur.
54 Die Bibel nach Martin Luthers Übersetzung, Stuttgart 2017.
55 Ferner verwendet *herchurch* für die Anbetung von *the Divine Feminine* den Titel *Shaddai* und folgt dabei der (in der Forschungsliteratur umstrittenen) Ableitung aus dem hebräischen שַׁד, was als Dual mit »Brüste« übersetzt werden kann und von Pastorin Boorn genutzt wird, um auf die topographische Umgebung der Twin Peaks, zwei Hügel in der Nachbarschaft der Kirche, zu verweisen.
56 https://www.herchurch.org/about/goddess-rosary (19.3.2025).
57 https://progressivechristianity.org/resources/hersay-songs-for-healing-and-empowerment (19.3.2025).

Divine Feminine künstlerisch hervorgebracht, beziehungsweise »geboren«. Dazu gehören Darstellungen Marias, etwa solche, die an Maria von Guadeloupe erinnern, und abstraktere Darstellungen, wie die *Madonna – nonbinary*, eine Konkretion von *the Divine Feminine*, die sich dadurch auszeichnet, dass sie sich der binären Geschlechterordnung von Mann und Frau entzieht.[58] Eine Ikone ist der demokratischen Präsidentschaftskandidatin Kamala Harris gewidmet, die sich bei der Wahl 2024 nicht durchsetzen konnte. Andere in *herchurch* verwendete Kunstwerke wie eine Figur, die an die kanaanitische Gottheit *Aschera* erinnert, berühren den Bereich paganer Ausdrucksformen, den ich im Folgenden behandeln möchte.

5. Christopagane Ausdrucksformen

Die Religionssoziologin Linda Woodhead rekapituliert in einem 1993 erschienenen Aufsatz feministische Formen neuer Spiritualität und stellt fest, dass diese häufig danach unterschieden würden, ob sie sich innerhalb der christlichen Tradition verorteten (»Christian feminist spirituality«) oder als »post-christlich« verstünden.[59] Sie kommt zu dem Schluss, dass der Unterschied zwischen reformorientierten, in der Kirche verorteten und post-christlichen Feminist_innen lediglich darin bestehe, inwieweit sie dafür offen seien, jüdische und christliche Traditionen, Schriften und Geschichten als fruchtbare Quelle ihrer Argumentation aufzunehmen.

Auch die Kulturanthropologin Victoria Hegner erklärt, dass im Zuge der zweiten Welle des Feminismus (sechziger bis achtziger Jahre des 20. Jahrhunderts) die Wahlverwandtschaft feministischer Theologie mit dem Neopaganismus entdeckt wurde, und beide bis zu einem bestimmten Punkt miteinander Synergien eingingen.[60] Auf die christopagane Praxis in *herchurch* bezogen stellt sich hier die Frage, inwieweit feministische Formen neuer Spiritualität christliche Palimpsestschichten produktiv rezipieren, transformieren oder recyceln.

58 Hieran zeigt sich auch, dass *herchurch* von der dritten Welle des Feminismus und queeren Ansichten beeinflusst ist.

59 Woodhead, Post-Christian Spiritualities.

60 Hegner, Hexen der Großstadt, 88.

Als revolutionären feministisch-theologischen Ansatz versteht die Religionswissenschaftlerin Mary Ann Beavis es, weibliche Sprache und Bilder des Göttlichen routinemäßig zu verwenden und teilweise Göttinnen nichtchristlicher Traditionen miteinzubeziehen, wie es auch Pastorin Boorn tut. Im Anschluss an ihre Kollegin und »Göttinnen-Forscherin« Johanna Stuckey[61] spricht Beavis von »paganem Christentum« bzw. »Christian Goddess Spirituality«.[62]

Einen Ursprung hat die christopagane Palimpsestschicht in *herchurch* in dem frühen Werk »Womanspirit Rising«, einem feministisch-theologischen Reader, in welchem schon 1979 die »essentielle Herausforderung« formuliert wurde, dass Theologie mit der Erfahrung von Frauen korrespondieren müsse.[63] Dort wird die These vertreten, dass alle Menschen Göttinnen anbeteten, bevor sie diese mit toxischen patriarchalen Palimpsestschichten überdeckten,[64] und dass Frauen Göttinnen aus psychologischen und politischen Gründen für ihre Emanzipation bräuchten.[65] Unter dem Stichwort »Thealogie« wurde der »Diskurs der Göttin« in der Theologiefachgeschichte verbreitet.[66]

Wenn sie auch von einem gänzlich anderen Standpunkt her argumentieren, so treffen sich doch die christlichen Verfasserinnen von »Womanspirit Rising« und die in der neopaganen Community des späten 20. Jahrhunderts populäre Hexe und Autorin *Starhawk* in der Idee der »Wiedergeburt der antiken Religion der großen Göttin«[67]. Es kommt nicht von ungefähr, dass aus *Ebenezer Lutheran Church* ausgerechnet in San Francisco, wo seit fünfzig Jahren eine umfangreiche spirituelle und neopagane Szene besteht, *herchurch* wurde.[68]

61 Johanna H. Stuckey, Women's Spirituality. Contemporary Feminist Approaches to Judaism, Christianity, Islam and Goddess Worship, Toronto 2010.

62 Mary Ann Beavis, Christian Goddess Spirituality. Enchanting Christianity, New York 2020.

63 Valerie Saving, The Human Situation. A Feminine View, in: Carol P. Christ/Judith Plaskow (Hg.), Womanspirit Rising. A Feminist Reader in Religion, San Francisco 2006, 25–42.

64 Stone, God was a Woman.

65 Carol P. Christ, Why Women Need the Goddess. Phenomenological, Psychological and Political Reflections, in: Dies./Judith Plaskow (Hg.), Womanspirit Rising, 273–287.

66 Melissa Raphael, Introducing Thealogy. Discourse on the Goddess, Sheffield 1999, 29–51.

67 Starhawk, The Spiral Dance. A Rebirth of the Ancient Religion of the Great Goddess, San Francisco 1979.

68 In jüngerer Zeit wird die These der »Resurrecting the Goddess« etwa in einem Online-Kurs wiederholt, der »feststellt, welchen Schaden das patriarchale Christentum angerichtet« hätte, und stattdessen dazu einlädt, das Konzept von *the Divine Feminine* kennenzulernen. Hier werden neopagane Vorstellungen von Muttergottheiten kreativ mit christlichen Gottesbildern verbunden – unter anderem wird Pastorin Stacy Boorn zu diesem Zweck interviewt, https://www.resurrectingthegoddess.com (19.3.2025).

Die Berufsausbildungen und Angebote der in *herchurch* Aktiven Stacy Boorn, Katie Ketchum, Jennifer Mantle und Christine Konkol tragen zu einem Palimpsest unterschiedlicher Strömungen von Christentum und Neuheidentum bei. Pastorin Mantle etwa hat einen Master-Abschluss in »Weiblicher Spiritualität« an der Sophia-Universität (San Francisco/Los Angeles), einer Einrichtung, die Robert Frager 1975 als erste Universität für transpersonale Psychologie gründete, und die unter anderem durch den Zen-Buddhismus und Sufismus beeinflusst ist.[69] Die *resident witch* Christine Konkol verteilt »magische Gaben« und hält Treffen ab, bei denen »Instinkt und Intuition helfen sollen, die Göttlichkeit der Natur und damit das Göttliche«[70] zu entdecken. Erwähnenswert ist auch eine von einem Gemeindemitglied hergestellte Puppe mit dem hawaiianischen Namen *I'Lana* (»verankern«), die aus einem tiefenpsychologischen Kunstprojekt hervorgegangen ist und in der Gemeinde zu verschiedenen Gelegenheiten Verwendung findet.[71] Sie repräsentiert gegenüber dem Archetyp der Jungfrau und der Mutter die weise alte Frau, eine dritte Form der Trinität weiblichen Lebens. Für die Feier des Wechsels von einer Form weiblichen Lebens in eine andere werden Übergangsrituale angeboten. Als Konsequenz des Angebotes von *herchurch* ist auch seine Klientel divers. Auf der Homepage wird verkündet, dass sowohl pagane, nicht-theistische, spirituell Suchende als auch lebenslange Lutheraner_innen unter den 115 Mitgliedern der Gemeinde sind.[72] Als einen Kulminationspunkt christopaganer Praxis in *herchurch* möchte ich im Folgenden das Göttinnen-Rosenkranzgebet analysieren, an welchem ich im November 2024 teilnehmen konnte.

6. *Sensational Forms*: Das Göttinnen-Rosenkranzgebet

Im Rekurs auf Benedict Andersons Konzept der *imagined communities* spricht die Religionswissenschaftlerin Birgit Meyer davon, dass sich vorgestellte Gemeinschaften dann real anfühlten, wenn sie sich in der gelebten Umgebung materialisierten und »in den Knochen wahrgenommen« würden.[73] Auch religiöses

69 https://www.sofia.edu/about-us (19.3.2025).
70 https://www.herchurch.org/priestexx (19.3.2025).
71 https://www.herchurch.org/about/ilana (19.3.2025).
72 https://www.herchurch.org/about/our-purpose (19.3.2025).
73 Meyer, Aesthetic Formations, 5.

Wissen bliebe bloße Repräsentation, solange es nicht ästhetisch erfahrbar gemacht würde.[74] Erst religiöse Performanz erzeuge das Gefühl von Zusammengehörigkeit und geteilter Sinnlichkeit. Ich möchte zeigen, inwiefern dies bei *herchurch* der Fall ist.

Nicht zufällig entwickelt Meyer ihre Theorie der *sensational form* in Anlehnung an Webers Idee vom »lustlosen Protestantismus«.[75] Während der traditionelle Protestantismus Körperlichkeit vernachlässige, rückt sie laut Meyer in anderen Konfessionen und Gemeinden, etwa in pfingstlerischen Kontexten, ins Zentrum. Auch das Göttinnen-Rosenkranz-Gebet lebt von einer erweiterten Performanz gegenüber dem bekannten Ritual. Auffällig ist die selbstverständliche Aneignung ritueller Formen aus anderen religiösen Traditionen: Römisch-katholisches Rosenkranzgebet, orthodoxe Ikonenmalerei, Klangschalen aus dem tibetischen Buddhismus und Symbole der griechischen Antike verschmelzen zu einer neuen, sinnlich aufgeladenen Liturgie.

Das Göttinnen-Rosenkranzgebet findet regelmäßig am ersten Donnerstagabend im Monat statt. Bis vor einiger Zeit wurde auf der Homepage der Gemeinde verkündet, dass dies ein günstiger Termin sei, sich selbst in hektischer Zeit zu fokussieren und es zuzulassen, dass »das Heilige einen umgibt und umarmt«[76]. Als ich am 7.11.2024 an dem Gebet teilnahm, war die Wiederwahl Donald Trumps gerade zwei Tage her. Es waren etwa zehn Personen anlässlich des Gebetes in das Sanktuarium der Kirche (*womb*) gekommen und verteilten sich in größerem Abstand in den Kirchenreihen.

Zentral für den Ablauf ist das materielle Ritualobjekt selbst: der *Goddess Rosary.* Anders als der katholische Rosenkranz, der meist aus standardisierten Perlen besteht, ist der *Goddess Rosary* ein individuelles Kunstwerk. Die Teilnehmer_innen erhalten diese Objekte vor Beginn des Gebetes oder bringen selbst gestaltete Exemplare mit. In der Berührung der Perlen beginnt das Ritual – das Durchgleiten wird zur leiblich-meditativen Technik. Nach Meyer sind es diese »materiellen Objektivationen«, die den Zugang zur Transzendenz nicht nur vermitteln, sondern hervorbringen.[77]

Es gibt vier Kategorien von Perlen im *Goddess Rosary*: Drei kleine Perlen, die für die Dreieinigkeit von Jungfrau, Mutter und alter Frau stehen, große Per-

74 Meyer, Aesthetic Formations, 7.
75 Meyer, Religious Sensations, 7–8.
76 Aldregde-Clanton, Changing Church, 21.
77 Meyer, Religious Sensations, 10.

len, die für *the Divine Feminine* stehen, mittelgroße Perlen, die die in *herchurch* entwickelte Variante des *Ave Maria* (*Hail Goddess*) hervorrufen, und einzelne kleine Perlen, bei denen einer der Namen der *Divine Feminine* (*Sophia*, *Shaddai*, *ah-she*) genannt werden soll. Während meines Besuches wurde die Liturgie mit einem *Our-Mother*-Gebet eingeleitet, welches bis zu einer Unterbrechung auf der Hälfte des Rosenkranzes noch zweimal auf je sieben Wiederholungen des *Hail Goddess* folgte. Dabei wurde das Gebet von Pastorin Boorn mit Gebärden untermauert, die jedoch nur bedingt von den Gemeindegliedern nachgeahmt wurden.

Nach Meyers Ansatz erzeugt die ständige Wiederholung anhand der Perlen des Rosenkranzes mithilfe einer Sakralisierung des Mediums das Gefühl, dem Transzendenten nahe zu sein. Die Teilnehmer_innen würden in eine kollektiv erzeugte Trancezone geraten, die das Heilige nicht nur beschreibt, sondern realisiert. Diese Art der Übertragung theologischer Inhalte ließ sich jedoch nur sehr bedingt beobachten. Ich erlebte die Performanz der einzelnen Gemeindeglieder eher als eine jeweils nach innen gerichtete. Dies änderte sich jedoch, als der Rosenkranz von Pastorin Boorn, wie zuvor angekündigt, auf der Hälfte unterbrochen wurde.

An dieser Stelle wurde Gelegenheit gegeben, vom räumlichen Angebot des »Mutterleibes« Gebrauch zu machen. In meiner Wahrnehmung wurden einige der Teilnehmenden erst in diesem Moment aktiv: Mehrere machten Gebrauch von dem zur Verfügung gestellten Öl, das zur Salbung und für »Heilungsgebete« verwendet wurde.[78] Auch tibetische Glocken und Klangschalen, die auf dem zentralen Altar platziert waren, fanden Verwendung. Sie sollten laut Homepage dazu dienen »die Stimme und Seele des *Holy Other*« im Gläubigen hervorzurufen.[79] Einzelne Personen entzündeten Kerzen, welche als »Lichter der Göttin im Leben und der Welt« und zur Erinnerung an Andere funktionierten.[80] Am interessantesten schien mir zu beobachten, dass eine Teilnehmerin speziell die über dem Seiteneingang angebrachte Ikone von Kamala Harris (die zwei Tage zuvor bei der Wahl unterlag) fokussierte und einen Räucherstab dreimal im Kreis schwenkte.

Nachdem die Gemeindeglieder ihre Aktivitäten während der Halbzeitpause des Rosenkranzes beendet hatten, wurde dieser in der genannten Form bis zum Ende fortgesetzt. Höhepunkt der Veranstaltung schien mir jedoch der anschlie-

78 https://www.herchurch.org/about/goddess-rosary (19.3.2025).
79 https://www.herchurch.org/about/goddess-rosary (19.3.2025).
80 https://www.herchurch.org/about/goddess-rosary (19.3.2025).

ßende Austausch in einem informellen Gespräch zu sein, welches sich um die individuelle und kollektive Gefühlslage im Anschluss an das Wahlergebnis drehte. Hier entstand ein Raum gemeinsamer Gefühle der Frustration und Enttäuschung. Einzelne Gemeindeglieder begannen zu weinen, andere drückten ihre Wut aus. Pastorin Boorn leitete alle dazu an, sich Erleichterung durch einen kollektiven Wutschrei zu verschaffen.

In dieser letzten und der mittleren Sequenz liegt meines Erachtens der Kern der sinnlichen Erfahrung von Gemeinschaft und Transzendenz im Sinne von Meyers *sensational forms*. Der *Goddess Rosary* ist mehr als ein Gebet – er ist ein Gesamtkunstwerk christopaganer Spiritualität. Kunstwerke, Musik, Farben und Gerüche, religiöse Performanz und gemeinschaftlicher Ausdruck innerer Gefühle verbinden sich zu einer sinnlich verdichteten Atmosphäre. Die Körper der Gläubigen werden, indem sie sakralisiert werden, in Verbindung mit dem Rosenkranz selbst zu jenem Medium, das Verbindung zum Transzendenten schafft.[81]

Der *Goddess Rosary* in *herchurch* stellt eine theologisch-rituelle Praxis dar, die das Göttlich-Weibliche nicht nur repräsentiert, sondern durch mediale, körperliche und emotionale Verfahren wirklich zu machen verspricht. Im Sinne Meyers ist er eine *sensational form par excellence*: ein kultisches Arrangement, das affektive Öffnungen zur Transzendenz schafft, Sakralität sinnlich materialisiert und kollektive Resonanz erzeugt. Dabei verschiebt er zugleich die religiöse Semantik des Christentums hin zu einer feministischen Spiritualität, die weibliche Körperlichkeit, Kreativität und Selbstreflexion als Quelle des Göttlichen affirmiert.

7. *herchurch* als Stein des Anstoßes

Es gibt natürlich auch Gegenstimmen, denen die Praxis von *herchurch* ein Dorn im Auge ist. Der Blogger Dan Skogen etwa betreibt eine Plattform, die sich ausschließlich zur Aufgabe gemacht hat, über die Häresien der liberalen Dachorganisation *ELCA* aufzuklären. *Exposing the ELCA* versteht sich auf einem »Kreuz-

81 Dabei traten während meines Besuches jene spezifisch weiblichen Elemente, die insbesondere Pastorin Mantle dem Rosenkranz attestiert, nicht in den Vordergrund. Nach ihrer Auffassung geht es beim Göttinnen-Rosenkranzgebet wesentlich um die »weiblichen Blutmysterien«, die als Menstruation, Geburt und Menopause definiert werden (Mantle, Circling the Goddess, 2–3).

zug, das Wort Gottes zu verteidigen«[82]. Auf dieser Webseite sind ca. 30 Artikel veröffentlicht, die verschiedene Praktiken in *herchurch* auf der Basis der eigenen orthodox-lutherischen Identität verurteilen. Besondere Verärgerung hatte 2010 ein Workshop hervorgerufen, bei dem Pastorin Boorn die Teilnehmer_innen dazu aufgefordert haben soll, aus Ton eine Statue der kanaanitischen Muttergottheit *Ascherah* zu formen. Unter Verweis auf Dt 12,3 wird diese Praxis von Seiten Skogens als Idolatrie bewertet und entsprechend verurteilt.[83]

Ein weiteres Beispiel ist ein Artikel im Blog *Unashamed of Jesus*,[84] in welchem die Praxis in *herchurch* als ein Beispiel »liberaler *churchianity*«, einer über das Maß gesteigerten Bezogenheit auf kirchliche Praxis einer bestimmten Gemeinde anstelle der allgemeinen Christenheit,[85] angeführt wird. Feminismus wird hier als im Satanismus begründete Praxis diffamiert[86] und der in *herchurch* angebetete »Dämon« *Sophia* in Christi Namen widerrufen.[87]

Die Dachorganisation *ELCA* toleriert die feministisch inspirierte, christopagane Praxis in *herchurch*. Dies mag einerseits an der Freiheit und finanziellen Unabhängigkeit einzelner Gemeinden gegenüber den religiösen Dachorganisationen liegen, die für die USA typisch sind. Sie kann aber auch im Rahmen einer Tendenz der Kirchenleitung in Chicago begriffen werden, das Verständnis, was in der Postmoderne unter einer »lutherischen Tradition« verstanden werden soll, zur Disposition zu stellen.[88]

Das Konzept des *Divine Feminine* ist sicherlich darauf ausgelegt, die als toxisch definierte Palimpsestschicht des *white savior* Jesus Christus zugunsten einer vermeintlich älteren Vorstellung göttlicher Weiblichkeit zu korrigieren. Das Verschmelzen beider Vorstellungen in der Figur von *Christ-Sophia*, wie sie unter anderem im Göttinnen-Rosenkranzgebet in Erscheinung tritt, zeigt jedoch, dass bestimmte Theologoumena nicht gänzlich überschrieben werden können, wenn man sich weiterhin im Kosmos der lutherischen *ELCA* bewegen und entsprechende Klientel anziehen möchte.

82 https://www.exposingtheelca.com (19.3.2025).
83 http://ichabodthegloryhasdeparted.blogspot.com/2010/11/notice-how-elca-treats-herchurch.html (19.3.2025).
84 https://unashamedofjesus.org/ (19.3.2025).
85 https://www.gotquestions.org/churchianity.html (19.3.2025).
86 https://www.youtube.com/watch?v=pbSA1ZqwK9U, 0:43–0:44 (19.3.2025).
87 https://www.youtube.com/watch?v=pbSA1ZqwK9U, 3:33–3:40 (19.3.2025).
88 Vgl. hierzu Russel E. Richey, Denominations, in: Philip Goff (Hg.), The Blackwell Companion to Religion in America, Malden 2010, 90–104.

Was die Befürwortung von queeren Themen in *herchurch* und die Frustration über die transfeindliche Politik der zweiten Trump-Administration anbelangt, so findet man sich in der *Sierra Pacific Synod* der *ELCA* mit dem ersten transidentifizierten Bischof in einträchtiger Gesellschaft. Einzelne Mitglieder benachbarter Gemeinden hatten in der Vergangenheit dennoch formale Beschwerden gegenüber der allzu liberalen Auslegung des Luthertums in *herchurch* beim zuständigen Regionalbischof eingelegt. Sie konnten aber lediglich eine Visitation erreichen. Diese stellte fest, dass *herchurch* sich an den Rändern des theologisch Zulässigen bewege, jedoch kein inhaltlicher Verstoß erkennbar sei, der ein Disziplinarverfahren rechtfertige.[89]

Eine schöne Zusammenfassung des feministisch-kritischen Ansatzes und Sinnbild der Palimpsestierung, also des Vermischens und der Priorisierung unterschiedlicher Schichten,[90] ist Boorns Aussage, dass das Evangelium und der Feminismus ein und dasselbe seien.[91] Im Sinne einer »liberating love«, für die die harmonisierende Figur von *Christ-Sophia* steht, ist keine Binnendifferenzierung der Palimpsestschichten nach übergeordnetem (*scriptio superior*) und untergeordnetem Text (*scriptio inferior*) notwendig.[92] Boorn schließt: »if this liberating love don't reach into all parts of our humanity, then we're missing the point. And that's part of my Lutheran tradition.«[93]

Im Sinne eines erweiterten Forschungsprogramms lädt *herchurch* dazu ein, lokale Netzwerke, milieuspezifische Anknüpfungspunkte, postkonfessionelle Aneignungen und die Entwicklung queerer Thealogien differenzierter zu untersuchen. Die Gemeinde steht exemplarisch für eine sich neuformierende, rituell wie ästhetisch experimentierfreudige spirituelle Landschaft, in der postmoderne Identitätskonzepte, feministische Kritik und sakrale Repräsentation ineinandergreifen. Gerade ihre Position an der Grenze zwischen institutioneller Bindung und spirituellem Experiment macht *herchurch* zu einem besonders aufschlussreichen Fall innerhalb der gegenwärtigen Debatte um die Zukunft progressiver religiöser Ausdrucksformen im westlichen Protestantismus.

89 Auch Pastorin Boorn stellt für sich selbst fest, dass sie für viele Lutheraner_innen nicht für höhere Ämter wählbar sei, weil sie »too out there« sei, was ihre Unterstützung für die feministische Sache anbelangt (Aldregde-Clanton, Changing Church, 21).

90 Malinowski u. a., Palimpsestierung.

91 Aldregde-Clanton, Changing Church, 21.

92 Malinowski u. a., Palimpsestierung, 202.

93 Interview mit Duffy-Burke, 15:17–15:50 (19.3.2025).

(Dr. Thorsten Wettich ist Wissenschaftlicher Mitarbeiter am Institut für Religionswissenschaft und Religionspädagogik an der Universität Bremen.)

ABSTRACT

This article explores *herchurch*, a Lutheran congregation in San Francisco, as a palimpsest of feminist, neopagan, and Christian-theological layers. Through aesthetic and liturgical innovations such as Goddess-inclusive language, iconography, and ritual practices like the Goddess Rosary, the church reinterprets and partly overwrites traditional Lutheran forms. Drawing on Birgit Meyer's concept of sensational forms, the study examines how embodied, artistic, and emotionally charged practices enable new experiences of *the Divine Feminine*. Theologically grounded in critiques of the *whitemalegod*, *herchurch* represents both continuity with and rupture from Christian traditions, making it a contested site of post-Christian spirituality, feminist reimagination, and theological experimentation within a liturgical framework. As such, it exemplifies how religious innovation can emerge through the creative negotiation of inherited forms, spiritual need, and socio-political critique.

Zwischen Tradition und Moderne

Die Textkultur orientalisch-orthodoxer Kirchen in Europa

Jan Gehm

Seit den 1970er Jahren sind Angehörige der orientalisch-orthodoxen Gemeinschaften[1] aus sozialen und wirtschaftlichen Gründen, aber auch wegen kriegerischer Auseinandersetzungen nach Europa migriert. Was mit einzelnen Menschen begonnen hat, hat sich zu großen etablierten Gemeinden entwickelt. Heute gibt es in ganz Europa verteilt Kirchengemeinden der Syrisch-Orthodoxen Kirche, der Koptischen Kirche, der Armenisch-Apostolischen Kirche, der Äthiopisch-Orthodoxen Kirche und der Eritreisch-Orthodoxen Kirche. Da die Zugehörigkeit zu Religionsgemeinschaften von den staatlichen Behörden nicht erfasst wird, gibt es nur Schätzungen zur Größe orientalisch-orthodoxer Gemeinschaften in Europa, die hauptsächlich auf den Selbstauskünften der Gemeinschaften beruhen. Man kann dementsprechend davon ausgehen, dass etwa zwei Millionen Gläubige der orientalisch-orthodoxen Kirchen in Europa leben.[2] Neben der Frage nach der Fortführung ihrer Tradition, die alle diese Gemeinschaften umtreibt, ist ein weiteres Schwerpunktthema die Verbreitung und Veröffentlichung von Texten. Diese Literatur beinhaltet sowohl religiöse Texte wie Liturgien, Gebets-

1 Der Begriff »orientalisch-orthodox« wird als Bezeichnung der Kirchenfamilie verwendet (Wolfgang Hage, Das orientalische Christentum, Stuttgart 2007, 129). Die Gemeinschaften selbst verwenden diese Bezeichnung häufig auch, oder sie bezeichnen sich nur als »orthodox«. Die Debatten rund um Orientalismus werden nicht weiter aufgegriffen, da es sich um eine kirchliche Zuordnung handelt, die nicht als Fremdbezeichnung oder Stigmatisierung dient.

2 Vgl. Heleen Murre van den Berg, Texts, Language, and Religion in the Making of Syriac Orthodox Communities in Europe, in: Birgit Meyer/Peter van der Veer (Hg.), Refugees and Religion, London 2021, 179–197, hier: 181.

bücher und Heiligengeschichten als auch weltliche Literatur wie Geschichtsbücher, Märchen und Bildungsmaterial. In diesem Artikel soll es darum gehen, wie sich diese schriftlichen Traditionen in den orientalisch-orthodoxen Gemeinschaften nach ihrer Migration nach Europa entwickelt haben und was sie über ihre jeweiligen Gemeinschaften aussagen. Die Ergebnisse basieren auf der Forschung des ERC-Projekts »Rewriting Global Orthodoxy. Oriental Christianity in Europe between 1970 and 2020« unter der Leitung von Heleen Murre-van den Berg (Nijmegen).[3] In diesem Projekt wurde die Vielfalt der Texte der orientalisch-orthodoxen Gemeinden und Kirchen in Europa durch ein interdisziplinäres Team aus drei Doktoranden und zwei Postdocs gesammelt, erfasst und analysiert.[4] Um die gesammelten Publikationen auch für die akademische Welt verfügbar zu machen, wurde zusätzlich eine digitale Datenbank durch das Projekt angelegt. Die Datenbank »Four Corners of the World Library« beinhaltet sämtliche Schriften, die das Projekt zusammengetragen hat, und kann für weitere Forschungszwecke genutzt werden.[5]

In einem ersten Schritt wird sich dem Thema Medien und Religion angenähert. Es sollen Ansätze des *material turn* und die Forschung des ERC-Projekts miteinander in Verbindung gebracht werden. Um sich dem Material der Texte zu widmen, ist es notwendig die Begrifflichkeiten und die Thematik der orientalisch-orthodoxen Gemeinschaften und der dazugehörigen Orthodoxie zu verorten und zu konkretisieren. Allgemein ist dieser Schritt wichtig, um eine begriffliche Eingrenzung vorzunehmen und sie dadurch deutlich von der weiter verbreiteten Forschung und Beschäftigung mit der östlichen Orthodoxie abzugrenzen.

3 https://www.ru.nl/en/research/research-projects/rewriting-global-orthodoxy (10.4.2025).

4 Der Autor dieses Artikels war als Doktorand Teil des ERC-Forschungsprojekts. Für das Projekt haben die Forschenden in unterschiedlichen europäischen Ländern Material gesammelt. Die geographischen Schwerpunkte lagen sowohl in Westeuropa, insbesondere in Frankreich, Großbritannien und den Niederlanden, als auch in Südeuropa, mit einem Fokus auf Spanien und Italien. Darüber hinaus wurden Materialien in Schweden und Deutschland gesammelt. Die Ergebnisse der Teilprojekte konnten mit anderen internationalen Forschungsnetzwerken ausgetauscht und evaluiert werden. Obwohl jede Forschung unterschiedliche Schwerpunkte hatte, arbeitete das Projektteam zusammen, um die Frage zu untersuchen, wie die Gemeinschaften sich in Europa etablieren konnten. Anhand ihrer Literatur war es möglich, verschiedene Aspekte der Integration dieser Gemeinschaften nachzuvollziehen.

5 Das ERC-Projekt »Rewriting Global Orthodoxy. Oriental Christanity in Europe between 1970 and 2020« unter der Leitung von Heleen Murre van den Berg mit Matija Milicic, Habtom Yohannes, Christopher Sheklian und Gaétan du Roy hat sich von 2020 bis 2024 diesem Thema gewidmet. Die Datenbank des Projektes https://fourcornersoftheworld.ptrs.ru.nl/ zeigt gesammeltes und erfasstes Material im Rahmen dieser Forschung.

Dazu werden unter anderem die geläufigen Bezeichnungen dieses Phänomens besprochen, und es wird in den gegenwärtigen Forschungsstand zu orientalisch-orthodoxen Kirchen eingeführt. Im Hauptteil sollen exemplarisch Publikationen der orientalisch-orthodoxen Gemeinschaften in Europa betrachtet werden unter der Fragestellung, welche Entwicklungen an ihnen sichtbar werden. Dazu werden Publikationen der Gemeinschaften aus verschiedenen europäischen Kontexten herangezogen und besprochen. Anhand dieser Beispiele soll veranschaulicht werden, welche Entwicklungen in den orientalisch-orthodoxen Gemeinschaften nach der Migration in Europa stattgefunden haben.

1. Medien und Religion

Zahlreiche wissenschaftliche Publikationen haben sich in der jüngeren Vergangenheit mit dem Zusammenhang von Medialität und Religion befasst. Neben den Kulturwissenschaften ist der *material turn* auch in den Religionswissenschaften stärker in die Forschung eingeflossen. Der Forschungsschwerpunkt des ERC-Projekts mit der Literatur orientalisch-orthodoxer Gemeinschaften spiegelt genau diesen Forschungstrend wider. Die Forschungen zu diesem Thema nehmen verschiedene Aspekte in den Blick. David Morgan hat sich in seiner Arbeit insbesondere mit der visuellen Kultur und Religion auseinandergesetzt. In seinem Werk »The Sacred Gaze. Religious Visual Culture«[6] beschreibt Morgan die religiöse Funktion von Bildern und die Werkzeuge, mit denen sie gedeutet werden können. Auch Manuel Vásquez setzt sich in seinem Buch »More than Belief. A Materialist Theory of Religion«[7] mit einem neuen Zugang zu Religion auseinander, indem er einen Schwerpunkt auf die materielle Perspektive legt. Für ihn sind der Körper, die Praxis und der Raum zentrale Dimensionen der religiösen Erfahrung und Performanz.

Eine weitere bekannte Vertreterin dieser Strömung ist die Religionswissenschaftlerin und Anthropologin Birgit Meyer. Sie legt in ihrem Ansatz den Schwerpunkt auf Medien und Religion. In ihrem Aufsatz »Religion as Mediation«[8] be-

6 David Morgan, The Sacred Gaze. Religious Visual Culture in Theory and Practice, Berkeley 2005.
7 Manuel Vásquez, More than Belief. A Materialist Theory of Religion, Oxford 2011.
8 Birgit Meyer, Religion as Mediation, in: Entangled Religions 11/3 (2020), Religion, Media, and Materiality, https://doi.org/10.13154/er.11.2020.8444.

tont sie die zentrale Rolle von Medien für religiöse Gemeinschaften. Sie argumentiert, dass Medien eine wesentliche Möglichkeit bieten, die Entwicklung dieser Gemeinschaften zu analysieren. Durch die Beschäftigung mit Konflikten über den Gebrauch von alten und neuen Medien lässt sich beispielsweise Neues über die Gemeinschaft erfahren. Meyer führt als Beispiel die Reformation an, welche die Ablehnung religiöser Bilder zugunsten der Bibellektüre betonte.[9] Laut Meyer hat zudem die Verfügbarkeit und Aushandlung von Medien einen erheblichen Einfluss auf den religiösen Wandel der Gemeinschaften. Gleichzeitig tragen diese Medien auch dazu bei, wie sich die jeweiligen Gruppen in der Gesellschaft ausgerichtet haben: »The availability and negotiation of media fuels processes of religious transformation, and shapes the ways in which religious groups are positioned in society.«[10] Die Grundannahme ist, dass durch materielle Ausdrucksformen der Religion, wie sie sich beispielsweise in Büchern, Broschüren oder Zeitschriften manifestieren, etwas Transzendentes im Immanenten Gestalt annimmt.[11] Die Materialität der Religion lässt sich also nicht auf ein bloßes Oberflächenphänomen reduzieren, sondern macht vielmehr sichtbar, wie das angenommene Transzendente im Immanenten materielle Form annimmt. Diese Medien bieten gleichzeitig einen Ort, um Aushandlungen von religiösen und säkularen Haltungen nachzuvollziehen. Mit dem Ansatz von Meyer eignen sich die Texte der orientalisch-orthodoxen Gemeinschaften in Europa in Form von Zeitschriften, Lehrbüchern, Geschichtsbüchern, Heiligengeschichten besonders als Forschungsgegenstand. Im Sinne des *material turn* sollen diese Texte durch die Arbeit zur Materialität in Religion als sozial eingebetteter, materiell vermittelter Praxis nicht nur eine systematische Erfassung und Analyse der von diesen Gemeinschaften über Jahrzehnte hervorgebrachten Schriften ermöglichen, sondern bieten darüber hinaus einen Einblick in die Aushandlungsprozesse und Dynamiken innerhalb der Gemeinschaften. Anhand dieser Texte lassen sich zudem weiterführende Rückschlüsse auf Integrationsprozesse sowie auf die Entwicklungen der orientalisch-orthodoxen Gemeinschaften nach ihrer Migration nach Europa ziehen.

9 Meyer, Mediation, 5.
10 Vgl. Meyer, Mediation, 6.
11 Vgl. Meyer, Mediation, 28.

2. Orientalische Orthodoxie

Orientalisch-orthodoxe Kirchen und ihre Gemeinschaften werden heute häufig im kirchenhistorischen Kontext betrachtet, insbesondere im Zusammenhang mit ihrer Ablehnung des Konzils von Chalcedon (451). Die Kernländer dieser Kirchenfamilie liegen im Nahen Osten und in Nordafrika. Die alten Bischofssitze in Antiochia (heute das türkische Antakya), Alexandria in Ägypten sowie in Armenien und Äthiopien beherbergen die orientalisch-orthodoxen Christentümer dieser Tradition. In der Kirchengeschichte und Konfessionskunde spricht man aufgrund der Ablehnung der Zwei-Naturen-Lehre (Dyophysitismus) des Konzils von Chalcedon bei diesen Kirchen von der nichtchalcedonensischen oder auch der vorchalcedonischen Orthodoxie.[12] Theologisch spricht man, entgegengesetzt zum vom Konzil von Chalcedon vertretenen Dyophysitismus, auch von der Strömung des Miaphysitismus, also der Lehre von der einen Natur Christi. Während ein starker Fokus dieser Glaubenstradition auf der Liturgie und der Frömmigkeit liegt, haben alle diese Traditionen auch ihre eigenen Sprachen, in denen sie ihre Gottesdienste feiern und ihre Geschichtsschreibung tradieren. Die koptischen Gläubigen sprechen viel Arabisch in ihren Kirchen, mit Anteilen von Koptisch. Die syrisch-orthodoxe Gemeinschaft hält ihre syrische Sprache in der Liturgie besonders hoch, die mit der Sprache Jesu in Verbindung gebracht wird. Aber auch armenische orthodoxe Christinnen und Christen verwenden ihr Altarmenisch im kirchlichen Raum, und die äthiopische Kirche verwendet ihre Kirchensprache Geez. Diese Sprachen sind trotz wechselvoller Geschichte der Region, besonders unter Einfluss der arabischen Eroberung und der arabischen Sprache, im kirchlichen Kontext bis heute ganz oder teilweise erhalten geblieben. Sie bilden einen wesentlichen Bestandteil der Identität dieser Gemeinschaften.[13]

Anders als die östliche Orthodoxie bzw. Ostkirchen des byzantinischen Ritus, die ein bekanntes Thema in der europäischen Wissenschafts- und Religionsgeschichte sind, ist das Phänomen der Orientalischen Orthodoxie in Europa in der

12 Vgl. https://www.pro-oriente.at/ostkirchen/orientalisch-orthodoxe-kirchen-einleitung (15.5.2025).

13 Vgl. Bert Groen, Orthodox Liturgy in the West. Identity Preservation and Acculturation, in: Herman Teule/Joseph Verheyden (Hg.), Eastern and Oriental Christianity in the Diaspora, Leuven 2020, 1–32, hier: 8.

Forschung bislang eher vernachlässigt.[14] In der jüngeren Forschung wird jedoch zunehmend der Begriff »Orientalische Orthodoxie« verwendet, um über diesen Zweig des Christentums zu sprechen.[15] Damit grenzt man sich neben den theologischen Traditionen auch begrifflich von der östlichen Orthodoxie ab. Im Zusammenhang mit dem Orientalischen Christentum werden jedoch auch oft Bezeichnungen wie »Kirchen des Orients«[16], »Oriens Christianus«[17], »altorientalische Kirchen«[18], »Das Christentum in Afrika und dem Nahen Osten«[19], »Christen in der islamischen Welt«[20] oder »Die Kirchen des christlichen Ostens«[21] verwendet. In dieser Arbeit verwende ich die Bezeichnung »orientalisch-orthodox« bzw. den Sammelbegriff »Orientalisches Christentum«, da diese die Kirchentradition umfasst und die Bezeichnung auch von den Gemeinschaften selbst als Selbstbe-

14 Vgl. Dyron B. Daughrity, Ignoring the East. Correcting a Serious Flaw in World Christianity Scholarship, in: Afe Adogame (Hg.), Religion on the Move! New Dynamics of Religious Expansion in a Globalizing World, Leiden 2013, 41–59. Wolfgang Hages Überblickswerk *Das Orientalische Christentum* (2007) ist das Grundlagenwerk für das Thema und die verschiedenen Kirchen. Aber auch Forschungen zur jüngeren Vergangenheit und der Missionsgeschichte befassen sich mit der Orientalischen Orthodoxie, wie die Arbeit des französischen Historikers Bernard Heyberger mit seiner Forschung zum Orientalischen Christentum im 17. und 18. Jahrhundert und dem Einfluss der katholischen Reformbewegung in Europa (Bernard Heyberger, Les chrétiens du Proche-Orient au temps de la réforme catholique, Paris 1994). Die Forschung der ev. Theologin Maibritt Gustrau hingegen befasst sich mit dem Orientalischen Christentum in Reiseberichten deutscher Theologen (Maibritt Gustrau, Orientalen oder Christen? Orientalisches Christentum in Reiseberichten deutscher Theologen, Göttingen 2016). Diese punktuellen Forschungsbeiträge zeigen, wie nachlässig sich bisher dem Thema gewidmet worden ist. Wissenschaftlich wurde sich mit dem Thema hauptsächlich in Disziplinen der Theologie wie der Ostkirchenkunde, dem Christlichen Orient oder auch der Philologie beschäftigt. In der Gegenwart zeigen sich jedoch auch Tendenzen, dass das Thema über diese klassischen Disziplinen hinaus größere Beachtung gewinnt. So findet sich das Thema in der neueren Forschung in verschiedenen Bereichen wie der Anthropologie, Soziologie, Psychologie, Religionswissenschaft und Migrationsforschung.

15 Hage, Das orientalische Christentum; Martin Tamcke/Egbert Schlarb, Überleben, Pilgern, Begegnen im orientalischen Christentum, Wiesbaden 2020; Maria Hämmerli/Jean-François Mayer, Orthodox Identities in Western Europe. Migration, Settlement and Innovation, London 2014.

16 Hage, Das orientalische Christentum.

17 Sabine Gralla (Hg.), Oriens christianus. Geschichte und Gegenwart des nahöstlichen Christentums, Münster u. a. 2003.

18 Christian Lange/Karl Pinggéra (Hg.), Die altorientalischen Kirchen. Glaube und Geschichte, Darmstadt 2010.

19 Klaus Hock, Das Christentum in Afrika und dem Nahen Osten, Leipzig 2005.

20 Martin Tamcke, Christen in der islamischen Welt. Von Mohammed bis zur Gegenwart, München 2008.

21 Johannes Oeldemann, Die Kirchen des christlichen Ostens. Orthodoxe, orientalische und mit Rom unierte Kirchen, Kevelaer 2016.

zeichnung akzeptiert und verwendet wird.[22] Forschungen zur »klassischen« Orthodoxie mit den östlich-orthodoxen Kirchen, der byzantinischen oder russisch-orthodoxen Tradition oder auch der Kontakt zwischen Europa und dem orthodoxen Osten sind keine Seltenheit. Beispielsweise beschäftigt sich Sebastian Rimestad in seinem Buch »Orthodox Christian Identity in Western Europe« mit Aspekten orthodoxer Identität in Europa.[23] Rimestad untersucht dazu Fallstudien wie zur Orthodoxie in Norwegen, aber beleuchtet auch orthodoxe Kirchenstrukturen in Schweden, Frankreich und Deutschland. Daneben gibt es Forschungen, die sich mit globaleren Themen wie der Globalisierung beschäftigen, und welche Auswirkungen sie auf die Orthodoxie hat. Ein Beispiel ist die Forschung von Victor Roudometof, der sich in seinem Buch »Globalization and Orthodox Christianity« mit der Orthodoxie unter dem Einfluss einer globalisierten Welt beschäftigt.[24]

3. Mündliche Tradition und Schriftlichkeit

Eine Gemeinsamkeit, die alle orientalisch-orthodoxen Gemeinschaften in ihren verschiedenen Herkunftsregionen teilen, sind mündliche Überlieferungen, die von Generation zu Generation weitergegeben werden. In der Liturgie und im Kirchenkalender gehören die Heiligen und kirchlichen Feiertage zum Alltag. Geschichte und Religion finden auch in den Kirchen ihren Raum, indem beispielsweise der Verfolgungen in Vergangenheit und Gegenwart gedacht oder lokale Anlässe begangen werden. Außerhalb des kirchlichen Raums werden die Geschichten von Heiligen, Märchen und Volksweisheiten mündlich von den Eltern an ihre Kinder weitergegeben. Darüber hinaus kommt in allen Gemeinschaften den Kirchen und Klöstern eine große Bedeutung als Orte der Bewahrung von Schriften wie Gebeten, Liturgien und Heiligengeschichten zu. Diese Orte dienen

22 Es kommt auch vor, dass sich die Angehörigen der Gemeinschaften nur als orthodox bezeichnen, ohne zwischen orientalisch-orthodox und der anderen Orthodoxie zu unterscheiden.

23 Sebastian Rimestad, Orthodox Christian Identity in Western Europe. Contesting Religious Authority, London 2020.

24 Victor Roudometof, Globalization and Orthodox Christianity. The Transformations of a Religious Tradition, New York 2014.

jedoch nicht nur als geistliche Stätten, sondern bieten seit jeher auch Raum für religiöse Unterweisung und Sprachunterricht.

Die Bildung in diesen Gemeinschaften war in der Vergangenheit unterschiedlich organisiert. In Ägypten war es insbesondere die Sonntagschulbewegung unter Habib Girgis, die ab 1918 zur Förderung der Bildung koptischer Jugendlicher innerhalb der Kirche beitrug.[25] Als Gegenbewegung zur protestantischen Mission sollte diese Bewegung die Erneuerung der Kirche vorantreiben. Auch in der Syrisch-Orthodoxen Kirche spielten die Madrashto (Kirchenschule) in der Türkei und im Irak eine zentrale Rolle für die religiöse und sprachliche Bildung im Leben der Gläubigen. In der Äthiopisch-Orthodoxen Kirche existiert ebenfalls ein traditionelles Bildungssystem, das aus einem gegliederten Schulsystem besteht. Hier fand das Lernen von Psalmen, Gesang, Literatur und religiösen Praktiken statt.[26] Die Kirche ist nicht nur Ort der Gemeinschaft der Gläubigen und der Feier der Liturgie, sondern auch der zentrale Ort für die Vermittlung von Bildung in diesen Gemeinschaften.

In allen orientalisch-orthodoxen Gemeinschaften sind handgeschriebene Manuskripte weit verbreitet. Der Buchdruck mithilfe professioneller Druckerpressen begann unter dem Einfluss katholischer und protestantischer Mission im 18. und 19. Jahrhundert. Eine der ersten arabischen Druckerpressen wurde bereits 1706 unter katholischem Einfluss von der melkitisch griechisch-katholischen Kirche in Aleppo eingerichtet.[27] In Ägypten wurden unter der Führung des koptischen Patriarchen Cyril IV., der 1854 ins Amt kam, durch den anglikanischen Missionar John Lieder Reformen in der Kirche angestoßen, die unter anderem auch zur Beschaffung einer Druckerpresse aus Österreich führten.[28] Das Syrisch-Orthodoxe Patriarchat erhielt seine erste Druckerpresse 1881 durch Unterstützung des Erzbi-

25 Vgl. Wolfram Reis, Erneuerung in der Koptisch-Orthodoxen Kirche. Die Geschichte der koptisch-orthodoxen Sonntagsschulbewegung und die Aufnahme ihrer Reformansätze in den Erneuerungsbewegungen der Koptisch-Orthodoxen Kirche der Gegenwart, Hamburg 1998.

26 Mehari Worku/Wendy Laura Belcher, Ethiopian Orthodox Church Educational System, https://pemm.princeton.edu/en-us/research/research-and-lessons/24 (2.5.2025).

27 Vgl. Bruce Masters, Aleppo. The Ottoman Empire's Caravan City, in: Edhem Eldem u. a. (Hg.), The Ottoman City Between East and West. Aleppo, Izmir, and Istanbul, Cambridge 1999, 56.

28 Vgl. Eleanor H. Tejirian/Reeva Spector Simon (Hg.), Conflict, Conquest, and Conversion. Two Thousand Years of Christian Missions in the Middle East, New York 2012, 149.

schofs von Canterbury und des anglikanischen Priesters Canon Liddon.[29] Die Beschaffung von Druckerpressen erleichterte die Vervielfältigung von schriftlichem Material der orientalisch-orthodoxen Gemeinschaften erheblich. Im Rahmen westlicher Missionsaktivitäten wurden neue Textformate wie Katechismen oder Lehrbücher eingeführt, die allerdings meist auf den kirchlichen und schulischen Bereich beschränkt blieben.[30] Im Zuge der Migration in den 1960er und 1970er Jahren fanden viele Gläubige der orientalisch-orthodoxen Gemeinschaften in Europa eine neue Heimat oder verstanden sich als Diaspora ihrer Kirche. Der Verlust der angestammten Heimat und der vertrauten kirchlichen Räume wurde von den Gemeinden teilweise durch den Bau neuer Gotteshäuser und Klöster in Europa kompensiert. Man widmete Kirchen den Heiligen der eigenen kirchlichen Tradition und kaufte ehemalige katholische Klöster auf, um sie zu Zentren der Kirche in Europa zu machen. Mit der Migration kamen jedoch nicht nur die Menschen und ihre jeweiligen Lebensgeschichten nach Europa, auch die Produktion und Verbreitung von Texten innerhalb dieser Gemeinschaften erlebte einen erheblichen Aufschwung.[31] In den Herkunftsländern war eine umfangreiche Publikationstätigkeit oftmals aus politischen, sozialen oder ökonomischen Gründen nicht möglich gewesen. Hinzu kam, dass die traditionelle handschriftliche Vervielfältigung sowie die Nutzung von Manuskripten und – vereinzelt – von gedruckten Materialien im kirchlichen Kontext bislang keine dringende Notwendigkeit zur Entwicklung einer breiten Textkultur entstehen ließ. Auch das Fehlen der technischen Ausstattungen war dabei ein Faktor. Zwar gewannen die Produktion und Verbreitung von Texten mit dem verstärkten Wirken katholischer und protestantischer Missionare im Nahen Osten an Bedeutung, insgesamt blieb diese jedoch marginal.

29 Vgl. Ahmet Taşğın/Robert Langer, The Establishment of the Syrian Orthodox Patriarchate Press, in: Geoffrey Roper (Hg.), Historical Aspects of Printing and Publishing in Languages of the Middle East. Papers from the Third Symposium on the History of Printing and Publishing in the Languages and Countries of the Middle East, University of Leipzig, September 2008, Leiden/Boston 2014, 181–192, hier: 185.

30 Ein Beispiel für die Erweiterung des traditionellen Textkorpus ist der Druck von Grammatikbüchern und Katechismen wie Yulfono Mshihoyo im Jahr 1888 im syrisch-orthodoxen Safrankloster (Deir ul-Zafaran) bei Mardin, dazu vgl. Taşğın/Langer, Patriarchate Press, 188.

31 Das sind die Ergebnisse des ERC-Projekts »Rewriting Global Orthodoxy«.

4. Das Aufblühen einer orientalisch-orthodoxen Textkultur

Neben der Suche nach neuen Gebäuden und Räumlichkeiten für religiöse und soziale Veranstaltungen war schriftliches Material nötig, um das gemeinschaftliche Leben fortzusetzen. In der Anfangszeit brachten die Priester nur in geringem Umfang liturgische Bücher mit nach Europa, um Gottesdienste für die ersten neu entstandenen Gemeinden feiern zu können.[32] Diese Priester besuchten die aus den Dörfern und Städten migrierten Menschen in Europa gelegentlich, um Sakramente zu stiften oder auch Liturgien zu feiern. Durch diese Liturgie-, aber auch Gebetsbücher, die häufig mit der Hand geschrieben wurden, war es möglich, den Bedarf an schriftlichem Material für das kirchliche Leben teilweise abzudecken. Nachdem sich einzelne Angehörige der Gemeinschaft nach Europa aufgemacht hatten und auch später ihre Familien nachgezogen waren, schickte die Mutterkirche gezielt Priester, um die geistliche Versorgung der Gemeinschaft außerhalb der Heimatländer zu gewährleisten.

Mit der Errichtung von kirchlichen Strukturen in Europa haben die orientalisch-orthodoxen Kirchenleitungen die veränderte Situation anerkannt, dass ihre Gläubigen nicht nur zeitlich begrenzt die Länder verlassen, sondern ihren Lebensmittelpunkt permanent nach Europa verlagert hatten. Für die geistliche Versorgung des in Europa neu gewachsenen Kirchenlebens reichten die Kirchenbücher aus der alten Heimat nicht mehr aus. Die Migration stellte die Gemeinschaften vor neue Herausforderungen, wie etwa die Organisation der Bildung der Jugend in einem fremden Umfeld. Aus diesem Grund brauchte man neben den klassischen Texten für die Gottesdienste auch Unterrichtsmaterial, um die Sprache und Religion zu unterrichten. Hinzu kamen Texte, die über die Geschichte und Tradition der Gemeinschaften informierten und sich auch an Außenstehende der Gemeinschaft richteten. Neben gedruckten Büchern entstanden auch weitere Formen wie Zeitschriften, die bereits in den Ursprungsländern existierten. Eine bekannte Zeitschrift der Syrisch-Orthodoxen Diözese in Mitteleuropa war *Kolo Suryoye* (Die syrische Stimme), die von 1978 bis 2005 in den Niederlanden herausgebracht wurde und die ganze Diözese mit Informationen über die Kirche in

32 Als Beispiel für diese Mitnahme von Büchern wird über die Syrisch-Orthodoxe Kirche in Schweden berichtet in: Gabriel Bar-Sawme, Den syrisk-ortodoxa liturgin i Sverige Om migration och liturgisk förändring [The Syrian Orthodox Liturgy in Sweden. On Migration and Liturgical Change], in: Gudstjänstens mening 94 (2019), 13–25, hier: 16.

Mitteleuropa versorgte.[33] Sie stellte ein wichtiges Medium der Kommunikation zwischen Kirche und Gläubigen dar: Sie diente zum einen dazu, die zerstreute Gemeinschaft innerhalb des neuen Kontextes in Verbindung zu halten, zum anderen sollte die Verbindung zwischen den migrierten Gläubigen in Europa und den Zurückgebliebenen in den Herkunftsländern gewahrt bleiben.[34] So wurde neben der traditionellen Autorenschaft aus den kirchlichen Kreisen damit begonnen, dass Einzelpersonen mit oder ohne Kirchenfunktion neue Textformate kreierten und veröffentlichten. In der Anfangsphase der Gemeinden finden sich häufig Transliterationen – also Texte, bei denen die ursprüngliche Sprache zusätzlich in lateinischer Umschrift wiedergegeben wird, um das Lesen und die Aussprache zu erleichtern. Kennzeichnend für die Anfangszeit sind auch die vorwiegend muttersprachlichen Schriften. Häufig bestand das Problem in den Gemeinschaften, dass die Mitglieder weder ihre Kirchensprachen noch ihre Muttersprachen richtig lesen und verstehen konnten. Stattdessen waren die Priester und Mönche in den Herkunftsländern der primäre Ansprechpartner für religiöse Fragen und die Sprache. Auch im Alltag zeigten sich Schwierigkeiten: Zunächst mussten die Menschen die Sprachen in den jeweiligen Ländern lernen, aber auch ihren eigenen Lebensunterhalt sichern. Somit war neben der gesellschaftlichen Integration auch die Vereinbarung von religiösem Leben und der neuen Realität in Europa eine Herausforderung. Neben dem Aufbau der kirchlichen Strukturen etablierten sich auch kirchennahe und säkulare Organisationen der Gemeinschaften, die die Mitglieder organisierten; in diesem Zusammenhang brachten sie auch Publikationen heraus, die eine ethnische oder auch nationale Identität bekräftigten.[35]

33 https://fourcornersoftheworld.ptrs.ru.nl/publication/1302/public/ (16.6.2025).
34 Unveröffentlichte Ergebnisse in der Dissertation von Jan Gehm.
35 In der syrisch-orthodoxen Gemeinschaft ist dieses Phänomen besonders ausgeprägt. Neben kirchlichen Strukturen haben sich auch politische und national ausgerichtete Vereine und Organisationen gegründet. Deren Sprachrohr waren oft Zeitschriften, die ihre Ideen in die Gemeinschaft trugen. Einige dieser Organisationen standen der Kirche nahe, andere hingegen waren sehr kirchenkritisch.

5. Fortschreibung der Literatur orientalisch-orthodoxer Gemeinschaften in Europa

Mit den klassischen Formaten der religiösen Literatur im kirchlichen Gebrauch waren es Unterrichtsmaterialien zum Erlernen der Sprachen der Gemeinschaften und der kirchlichen Tradition, die bis heute eine wichtige Rolle in den Gemeinschaften spielen. In der Arbeit des ERC-Projektes wurde deutlich, dass es sich bei dem erfassten Material nicht nur um Reproduktionen von traditionellem Material handelt, sondern auch häufig um Weiterentwicklungen von Inhalten in neuen Formaten. So entstanden unter anderem Bücher zur Geschichte oder über die Herkunftsregionen einzelner Gemeinschaften, die nicht nur die Bedeutung der eigenen Konfession betonen, sondern auch die Erinnerung an die alte Heimat verschriftlichen. Sie wenden sich an die Leserschaft derjenigen, die bereits außerhalb der historischen Kernregionen ihrer Kirchen geboren wurden.

Aber auch die Entwicklung von mehrsprachigen Formaten und Zeitschriften knüpfte an die veränderte Situation in Europa an. Durch Kettenmigration und die Familien- und Clanstrukturen waren die Angehörigen der Gemeinschaften häufig in ähnlichen Gegenden angesiedelt, wenn auch teilweise nicht mehr miteinander verbunden. Während syrisch-orthodoxe Christinnen und Christen sich in den Niederlanden, Deutschland und Schweden niedergelassen hatten, sind koptische Gemeinschaften besonders in Großbritannien und Frankreich beheimatet.[36] Äthiopische Gläubige verteilen sich größtenteils auf Großbritannien, Deutschland und die Niederlande. Die armenische Kirche ist besonders durch ihre Gläubigen in Frankreich vertreten, wenngleich auch in Großbritannien und Deutschland größere Gemeinschaften zu finden sind. Diese Verteilung und die jeweiligen nationalen Kontexte haben die Entwicklung von kirchlichen und weltlichen Zeitschriften vorangetrieben, die in Europa entwickelt wurden und auch oft mehrsprachig erschienen sind.

Im Folgenden werden die Weiterentwicklungen der textuellen Kultur unter orientalisch-orthodoxen Gemeinschaften in Europa nachgezeichnet und anhand ausgewählter Fallbeispiele veranschaulicht. Die ausgewählten Beispiele sollen sowohl verschiedene Textformate als auch verschiedene Kontexte, in denen sie

36 Matija Milicic, Coptic Orthodox Communities in Europe. An Overlooked Diaspora, https://egyptmigrations.com/2021/07/09/coptic-orthodox-communities-in-europe-an-overlooked-diaspora/ (10.5.2025).

entstanden sind, darstellen. Es werden dabei auch Beispiele von verschiedenen orientalisch-orthodoxen Gemeinschaften ausgewählt, um der Vielfalt der Gemeinschaften gerecht zu werden. Dabei liegt der Fokus sowohl auf den Entstehungsbedingungen der jeweiligen Publikationen als auch auf deren Ausrichtung.[37]

5.1 Das Magazin *Al-Tariq/De Weg* der koptischen Kirche in den Niederlanden und Belgien

Ein Publikationsbeispiel für die Mehrsprachigkeit der orientalischen Orthodoxie in Europa ist das zweisprachige Magazin der koptischen Kirche in den Niederlanden und Belgien *al-Tariq/De Weg.*[38] Der arabische und niederländische Titel bedeutet »der Weg«. Der Titel ist an die Stelle aus Joh 14,3 (»Ich bin der Weg, die Wahrheit und das Leben«) angelehnt. Seit der Gründung der koptischen Gemeinschaft in den Niederlanden im Jahr 1985 erscheint das Magazin in Arabisch und Niederländisch.[39] Bis heute existiert dieses Magazin sowohl als Printversion als auch digital und wird auch auf der Facebookseite der koptischen Kirche bereitgestellt. Die Zeitschrift wird Mitgliedern der Gemeinschaft kostenlos nach Hause geschickt. Bis 2024 sind um die 180 Ausgaben von *al-Tariq* erschienen.[40] Der Bischof der niederländischen-koptischen Kirche ist der Herausgeber des Magazins und verfasst das Vorwort. Meist behandelt er dabei geistliche oder soziale Themen, wie christliche Werte, die Familie, zwischenmenschliche Beziehungen und die richtige Durchführung von religiösen Festen. Inhaltlich deckt das Magazin sowohl geistliche, hauptsächlich von Priestern verfasste Beiträge ab als auch solche von Laien mit koptischem als auch nicht-koptischem Hintergrund. Diese Beiträge sind meist von innerhalb und außerhalb der Niederlande lokalisierten Expertinnen und Experten in einem Gebiet verfasst oder auch von promovierten Hochschulabsolventen. Thematisch variieren die Beiträge sehr und umschließen

37 Die hier aufgeführten Beispiele wurden von Mitgliedern der ERC-Forschungsgruppe bereits umfassend analysiert. An dieser Stelle dienen sie exemplarisch der Veranschaulichung für die vorliegende Untersuchung.

38 https://fourcornersoftheworld.ptrs.ru.nl/publication/294/public/ (15.5.2025).

39 Die folgenden Angaben zum Magazin *al-Tariq/De Weg* stammen aus den Forschungsergebnissen von Matija Milici und seiner Dissertation: Matija Milici, Boundary-Making, Belonging, and Continuity. The Rewriting of Coptic Orthodox Communities in Europe, Nijmegen 2025, 190–201.

40 Milici, Boundary-Making, 191.

Bereiche wie Geschichte, Theologie, Spiritualität, Heiligengeschichten, beinhalten aber auch Bildungstexte sowie Texte zu sozialen und familiären Angelegenheiten. Das Magazin *Al-Tariq* ist nicht nur ein Kommunikationsmedium, um über Neuigkeiten in der Diözese zu berichten, sondern reagiert auch auf die veränderte Lebenswirklichkeit der koptischen Gemeinschaft in den Niederlanden. Indem die traditionelle religiöse Lehre auf die gesellschaftliche Wirklichkeit angewendet wird, entstehen neue Texte, die auf die europäische Situation reagieren. Die koptische Kirchenleitung will dadurch nicht nur die Wissensvermittlung von theologischer Bildung und Kirchengeschichte sicherstellen, sondern versucht auch, die richtige Durchführung religiöser Praktiken und ihre moralischen Standpunkte und Weltsichten unter ihren Gläubigen zu verbreiten.[41] Somit dient das Magazin als Medium, um die Integration der Gemeinschaft unter Leitung der Kirche in der Gesellschaft sicherzustellen. Gleichzeitig soll damit auch der Kontakt zu den Gläubigen gehalten und der Traditionsabbruch in der westlichen Gesellschaft verhindert werden. Die Materialität des Magazins in den gedruckten und digitalen Formen spiegeln diese Aushandlungen in der neuen gesellschaftlichen Realität wider und schaffen gleichzeitig eine Normativität für die Gläubigen.

5.2 Die Schrift *Zeugen Jehovas und ihre Irrlehren* von Papst Schenuda III. in Schweden

Die seit den 1970er Jahren etablierte Syrisch-Orthodoxe Kirche in Schweden zählt heute als größte Migrationskirche im Land, und auch global hat die Kirche dort eine der größten Diasporagruppen.[42] Neben der Konsolidierung der eigenen Gemeinden hatten orientalisch-orthodoxe Gemeinschaften in Europa immer wieder mit Anfechtungen auch von außen zu kämpfen. Die Bewegung der Zeugen Jehovas wurde in den Gemeinschaften als eine Gefahr für die eigene Kirche gesehen, weil sie aktiv öffentlich missionierten. Als Reaktion auf die Aktivität und Missionstätigkeit von Zeugen Jehovas in Schweden veröffentlichte 1996 eine syrisch-orthodoxe Studiengruppe der Gemeinde in Södertälje (in der Nähe von Stockholm) einen Text des koptischen Papstes Schenuda III. (1923–2012).[43] Um ihre

41 Vgl. Milici, Boundary-Making, 193.
42 Magdalena Nordin, Family and the Transmission of Traditions in the Syriac Orthodox Church in Sweden, in: Nordic Journal of Religion and Society 36/1 (2023), 19–32, hier: 21.
43 Diese Ergebnisse basieren auf unveröffentlichtem Material aus der Feldforschung von Jan Gehm.

Mitglieder vor der Gruppe zu warnen, bildete sich eine Aktionsgruppe. Einen Teil dieser Aufklärungsarbeit bildete die Veröffentlichung der Schrift einer koptischen Autorität. Die syrisch-orthodoxe Gemeinde in Södertälje brachte den fünfunddreißigseitigen Text des koptischen Papstes, »Jehovah's Witnesses and their Heresy. A Collection of Articles«[44], der bereits seit 1993 auf Englisch existierte, auf Schwedisch heraus.[45] Um diese Schrift auf die Situation der syrisch-orthodoxen Gemeinschaft anzuwenden, beauftragte die Studiengruppe einen schwedischen Übersetzer, der die schwedische Publikation ermöglichte. Schließlich wurde die betreffende Veröffentlichung als Instrument im Diskurs gegen die Bewegung der Zeugen Jehovas verwendet. Die Besonderheit dieser Publikation besteht darin, dass es sich hierbei ursprünglich um einen koptischen Text einer koptischen religiösen Autorität handelt, der später in den syrisch-orthodoxen Kontext übernommen und dort weiterverwendet wurde. Damit erfährt der Text einen interkonfessionellen Gebrauch und zeugt von der wechselseitigen Rezeption religiöser Traditionen über Konfessionsgrenzen hinweg: Schließlich kann angenommen werden, dass die syrisch-orthodoxe Gemeinschaft in Schweden entweder über ihre transnationalen Netzwerke Kenntnis von der Schrift des koptischen Papstes über die Zeugen Jehovas erlangte oder durch Kontakte zu lokal ansässigen koptischen Gläubigen in Schweden in den Besitz dieses Textes gelangte. Ungeachtet der genauen Übertragungswege stellt die Publikation ein Beispiel für eine Reaktion der syrisch-orthodoxen Gemeinde in Schweden auf eine äußere Bedrohung dar, wobei bereits vorhandenes Material angepasst und für die eigenen Zwecke verwendet wird. Damit wird zugleich ein gemeinsames Verständnis innerhalb der orientalisch-orthodoxen Kirchen demonstriert, das es ermöglicht, Autoritäten und Stellungnahmen aus jeweils anderen kirchlichen Traditionen trotz Unterschieden zu übernehmen und einzusetzen. Auch sieht man an dem Beispiel deutlich, dass ein Text als effektives und passendes Mittel angesehen wird, um der Bewegung der Zeugen Jehovas etwas entgegenzusetzen: Die Kirche könnte auch nur in ihren Gottesdiensten und Veranstaltungen über die Missionierungsversuche aufklären und davor warnen; stattdessen wählt man gezielt eine Publikation in der Landessprache Schwedisch als Mittel, von der man überzeugt ist, dass sie der Bewegung etwas entgegensetzen kann. Das Medium der

44 Pope Shenouda III, Jehovah's Witnesses and their Heresy. A Collection of Articles Published in ›El-Keraza‹ English Magazine, Baramous 1993.

45 https://fourcornersoftheworld.ptrs.ru.nl/publication/1356/public/ (15.5.2025).

Publikation wird von der schwedischen Studiengruppe bewusst verwendet, um den Zeugen Jehovas etwas entgegenzusetzen. Da man nicht über ein solches Material verfügt, nimmt man das koptische Material. Man passt es dem schwedischen Kontext an und materialisiert den Protest gegen diese Bewegung in der Verbreitung der Publikation. Abgesehen davon, wie erfolgreich die Publikation gegen die Aktivität der Zeugen Jehovas gewirkt hat, ist dieses Material an sich als Missbilligung der Situation zu betrachten. Die koptische theologische Schrift wird als syrisch-orthodoxes Heft veröffentlicht und übernimmt die Argumentation der koptischen Kirche zu der globalen Bewegung der Zeugen Jehovas. An dieser Stelle ist es nicht die Kirchenleitung, die die Publikation herausgibt, sondern eine lokale schwedische Studiengruppe. Anhand dieses Heftes zeigen sich beispielhaft Entwicklungen der syrisch-orthodoxen Gemeinschaft in Schweden. Zusammenfassend lässt sich sagen, dass die Veröffentlichung und Verbreitung der Schrift »Zeugen Jehovas und ihre Irrlehren« durch die syrisch-orthodoxe Gemeinde in Schweden ein eindrucksvolles Beispiel für das Zusammenspiel von Mehrsprachigkeit, interkonfessioneller Rezeption und Laienengagement angesichts spezifischer Herausforderungen in der Diaspora ist. Zudem illustriert die Fallstudie, wie bestehende theologische Ressourcen aus verwandten Konfessionen zum Schutz der eigenen Glaubenstradition verwendet und produktiv gemacht werden.

5.3 Die Heiligengeschichte *Saint Servatius d'Arménie* über den Bischof aus Armenien in Maastricht

Eine Besonderheit, die die armenische Kirche von den anderen orientalisch-orthodoxen Gemeinschaften in Europa unterscheidet, ist deren jahrhundertelange Existenz in Europa, die bis ins 12. Jahrhundert zurückreicht.[46] In dieser Zeit waren es armenische Händler, die bereits in die heutigen Gebiete von Belgien und den Niederlanden vorgedrungen sein sollen. Nachweise für armenische Präsenz

46 Dieser Abschnitt basiert auf der Forschung von Christopher Sheklian im ERC-Projekt »Rewriting Global Orthodoxy«. Sein Artikel *»Their Compatriot St. Servatius.« Armenian Emplacement in Maastricht* befasst sich mit dem Heiligen Servatius mit armenischem Hintergrund und seiner Verehrung im niederländischen Maastricht (Christopher Sheklian, »Their Compatriot St. Servatius.« Armenian Emplacement in Maastricht, in: Martin Tamcke [Hg.], Europe and the Migration of Christian Communities from the Middle East, Wiesbaden 2022, 111–124).

in Amsterdam finden sich bereits im 16. Jahrhundert. Mit der Zunahme der Migration in den sechziger Jahren wuchs auch die armenische Gemeinschaft in den Niederlanden.[47] Der Heilige Servatius (gest. ca. 384), auch bekannt als Servatius von Tongern (Stadt in Belgien), ist für die armenische Gemeinschaft in Europa ein wichtiger Heiliger geworden. Servatius soll in Armenien geboren sein und nach seiner Zeit als Bischof in Tongern im niederländischen Maastricht gewirkt haben. Seine Überreste finden sich heute in der Servatiusbasilika in Maastricht, auf dessen Grab die Basilika errichtet wurde. Ein Heiliger mit armenischen Wurzeln wird nicht nur von den ansässigen Katholikinnen und Katholiken verehrt, sondern auch von den armenischen Christinnen und Christen in den Niederlanden und darüber hinaus. Anlässlich des Gedenktages des Heiligen Servatius (13. Mai) widmete die armenische Gemeinschaft am 15. Mai 2016 dem Heiligen Servatius einen Kreuzstein (armenisch: Khatchkar) vor der katholischen Basilika. Interessanterweise wird der Heilige Servatius in der Armenisch-Apostolischen Kirche selbst nicht verehrt. Er ist weder in der armenischen Frömmigkeit noch in der Literatur zu finden.[48] Aber in der europäischen Diaspora der armenischen Gemeinschaft hat seine Person an Bedeutung gewonnen und erfährt eine neue Verehrung.

Mit den armenischen Wurzeln des Heiligen Servatius und seiner Verbindung zu der Stadt Maastricht befassen sich auch in Europa veröffentlichte Texte. Ein Beispiel für Publikationen ist das französischsprachige Buch *Saint Servatius d'Arménie. 1er évêque de Maastricht* (Trésors d'Arménie) [Sankt Servatius der Armenier: Erster Bischof von Maastricht (Schätze von Armenien)].[49] Dieses Buch ist keine klassische Heiligengeschichte, sondern verbindet die europäischen Traditionen, die sich um den Heiligen ranken, mit der niederländischen Stadt Maastricht. Das Buch beinhaltet neben Fotos eine französische Einleitung zu St. Servatius und die Traditionen, die um ihn kursieren. Aber auch seine Vergangenheit mit den armenischen Ursprüngen und die gegenwärtige Verehrung seiner Person in Maastricht sind Gegenstand des Buchs. Der Heilige, der in der armenischen Tradition unbekannt ist, wird durch ansässige armenische Gemeinschaften wegen seiner armenischen Herkunft verehrt und besonders bedacht. Ihm werden Publikationen gewidmet, sein Gedenktag wird in der Stadt gefeiert, und die ka-

47 Sheklian, Armenian Emplacement, 118.
48 Sheklian, Armenian Emplacement, 111.
49 Saint Servatius d'Arménie, 1er évêque de Maastricht, Trésors d'Arménie, Marseille 2002, https://fourcornersoftheworld.ptrs.ru.nl/publication/900/public/ (15.5.2025).

tholische Basilika wird zum Verehrungsort für armenisch-orthodoxe Gläubige. Die Publikation über den Heiligen ist wie die Errichtung des Kreuzsteines ein Zeichen, wie die katholische Heiligenverehrung von der lokalen armenischen Gemeinschaft übernommen wird. Mit der Herkunft des Heiligen schreibt sich die armenische Gemeinschaft in die Stadt Maastricht ein.[50] Die Gegenstände wie der Kreuzstein oder die Publikation *Saint Servatius d'Arménie* zeigen, wie das armenische *emplacement*[51] in der niederländischen Stadt stattfindet. Das Buch ist nicht nur Informationsmaterial, sondern es verbindet materiell die Person Servatius und den Ort mit der Gemeinschaft und schafft dadurch eine Verbundenheit mit der Region. Die Publikation verkörpert nicht nur eine in der Diaspora entwickelte neue Heiligenverehrung, sondern steht dafür, wie diese in einer Publikation festgeschrieben wird und damit eine Verstärkung erfährt. Die Materialität der Heiligengeschichte unterstreicht die praktizierte Heiligenverehrung in der Region. Somit greift die Publikation die praktizierte Heiligenverehrung der armenischen Diaspora auf und materialisiert diese in der Veröffentlichung. Sie verleiht der Heiligenverehrung Ausdruck und fixiert diese schriftlich. An dieser lässt sich eine neue Frömmigkeit der europäischen Diaspora beobachten, die die traditionelle Verehrung von Heiligen in der armenischen Kirche nicht nur in der Praxis erweitert, sondern auch schriftlich festhält.

5.4 Das syrisch-orthodoxe Schulbuch *Auf dem Weg zum Glauben* in Deutschland

Neben Magazinen und Heiligengeschichten ist es ein großes Anliegen aller Gemeinschaften, ihre Jugendlichen in der Religion zu unterrichten. Früher war der Ort des Unterrichts hauptsächlich in den Kirchen und den Klöstern zu finden. Mit der Migration der Gemeinschaften wird diese Tradition mit Sonntagsschulen besonders in der koptischen Kirche teilweise fortgesetzt, aber man hat sich auch den europäischen Kontexten angepasst. So ist in mehreren Bundesländern in Deutschland syrisch-orthodoxer Religionsunterricht an staatlichen Schulen möglich. In zahlreichen Bundesländern gibt es dazu auch Lehrpläne für die verschiedenen Klassenstufen und entsprechende Materialien. Das Lehrbuch für den sy-

50 Vgl. Sheklian, Armenian Emplacement, 122.
51 Sheklian, Armenian Emplacement, 122.

risch-orthodoxen Religionsunterricht »Auf dem Weg zum Glauben. Syrisch-Orthodoxe Religionslehre« ist ein Beispiel dafür; es ist 2020 für die fünfte und sechste Klasse erschienen.[52] Dieses Buch ist neben einer anderen Reihe offiziell für den Gebrauch im Schulunterricht zugelassen.[53] Das Vorwort zum Schulbuch schreibt der Bischof der Syrisch-Orthodoxen Kirche von Deutschland, Mor Philoxenus Mattias Nayis, und führt in das Buch ein. Die folgenden Themen finden sich im Buch: Beten, Mensch, Welt und Verantwortung, Gott, Jesus Christus, Bibel und Tradition, Kirche und Religion und Weltanschauungen. Dieses Lehrwerk ist in seinem Aufbau deutlich von katholischen und evangelischen Lehrwerken geprägt, was in der Wahl der Literatur für das Buch sichtbar wird. Thematisch befasst sich das Buch mit klassischen Themen der Syrisch-Orthodoxen Kirche, etwa wie man betet und was das kirchliche Leben in der alten Heimat und der Gegenwart in Deutschland ausmacht. Anders als in der traditionellen Lehre widmet sich ein Kapitel auch dem Judentum und dem Islam, was nicht nur auf Zustimmung innerhalb der Gemeinschaft gestoßen ist.[54] An dieser Stelle wird deutlich, dass das Lehrwerk ein Buch ist, das einen pluralen Kontext in Deutschland anspricht und nicht nur eine Religionsgemeinschaft repräsentiert, die vormals nur auf ihre kirchlichen Inhalte bedacht war. Obwohl die syrisch-orthodoxe Gemeinschaft eine wechselvolle Geschichte besonders im muslimischen Kontext im Nahen Osten aufweist, die auch mit Verfolgung und Gewalt im Zusammenhang steht, wird der Islam im Schulbuch als eine gleichberechtigte Religion dargestellt. Auch die Beziehung mit dem Judentum wird im Schulbuch neu bewertet. Die Überschrift »Unsere älteren Geschwister feiern den Sabbat«[55] stellt eine klare Verbindungslinie zwischen beiden Religionen her und beschreibt diese Beziehung als Geschwisterlichkeit. Der Inhalt des Buches bricht somit mit traditionellen kirchlichen Narrativen, die sich häufig durch eine klare Abgrenzung vom Judentum auszeichnen und sich auch in polemischen Schriften von Kirchenvätern niederschlagen.[56] Das Lehrwerk orientiert sich stattdessen an den Anforde-

52 https://fourcornersoftheworld.ptrs.ru.nl/publication/1448/public/ (12.5.2025).

53 Die Forschung zu diesem Thema basiert auf unveröffentlichten Ergebnissen der Arbeit von Jan Gehm.

54 Im Rahmen des ERC-Forschungsprojekts wurde in Gesprächen und Interviews mit Gemeindemitgliedern deutlich, dass das Vorkommen anderer Religionen im Lehrwerk für den Syrisch-Orthodoxen Religionsunterricht unterschiedlich bewertet wird.

55 Josef Önder, Auf dem Weg zum Glauben. Syrisch-orthodoxe Religionslehre, Glane-Losser 2020.

56 Vgl. Christine Shepardson, Anti-Judaism and Christian Orthodoxy. Ephrem's Hymns in Fourth-Century Syria, Washington 2008.

rungen einer pluralen Gegenwartsgesellschaft, in der alle Religionen gleichwertig zu behandeln sind. Gleichzeitig legt das Lehrwerk großen Wert darauf, den Jugendlichen die Gebete und kirchlichen Gepflogenheiten näherzubringen, etwa durch Gebetsauszüge auf Syrisch oder praktische Anweisungen, wie man sich in der Kirche verhält. Die Autorinnen und Autoren der Schulbuchreihe verfolgen mit dieser Publikation das Ziel, eine Brücke zwischen der syrisch-orthodoxen Kirche und der gesellschaftlichen Realität in Deutschland zu schlagen – im Bewusstsein, dass religiöse Unterweisung nicht nur auf staatlicher Ebene erteilt, sondern auch mit zeitgemäßem Material begleitet werden muss. Anstelle der ausschließlichen Verwendung traditioneller Katechismen oder der Schriften der Kirchenväter wurde ein Lehrwerk für das deutsche Bildungssystem entwickelt, das sich am Vorbild katholischer und evangelischer Schulbücher orientiert. Im Medium Schulbuch werden nicht nur Inhalte präsentiert, sondern es findet eine Aushandlung zwischen kirchlicher Tradition und gesellschaftlicher Realität statt. Das Schulbuch materialisiert diese Aushandlungen und bietet der syrisch-orthodoxen Jugend einen neuen Zugang zu den Lehren und Traditionen ihrer Kirche. Mit dem neuen Bildungsmedium erfahren die Inhalte der Gemeinschaft eine Aktualisierung und werden angepasst. Die Tradition erfährt mit dem Medium eine Fortschreibung, die an die neue Generation herangetragen wird.

6. Fazit

Die im Rahmen des Projekts »Rewriting Global Orthodoxy« gesammelten Publikationen und für diesen Beitrag analysierten Fallbeispiele verdeutlichen, dass Publikationen orientalisch-orthodoxer Gemeinschaften in Europa nicht lediglich reproduziert, sondern in hohem Maße an die lokalen Kontexte und spezifischen Umstände angepasst wurden. Sie dienen somit nicht mehr ausschließlich der Wissensvermittlung und der Bewahrung traditioneller Praktiken, sondern fungieren zunehmend als Mittel zur Aushandlung neuer Identitäten im Spannungsfeld zwischen kirchlicher Tradition und den Gegebenheiten der jeweiligen Aufnahmegesellschaft. Die untersuchten Publikationen spiegeln einen dynamischen Prozess wider, in dem religiöse Gemeinschaften auf gesellschaftliche, religiöse und politische Veränderungen in ihren Publikationen reagieren. Die Notwendigkeit, jahrhundertealte Texte und Traditionen in die veränderten sozio-kulturellen

Kontexte Europas einzubetten, führen zu neuen Ausdrucksformen: Zum einen findet sich eine zunehmende Mehrsprachigkeit, die als Vermittlung zwischen den Herkunftssprachen der Gläubigen und den Sprachen der neuen Heimatländer fungiert. Zum anderen zeigen sich Veränderungen in der Formatvielfalt der Publikationen, die eine Wandlung der textuellen Kultur zur Folge haben. Beispielhaft sei die Aneignung und Verehrung eines katholischen Heiligen aus dem niederländischen Kontext durch die armenische Gemeinde genannt, wie sie in Publikationen thematisiert wird. Ebenso steht die didaktische Aufbereitung des traditionellen Lehrkorpus der syrisch-orthodoxen Kirche für den staatlich organisierten Religionsunterricht in deutschen Schulen für eine Neuverhandlung des Verhältnisses von religiöser Tradition und säkularer Öffentlichkeit. Während in der Vergangenheit das Hauptaugenmerk vielfach auf Abgrenzung und Traditionsbewahrung lag, dokumentieren die vorgestellten Publikationen einen Prozess der Annäherung und Integration. Aber es entstanden auch Publikationen als direkte Reaktionen auf die veränderten Umstände, wie mit dem koptischen Text gegen die Lehren der Zeugen Jehovas in Schweden oder auch die Zeitschrift der koptischen Kirche in den Niederlanden, in denen konkrete Handlungsanweisungen zum Leben in einer zunehmend säkularisierten Gesellschaft und einem multireligiösen Umfeld vom Bischof gegeben werden.

Auch wenn die Beispiele die vorliegende Forschung zur Vielfalt der Publikationen orientalisch-orthodoxer Gemeinschaften nur in begrenztem Umfang abbilden konnte, lassen sich deutliche Tendenzen erkennen, die sowohl die Anpassungsleistungen als auch Integrationsprozesse dieser Gemeinschaften in Europa bezeugen. Insgesamt zeigt die Beschäftigung mit orientalisch-orthodoxen Publikationen in Europa, dass diese Gemeinschaften keineswegs starre oder rückständige Gemeinschaften sind, sondern aktiv an der Gestaltung und Verhandlung religiöser und kultureller Identität in ihren jeweiligen neuen Lebenswelten mitwirken. Dies trägt nicht zuletzt zu einem besseren Verständnis der Gemeinschaften und andererseits auch zum Abbau von Fremdheitswahrnehmungen innerhalb der europäischen Mehrheitsgesellschaften bei. Meyers These, dass man anhand der Materialität bzw. der Publikationen ein Verständnis über die religiösen Gemeinschaften gewinnen kann, wurde durch die besprochenen Beispiele deutlich bestätigt. Im neuen Kontext Europa sind frühere Textgrundlagen neu aufgelegt, übersetzt, überarbeitet, ergänzt, oder es sind völlig neue Formate entwickelt und geschrieben worden. Dieser Aushandlungsprozess zwischen alter und neuer Heimat findet sich auch in der Materialität der Texte der orientalischen Orthodoxie in Europa wieder. Die religiöse Veränderung, die damit einhergeht, bedarf weiterer Forschungsarbeiten. Die als Publikationen vorliegenden Medien veranschaulichen anhand der analysierten Beispiele das Potenzial, das in diesen zunächst unscheinbaren kirchlichen Schriften steckt.

(Jan Gehm ist wissenschaftlicher Mitarbeiter am Bayerischen Forschungsinstitut für Interreligiöse Diskurse an der FAU Nürnberg-Erlangen. Er vertrat von 2024 bis 2025 die Juniorprofessur für Interkulturelle Theologie und Religionswissenschaft an der Universität Hamburg. Von 2020 bis 2024 arbeitete er im ERC-Projekt »Rewriting Global Orthodox« unter der Leitung von Prof. Heleen Murre van den Berg an der Radboud University Nijmegen.)

ABSTRACT

Since the 1970s, Oriental Orthodox communities like the Syriac, Coptic, Armenian, Ethiopian, and Eritrean Churches have established vibrant diasporas across Europe. This article explores how their textual culture has evolved post-migration, focusing on the production and adaptation of religious and secular texts such as liturgies, educational materials, and magazines. Drawing on findings from the ERC project »Rewriting Global Orthodoxy,« the study demonstrates how these materials serve not only to preserve heritage but also to negotiate identity in new sociocultural contexts. Case studies on Coptic publications in the Netherlands and Belgium, adapted hagiographies within Armenian communities, interconfessional reception of a Coptic text in Sweden and Syriac Orthodox textbooks for German schools highlight increasing multilingualism, new content formats, and the interplay between tradition and modernity. Ultimately, the development of Oriental Orthodox textual culture in Europe reflects dynamic processes of integration, innovation, and identity formation, challenging assumptions of insularity within these communities.

Rosenkranz und Macht

Zur politischen Semiotik religiöser und materieller Objekte im Fall Vital Kamerhe

Égide Pèlerin Muziazia

Einführung

Die Materialwende – *Material Turn* – in den Geistes- und Sozialwissenschaften stellt einen Paradigmenwechsel dar, der die Bedeutung materieller Objekte und ihre aktive Rolle in sozialen, kulturellen und religiösen Prozessen zunehmend ins Zentrum rückt. Diese Entwicklung hinterfragt bislang vorherrschende Theoriemodelle, die menschliche AkteurInnen als alleinige TrägerInnen von Wissen und Handeln verstanden. Im Kontext des material turn werden materielle Dinge als Akteure mit eigenem Handlungspotenzial verstanden, als »Agenten«, die mit Menschen und sozialen Strukturen interagieren.

Materielle Objekte sind insbesondere in afrikanischen Religionen von zentraler Bedeutung, da sie in vielen religiösen Praktiken eine Brücke zwischen der sichtbaren und der unsichtbaren Welt bilden. Sie sind Träger spiritueller Kräfte, die den Gläubigen Trost und Schutz spenden und zugleich eine aktive Rolle für den sozialen Zusammenhalt und die Bildung einer Gemeinschaftsidentität spielen.

Der Rosenkranz, ein zentrales Andachtsobjekt des katholischen Glaubens, ist ein ebensolches faszinierendes Beispiel für die Rolle materieller Objekte in religiösen und politischen Kontexten. Seine Geschichte als Gebetsinstrument ist eng mit der katholischen Frömmigkeit verbunden und hat eine lange Tradition, die bis ins Mittelalter zurückreicht. Im Kontext der Demokratischen Republik

Kongo erhält der Rosenkranz jedoch eine zusätzliche Dimension. Hier ist er nicht nur Ausdruck individueller Frömmigkeit. Er wird zunehmend als politisches Instrument eingesetzt, insbesondere in Zeiten politischer Instabilität und sozialer Ungerechtigkeit. In einem Land mit einer Geschichte kolonialer Ausbeutung, politischer Unterdrückung und tief verwurzelter Korruption bietet die katholische Kirche als moralische Autorität den Gläubigen einen Raum, um ihre politische und soziale Unzufriedenheit auszudrücken. Der Rosenkranz wird zum Symbol des Widerstands und dient als Mittel des politischen Protests auf individueller und kollektiver Ebene.

Der vorliegende Beitrag widmet sich der Untersuchung der komplexen religiösen Funktion materieller sakraler Objekte sowie deren symbolischer und performativer Präsenz innerhalb kongolesischer politischer Kontexte. Im ersten Teil wird ein systematischer Überblick über die Bedeutung, Funktion und rituelle Einbindung materieller Objekte in afrikanischen Religionssystemen gegeben. Im weiteren Verlauf wird der Fokus auf den Rosenkranz als sakrales Objekt des Christentums und dessen Repräsentation im Rahmen politischer Protestbewegungen und gesellschaftlicher Aushandlungsprozesse gerichtet.

1. Material Turns im Kontext der afrikanischen Religion

Der *Material Turn* lenkt die Aufmerksamkeit auf die materielle Kultur und die Rolle von Objekten in der Wissensproduktion. Diese Entwicklung steht in Analogie zu anderen wissenschaftlichen »Turns«, wie dem *Linguistic Turn* oder dem *Iconic Turn*,[1] und markiert eine Verschiebung hin zur Erforschung der Bedeu-

1 Der von Doris Bachmann-Medick beschriebene »Iconic Turn« bezeichnet eine grundlegende Verschiebung innerhalb der Kulturwissenschaften, die den Fokus von sprachlichen auf visuelle Ausdrucksformen verlagert. Bachmann-Medick betont, dass Bilder eine eigene Logik und Wirkung haben, die sich der Sprache entziehen können und somit als eigenständige Wissensquelle fungieren. Diese Annährung stellt das traditionell textbasierte hermeneutische Paradigma in Frage und fordert eine Erweiterung der Methoden um visuelle Argumentationsweisen. Der »Iconic Turn« führt zu einer starken interdisziplinären Vernetzung und öffnet die Kulturwissenschaften für bildzentrierte Ansätze, die die aktive Rolle von Bildern in der Wissensproduktion und in sozialen Prozessen betonen, vgl. Doris Bachmann-Medick, Cultural Turns. Neuorientierung in den Kulturwissenschaften, Reinbek bei Hamburg [5]2006, 330 ff.

tung von Dingen und Materialien im sozialen und kulturellen Kontext.[2] Diese theoretische Neuorientierung geht mit einer Anerkennung der Handlungsmacht, der »Agency«, von Dingen einher und betont die relationalen Verflechtungen zwischen Menschen, Artefakten und materiellen Strukturen. Claudia Jahnel, eine wichtige Stimme in der interkulturellen Theologie und postkolonialen Forschung, hat den Begriff der *Agency* als Handlungsmacht und Handlungsfähigkeit in ihrer Arbeit über die afrikanische Theologie intensiv reflektiert.[3] Sie betrachtet Agency als Schlüssel zur Selbstbestimmung marginalisierter AkteurInnen, insbesondere im Kontext von postkolonialen Machtverhältnissen. Agency wird dementsprechend sowohl als individuelle Fähigkeit, als auch als kollektiver und relationaler Prozess verstanden, der es ermöglicht, soziale und epistemologische Hierarchien in Frage zu stellen und alternative Wissens- und Lebensformen zu schaffen.

> »*Agency* berührt existenzielle Fragen der Macht und Ohnmacht, der individuellen und gemeinschaftlichen Einflussnahme auf soziokulturelle und politische Prozesse, der kreativen und innovativen Gestaltungsmöglichkeiten, der Selbstbestimmung als einzelne, Gruppe oder Zivilgesellschaft, der Identität, Subjektivität und des freien Willens.«[4]

In Anlehnung an Jahnels Verständnis[5] von Agency lässt sich festhalten, dass Individuen und Gruppen sowie religiöse Objekte in den afrikanischen Religionen eine aktive Agency besitzen, die weit über ihre symbolische Funktion hinaus-

2 Vgl. Peter J. Bräunlein, Thinking Religion Through Things. Reflections on the Material Turn in the Scientific Study of Religion, in: Till Mostowlanksky/Andrea Rota (Hg.), Method & Theory in the Study of Religion, Vol. 28, N° 4/5, Leiden/Boston 2016, 365.

3 Vgl. Claudia Jahnel, Interkulturelle Theologie und Kulturwissenschaft. Untersucht am Beispiel afrikanischer Theologie, Stuttgart 2016, 276f.

4 Jahnel, Interkulturelle Theologie, 285.

5 Jahnel fragt auch nach der Rolle von Agency in der Repräsentation und Deutung von afrikanischer Kultur und Religion. Eine postkoloniale Theologie muss ihrer Meinung nach die Handlungsmacht der Betroffenen anerkennen und ihnen Raum geben, ihre Erfahrungen selbst theologisch zu deuten. Dies erfordert eine radikale Verschiebung hin zu einer »Wiederentdeckung von Agency in der afrikanischen Theologie«, die sich nicht auf universelle Wahrheitsansprüche stützt, sondern auf die spezifischen Kontexte und Praktiken der Marginalisierten. Für sie geht es hier darum, »ein neues – ›weniger schizophrenes‹ – Verhältnis zum Christentum zu gewinnen, indem AfrikanerInnen als Akteure der Missions- und Christentumsgeschichte Afrikas wahrgenommen werden und das Christentum nicht mehr als fremde, sondern als ›afrikanische Religionen‹ anerkannt wird.« (Jahnel, Interkulturelle Theologie, 289).

geht. Sie spenden Trost, indem sie spirituelle Nähe herstellen, und ermächtigen marginalisierte Gruppen, indem sie Schutz und Handlungsfähigkeit bieten.[6]

Die Ahnen spielen in dieser materiellen und sakralen Welt eine Mittlerrolle zwischen den Menschen und den Göttern. Ihnen werden materielle Gegenstände dargebracht, um sich ihres Schutzes zu versichern. Dabei bleiben sie als vertraute Figuren in Masken oder materielle Repräsentationen präsent, während Gott oft als transzendentes Wesen wahrgenommen wird.[7] Materielle Objekte und Repräsentationen werden häufig als Manifestationen von Ahnen oder göttlichen Kräften angesehen. Ihre Verehrung dient der spirituellen Kommunikation, aber auch dem Schutz und der Stärkung des sozialen Zusammenhalts innerhalb einer Gemeinschaft.[8]

Materielle Objekte sind in den afrikanischen Religionen nicht rein dekorativ. Sie verbinden das Diesseits mit dem Jenseits. Sie verkörpern Lebenskraft[9] und machen die Anwesenheit von Göttern oder Geistern spürbar. Durch Rituale wie Tänze, Gesänge oder Trancezustände werden diese Objekte animiert und ihre Kräfte entfaltet. Sie ermöglichen es den Gläubigen, das Göttliche in ihrer physischen Welt zu erfahren und eine enge Beziehung zu den spirituellen Kräften aufzubauen. Die Rituale der Ahnenverehrung sind nicht nur religiöse Praktiken. Sie sind auch Ausdruck des sozialen Zusammenhalts und der kulturellen Identität. Die Ahnen gelten als Mittler zwischen den Lebenden und dem Göttlichen; ihre Verehrung dient dem Schutz vor Unheil und der Harmonie in der Gemeinschaft.[10]

6 Franz Josef Thiel, Religionsethnologie. Grundbegriffe der Religion schriftloser Völker, Berlin 1984, 60.

7 Thiel, Religionsethnologie, 61.

8 Thiel, Religionsethnologie, 33.

9 Bénézet Bujo beschreibt die Lebenskraft als eine dynamische und allgegenwärtige Energie, die das Leben in seiner Gesamtheit durchdringt und die sichtbare mit der unsichtbaren Welt verbindet. Sie ist die Quelle des Lebens und zugleich das Medium, durch das Gemeinschaft, Spiritualität und Ethik in der afrikanischen Kultur verstanden werden. Die Lebenskraft existiert nicht isoliert, sondern zirkuliert in einem Netz von Beziehungen. Sie fließt zwischen Individuen, Ahnen, Natur und Gott. Diese Vorstellung spiegelt die afrikanische Anthropologie wider, in der der Mensch als Teil eines größeren kosmischen Gefüges gesehen wird. Die Lebenskraft wird durch Rituale, Opfergaben und soziale Interaktion genährt und weitergegeben, Bénézet Bujo, Afrikanische Theologie in ihrem gesellschaftlichen Kontext, Düsseldorf 1986, 24.

10 Vgl. Walter E. A. van Beek/Harrie M. Leyten, Masquerades in African Society. Gender, Power, and Identity, Oxford 2023, 57f.

2. Funktion, Bedeutung und Kontextualisierung materiell-sakraler Objekte in afrikanischen Religionen

Materielle Objekte nehmen innerhalb afrikanischer Religionen eine zentrale Funktion ein, da sie als Vermittlungsinstanzen zwischen der physischen und der metaphysischen Sphäre agieren. Ihnen wird die Qualität zugeschrieben, Träger und Manifestationen spiritueller Energie zu sein, die sowohl in rituellen Vollzügen als auch in den alltäglichen Lebensvollzügen eine tiefgreifende Bedeutung entfaltet.[11]

2.1 Statuen und Masken als Verkörperung spiritueller Kräfte

Diese Objekte fungieren als Verkörperungen von Ahnen, göttlichen Wesenheiten oder Schutzgeistern. Sie sind in komplexe rituelle Praktiken eingebunden. Besonders Statuen und Masken nehmen innerhalb der religiösen und sozialen Ordnungen west- und zentralafrikanischer Gesellschaften eine herausragende Stellung ein.[12] Im religiösen Kontext der Yoruba in Nigeria etwa finden sich Skulpturen, die die Orishas repräsentieren. In der spirituellen Hierarchie nehmen diese göttlichen Wesen eine vermittelnde Position zwischen den Menschen und dem höchsten Gott Olodumare ein. Demgegenüber entfalten Masken ihre Wirkmacht insbesondere in Initiationsriten oder rituellen Tänzen, in denen sie der spirituellen Transformation dienen.[13]

Bei den Baoulé – Elfenbeinküste – werden Masken als Träger übernatürlicher Kräfte betrachtet. Ihre Handhabung unterliegt strengen Regularien und ist ausschließlich spezialisierten Priestern oder Tänzern vorbehalten. Masken repräsentieren folglich nicht lediglich Kunstobjekte, sondern sind konsequent funktional ausgerichtet und dienen spezifischen religiösen oder gesellschaftlichen Zwecken.[14] Masken sind immer zweckgebunden. Sie haben eine Funktion zu erfüllen:

11 Vgl. van Beek/Leyten, Masquerades, 63.
12 Vgl. Gary Edson, Masks and Masking. Faces of Tradition and Worldwide, Jefferson, NC 2009, 192.
13 Vgl. Beek/Leyten, Masquerades, 15.
14 Vgl. Edson, Masks, 192.

> »Aber eine Maske ist in Afrika in einen dynamischen sozio-religiösen Prozess eingebunden: Sie tritt auf bei Begräbnissen, bei Aussaat und Ernte, bei Inthronisation und Beschneidung und bei allen möglichen zyklischen Jahresfesten. Die Maske lebt wirklich inmitten der Lebenden.«[15]

Die körperliche Interaktion mit der Maske wird als eine Form der spirituellen Inbesitznahme betrachtet, durch die sich der Träger mit der Kraft des dargestellten Wesens verbindet.

2.2 Kraftspendende Objekte als materielle Manifestationen spiritueller Energie

Kraftspendende Objekte werden mit besonderen spirituellen Energien in Verbindung gebracht, wobei es sich um Gegenstände aus Holz, Metall, Knochen oder Textilien handeln kann.[16] In rituellen Kontexten werden die symbolischen Qualitäten und materiellen Eigenschaften dieser Objekte bewusst hervorgehoben und transformiert. Erst durch komplexe Aktivierungsrituale – wie etwa Beschwörungen, Opferhandlungen oder Segensformeln – werden diese Objekte in einen Zustand versetzt, in dem sie als wirkmächtige Medien zwischen der menschlichen und der transzendenten Sphäre fungieren.

Im Kontext der afrikanischen Religionen kommt den sogenannten *Nkisi* eine paradigmatische Funktion zu. Diese aus diversen Substanzen bestehenden Objekte – häufig mit Nägeln, Spiegeln, Erde oder Kräutern versehen – sind im Kongo-Raum nicht lediglich symbolische Artefakte, sondern ontologisch wirksame Agenten. Es wird die Hypothese aufgestellt, dass sie die Macht der Ahnengeister und anderer spiritueller Mächte vergegenwärtigen, indem sie als Speicher und Kanal für deren Energie fungieren.[17] Nkisi nehmen eine bedeutende Rolle im religiösen und sozialen Leben ein, indem sie Heilung, Schutz und Gerechtigkeit gewährleisten, aber auch Sanktionen vollziehen und die soziale Ordnung stabilisieren. Sie operieren somit an der Schnittstelle zwischen Immanenz und Transzendenz und übernehmen eine Vermittlungsfunktion, die über das Individuum

15 Thiel, Religionsethnologie, 62.
16 Vgl. Toni Pressley-Sanon, Istwa across the Water. Haitian History, Memory, and the Cultural, University Press of Florida 2017, 91.
17 Vgl. Pressley-Sanon, Istwa, 81f.

hinaus in die kollektive Dimension von Gemeinschaft, Recht und politischer Legitimation hineinreicht.[18]

Diese Figuren werden mit Nägeln versehen, um symbolisch einen spirituellen Vertrag zu besiegeln. Sie dienen unter anderem als Schutzobjekte, Heilinstrumente oder rituelle Waffen gegen Feinde.[19] Die Funktion dieser Kraftobjekte ist kontextabhängig: Während einige als Heiligtümer in Schreinen verbleiben, werden andere als tragbare Talismane verwendet, die ihren Träger vor bösen Geistern oder negativen Energien schützen sollen.[20] Die rituelle Beseelung und Pflege der Objekte erfordert das Wissen spezialisierter spiritueller Akteure, die in einer langen Tradition im Umgang mit diesen Materialien geschult sind.

2.3 Amulette und Talismane als Schutz- und Heilungsgegenstände

Als Kind wuchs ich mit Freunden auf, die Amulette aus Tier- und Schlangenknochen trugen, um sich vor dem Bösen zu schützen. Diese tief in ihren traditionellen Weltanschauungen verwurzelten Amulette sind Medien, die Verbindungen zwischen der sichtbaren und der unsichtbaren Welt herstellen. In diesem Zusammenhang wird deutlich, wie Kinder sehr früh in ein kulturelles und religiöses Weltbild eingebunden werden, das das Leben als ein ständiges Wechselspiel von Schutz und Bedrohung begreift. Das Tragen solcher Amulette vermittelte den Internatsschülern, die aus dem gleichen Dorf stammten, eine kollektive Identität und ein Gefühl der Geborgenheit in der Gemeinschaft. Kinder lernen durch diese Traditionen schon früh die Bedeutung von Ritualen, Symbolen und die Verbundenheit mit der Natur.[21]

Amulette wirken sowohl physisch als auch psychisch – sie sind Träger der Hoffnung, des Glaubens und der Vorstellung, dass Menschen mit höheren Mächten verbunden sind. Ihre Bedeutung und Kraft gehen nicht nur von den verwendeten Materialien aus. Es ist vor allem die Absicht, mit der sie getragen werden.

18 Thiel, Religionsethnologie, 62f.
19 Thiel, Religionsethnologie, 63.
20 Vgl. Aribedesi A. Usman, The Ninenteenth-Century Black Atlantic, in: Toyin Falola/Kevin D. Roberts (Hg.), The Atlantic World 1450–2000, Indiana 2008, 122f.
21 Usman, Black Atlantic, 72.

Sie werden zu persönlichen Schutzschilden, die den Träger durch schwere Zeiten begleiten und ihm das Gefühl geben, nicht allein zu sein:

> »Die Anziehungskraft der Amulette auf den Menschen ist sehr stark. Auch in christlichen Kreisen sind sie weit verbreitet. In den Kirchen, in denen ihr Gebrauch legitim ist, dürften oft magische Vorstellungen mit ihnen verbunden sein. Wie stark die Nachfrage nach ihnen ist, geht auch daraus hervor, dass ein lebhafter Import von Talismanen u. a. aus Indien nach Afrika erfolgt.«[22]

Materielle religiöse Objekte – wie Amulette – erfüllen in traditionellen Glaubenssystemen eine Doppelfunktion: Sie sind sowohl physische Manifestationen kultureller Werte als auch aktive Werkzeuge des spirituellen Lebens.

3. Material Turns im katholischen Glauben: Der Rosenkranz

Der Rosenkranz nimmt innerhalb der katholischen Andachtspraxis eine besondere Stellung ein und wird in der Regel den sogenannten Devotionalien[23] zugeordnet. Der Rosenkranz lässt sich sowohl als Gebet als auch als materieller Gegenstand definieren. Er stellt eine Verbindung aus Ritual, Symbolik und Materialität dar, die in der katholischen Religionskultur verankert sind und deren Ursprünge sich bis ins Mittelalter zurückverfolgen lassen.

Die Ursprünge des Rosenkranzes sind eng mit der klösterlichen Gebetstradition assoziiert. Im Hochmittelalter etablierte sich in benediktinischen und später zisterziensischen Kontexten die Praxis, Psalmen als strukturierte Gebetsform zu rezitieren.[24] Ursprünglich wurde der Rosenkranz als ein 150 Mal wiederholtes Gebet praktiziert, wobei sich die Wiederholungen mit den Gebeten »Vaterunser«

22 Usman, Black Atlantic, 104.

23 Der Begriff »Devotionalien« leitet sich etymologisch vom lateinischen Wort »Devotio« ab und kann mit den Begriffen Andacht oder Frömmigkeit übersetzt werden. An Wallfahrtsstätten werden Devotionalien erworben, die von Pilgernden als Andenken, Erinnerungsstücke oder Pilgerzeichen mit nach Hause genommen werden. Im katholischen Glauben werden Devotionalien als Andachtsgegenstände definiert. Hierzu zählen Weihwasserbecken, Pilgerzeichen, Plaketten, Amulette, Andachtsbilder, Ikonen, Heiligenfiguren, Rosenkränze, Kruzifixe sowie Kerzen in Form von Anhängern, kleinen Figuren oder Abbildungen.

24 Miri Rubin, Mother of God. A History of the Virgin Mary, New Haven 2009, 332.

und »Ehre sei dem Vater« abwechselten.[25] Die Überlieferung, dass der Heilige Dominikus den Rosenkranz als Offenbarung der Gottesmutter Maria empfangen habe, erfuhr im 15. Jahrhundert eine deutliche Konsolidierung.[26] Die entscheidende Institutionalisierung erfuhr der Rosenkranz im 16. Jahrhundert durch Papst Pius V., der ihn nach dem Sieg der christlichen Flotte über die Osmanen in der Schlacht von Lepanto 1571 zum »Gebet der Christenheit erklärte.«[27] Die Errichtung des Festes »Unserer Lieben Frau vom Rosenkranz« am 7. Oktober durch denselben Papst bezeugt die kirchlich-theologische Anerkennung und Förderung dieser Gebetsform.[28]

Die primäre Bedeutung des Rosenkranzes liegt in der Praxis und Vertiefung christologischer Glaubensgeheimnisse. Die wiederholte Anrufung Mariens im »Ave Maria« dient der Marienverehrung und enthält auch eine theologisch tiefgründige Erinnerung an zentrale Ereignisse im Leben Jesu Christi.[29] Diese Ereignisse werden in den sogenannten freudenreichen, schmerzhaften, glorreichen und lichtreichen Geheimnissen zur geistlichen Betrachtung angeboten.[30] Demzufolge dient der Rosenkranz nicht nur als Mittel der persönlichen Andacht. Vielmehr ist er eine rituell strukturierte Form der Ausübung des christlichen Lebens. Die Wiederholung, die oft fälschlicherweise als bloße mechanische Wiederholung verstanden wird, wirkt als eine Form der meditativen Kontemplation. Sie ermöglicht es den Gläubigen, eine affektive, emotionale und theologisch begründete Beziehung zum Leben, Leiden, Tod und Auferstehung Jesu Christi aufzubauen:

> »Der Rosenkranz wählt einige Momente der Passion aus und veranlasst so den Betenden, den Blick seines Herzens darauf auszurichten und danach zu leben. Der betrachtende Weg öffnet sich mit Getsemani, dort wo Jesus einen besonders angstvollen Moment gegenüber dem Willen des Vaters durchlebt, dem die Schwachheit des Fleisches sich zu widersetzen versucht wäre.«[31]

25 Vgl. Rubin, Mother of God.
26 Vgl. Rubin, Mother of God, 333.
27 Vgl. Rubin, Mother of God, 401.
28 Vgl. Rubin, Mother of God.
29 Vgl. Papst Johannes Paul II., Apostolisches Schreiben Rosarium Virginis Mariae, Vatikan 2002, N18.
30 Vgl. Papst Johannes Paul II., Apostolisches Schreiben, N19 ff.
31 Papst Johannes Paul II., Apostolisches Schreiben, N22.

In der Geschichte der katholischen Kirche hatte der Rosenkranz immer eine apotropäische, d. h. abwehrende und schützende Funktion. Dies zeigt sich z. B. in seiner Verwendung als geistliche Waffe gegen Versuchung, Sünde und sogar politische Bedrohung, wie in der marianischen Darstellung der Schlacht von Lepanto (1571). Diese Schlacht wurde von Papst Pius V. ausdrücklich mit dem Rosenkranzgebet in Verbindung gebracht und damit ein Narrativ des geistlichen Widerstandes und der göttlichen Intervention begründet, das bis heute in marianischen Frömmigkeitsformen nachklingt.[32]

Ferner verweist die Verwendung des Rosenkranzes auf eine charakteristische Form des physischen Gebets im katholischen Glauben, bei der die taktile Wahrnehmung der Perlen den Akt des Gebets symbolisiert. Dadurch erhält das spirituelle Leben eine konkrete, sinnlich wahrnehmbare Dimension und unterstreicht die in der zeitgenössischen Religionswissenschaft erkennbare Hinwendung zum Materiellen.[33] Der Rosenkranz ist ein sakrales Objekt, das symbolische Bedeutung trägt und ein Medium religiöser Praxis. Er verdichtet Glaubensausübung, Dogma, Ritual und Emotion in einer einzigen Handlung.

Im katholischen Glauben kommt dem Rosenkranz eine komplexe Funktion zu, die weit über die Form eines Gebets hinausgeht. Tatsächlich wird argumentiert, dass diese Praxis von theologischer, historischer, ritueller und emotionaler Bedeutung ist und somit zur Bildung der katholisch-christlichen Identität sowie zur persönlichen spirituellen Vertiefung des Einzelnen in der Ausübung seines Glaubens beiträgt.

4. Katholische Kirche und Politik in der Demokratischen Republik Kongo

Im Kontext der Demokratischen Republik Kongo, die weithin als einer der politisch fragilsten Staaten im subsaharischen Afrika gilt, kommt der katholischen

32 Vgl. Damaris Grimmsmann, Krieg mit dem Wort. Türkenpredigten des 16. Jahrhunderts im Alten Reich, Berlin 2016, 244f.

33 Vgl. Birgit Meyer/Dick Houtman (Hg.), Things. Religion and the Question of Materiality, New York 2012, 7f.

Kirche[34] mit ihren rund 60 Millionen Gläubigen eine besondere und in vielerlei Hinsicht paradoxe Funktion zu. Die Kirche hat sich im Laufe der Jahre als religiöse Autorität und zentrale gesellschaftliche Kraft profiliert, die, wie Nzongola-Ntalaja treffend bemerkt, als »einzige glaubwürdige nationale Institution«[35] angesehen wird.

Wurzeln dieser bedeutsamen Stellung lassen sich bis in die Kolonialzeit zurückführen, als die katholische Kirche als Instrument der belgischen Verwaltung agierte.[36] Im Zuge der Entkolonialisierung entwickelte sich die Kirche jedoch zunehmend zu einer treibenden Kraft der politischen und sozialen Emanzipation.[37] Seit den 1990er Jahren, als das autoritäre Regime von Mobutu zu bröckeln begann, hat die katholische Kirche eine initiierende Rolle im Demokratisierungsprozess übernommen.[38] Dies erfolgte durch die offene Stellung gegen politische Korruption, soziale Ungleichheit und staatliche Gewalt. Infolgedessen wurde der Kirche eine Funktion als Stimme des Volkes in einer von struktureller Schwäche und politischer Instabilität geprägten Gesellschaft zugewiesen.

Die Konferenz der Bischöfe der Katholischen Kirche im Kongo, die unter dem Namen Conférence Épiscopale Nationale du Congo (CENCO) bekannt ist, hat sich wiederholt als moralische Autorität erwiesen. Ein Beispiel hierfür ist ihre Vermittlung in politischen Kreisen, wie den Verhandlungen 2016/2017, die zu einem Übergangsabkommen zwischen der Regierung und der Opposition führ-

34 Seit der Unabhängigkeit der Demokratischen Republik Kongo im Jahr 1960 hat sich die katholische Kirche, die bereits während der Kolonialzeit eine zentrale Rolle bei der Gestaltung der Gesellschaft spielte, zunehmend als eine der wenigen konstanten moralischen Autoritäten etabliert, die – trotz ihrer eigenen Verstrickung in koloniale und postkoloniale Machtstrukturen – gegen die oft autoritären und korrupten politischen Regime Stellung bezog. Nicht nur in Predigten und öffentlichen Stellungnahmen, sondern auch durch soziale Initiativen, Bildungsarbeit und die Unterstützung demokratischer Basisbewegungen setzte sie sich für das Recht auf politische Partizipation, Menschenrechte und soziale Gerechtigkeit ein. Damit wurde sie zu einer wichtigen Akteurin des zivilgesellschaftlichen Widerstands, insbesondere in den Krisenjahren unter der Diktatur Mobutu Sese Sekos und in den Umbruchs- und Konfliktphasen der 1990er und 2000er Jahre. Sie wurde zu einer wichtigen Akteurin im zivilgesellschaftlichen Widerstand, deren Einfluss bis heute in politischen Auseinandersetzungen spürbar ist, etwa bei Wahlbeobachtungen, Protestbewegungen und Vermittlungsversuchen im nationalen Dialog.

35 Georges Nzongola-Ntalaja, The Congo. From Leopold to Kabila. A People's History, London 2002, 20.

36 Vgl. David Van Reybrouck, Kongo. Eine Geschichte, Berlin [4]2012, 78f.

37 Vgl. Van Reybrouck, Kongo, 271f.

38 Vgl. Van Reybrouck, Kongo, 468.

ten.[39] Die Kirche nahm in diesen Prozessen nicht nur die Rolle einer neutralen Vermittlerin ein. Sie stellte auch explizite Forderungen nach Rechtsstaatlichkeit, sozialer Gerechtigkeit und demokratischer Partizipation, was sie zunehmend in Konfrontation mit der politischen Elite brachte.

Trotz dieser konfrontativen Haltung bleibt das Verhältnis zwischen katholischer Kirche und Politik ambivalent. Selbst wegen Korruption verurteilte hochrangige Politiker bedienen sich religiöser Symbole, indem sie mit Rosenkränzen, Kruzifixen oder Heiligenbildern in der Öffentlichkeit auftreten, um – zumindest symbolisch – ihre Unschuld und moralische Integrität zu demonstrieren.[40] Dieses Phänomen ist bezeichnend für die tiefe kulturelle Verwurzelung des Katholizismus im kollektiven Bewusstsein der kongolesischen Gesellschaft, in der religiöse Legitimität oft wichtiger ist als juristische Verfahren oder politische Programme. Die sakrale Konnotation der Politik wird auch in der Praxis evident, in der Wahlkampfveranstaltungen mit religiösen Zeremonien oder Pilgerfahrten kombiniert werden, wodurch die Grenze zwischen religiöser Zugehörigkeit und politischer Loyalität zunehmend verschwimmt. Didier Gondola gelangt zu der Schlussfolgerung, dass Akteure des politischen Lebens religiöse Symbolik als Mittel einsetzen, um sich eine Aura der Unantastbarkeit zu verschaffen und sich folglich gegen Kritik und soziale Feindseligkeiten immunisieren.[41]

Angesichts dieser Entwicklungen wird deutlich, dass die katholische Kirche im Kongo nicht nur als externe Kritikerin der politischen Ordnung fungiert, sondern vielmehr integraler Bestandteil eines komplexen Symbolsystems ist, in dem Macht, Moral und Religion untrennbar miteinander verwoben sind. Trotz wiederholter Forderungen nach politischer Neutralität und bewusster Distanzierung von parteipolitischen Strukturen bleibt die Kirche unweigerlich in gesellschaftliche Aushandlungsprozesse involviert, die sie sowohl stärken als auch gefährden. Wie Mudimbe treffend bemerkt, befindet sich die Kirche in einem Spannungsfeld zwischen prophetischer Distanz und pragmatischer Komplizenschaft.[42] Diese Konstellation verleiht ihr die Stellung einer bedeutenden moralischen Autorität,

39 Vgl. CENCO, Accord politique global et inclusif du Centre interdiocésain de Kinshasa, Kinshasa 2017.

40 Vgl. Congo Research Group, The Catholic Church in the DRC, Kinshasa 2022, 9.

41 Charles Didier Gondola, The History of Congo, Westport 2002, 167.

42 Valentin Y. Mudimbe, Tales of Faith. Religion as Political Performance in Central Africa, London 1997, 199f.

setzt sie jedoch auch wiederholt der Gefahr der Kooptierung durch die politische und kulturelle Ordnung aus.

In der Demokratischen Republik Kongo nimmt die katholische Kirche gegenwärtig eine zentrale Rolle im Kampf für politische Erneuerung und soziale Gerechtigkeit ein. Sie stützt sich dabei auf ihre spirituelle Glaubwürdigkeit und ihre historische Rolle als Trägerin sozialer Infrastruktur. Ihre Zukunftsfähigkeit als glaubwürdige moralische Autorität wird jedoch davon abhängen, ob es ihr gelingt, ein nachhaltiges Gleichgewicht zwischen sozialem Engagement und spiritueller Integrität zu wahren.

5. Rosenkranz als Protestwaffe

Die symbolisch-praktische Funktion religiöser Devotionalien, allen voran des Rosenkranzes, im Kontext katholisch-kirchlicher Protestbewegungen im Kongo steht nicht zuletzt für eine spirituelle Verankerung politischen Handelns. Darüber hinaus stellt sie eine performative Sakralisierung öffentlichen Widerstands dar, die die Grenzen zwischen liturgischer Praxis und zivilem Ungehorsam systematisch überschreitet. So entsteht eine Form der politischen Intervention, die sich durch Unabhängigkeit und theologische Fundierung auszeichnet.

Am 16. Februar 1992 organisierten Christen in Kinshasa, unterstützt von der katholischen Bischofskonferenz, den friedlichen »Marche des Chrétiens«, um die Wiederaufnahme der Conférence Nationale Souveraine zu fordern. Sicherheitskräfte des Mobutu-Regimes reagierten mit brutaler Gewalt, töteten Dutzende Menschen und verletzten oder verhafteten Hunderte.[43] Der Tag gilt seither als »Tag der Märtyrer der Demokratie«[44] und bleibt ein Symbol für den Mut im Kampf gegen Unterdrückung.

In den letzten Jahren der Herrschaft von Mobutu Sese Seko etablierte sich die katholische Kirche als moralische Autorität des Landes. Dank ihrer umfangreichen pastoralen Infrastruktur war sie in der Lage, Kräfte zu mobilisieren, denen weder politische Parteien noch andere soziale Organisationen etwas ent-

43 Vgl. Amnesty International, Zaire. At least 13 People killed by Government Troops during Religious Demonstration, https://www.amnesty.org/es/wp-content/uploads/2021/06/afr620031992en.pdf (18.8.2025).

44 Vgl. Amnesty International, Zaire.

gegenzusetzen hatten.[45] Im Zuge der Konflikte um die Machtübernahme durch Laurent-Désiré Kabila und später unter dessen Sohn Joseph Kabila gewann die Kirche erneut an politischer Bedeutung, insbesondere durch die Aktivitäten der Conférence Épiscopale Nationale du Congo (CENCO) und Laienorganisationen wie dem Comité Laïc de Coordination (CLC).

Zwischen 2017 und 2018 organisierten katholische Laien im Kongo friedliche Protestmärsche gegen die Amtsverlängerung von Präsident Joseph Kabila. Nach der Sonntagsmesse gingen Gläubige mit Bibeln und Rosenkränzen auf die Straße. Sicherheitskräfte reagierten mit Tränengas und scharfer Munition, auch in Kirchen. Mehrere Menschen starben, darunter Thérèse Déchade Kapangala, eine 24-jährige angehende Ordensschwester, die am 21. Januar 2018 vor ihrer Pfarrkirche erschossen wurde.[46] Rossy Mukendi Tshimanga, ein kongolesischer zivilgesellschaftlicher Aktivist, wurde am 25. Februar 2018 in Kinshasa während einer gewaltlosen Demonstration, die sich für freie und faire Wahlen in der Demokratischen Republik Kongo einsetzte, von einer Polizistin erschossen. Mukendi wurde in unmittelbarer Nähe der Kirche St. Benoît in Kinshasa tödlich getroffen, als er versuchte, mit seinem Rosenkranz in der Hand in der Kirche Zuflucht zu finden. Sein gewaltsamer Tod entwickelte sich zu einem Sinnbild für die systematische Repression und exzessive Gewaltanwendung durch staatliche Sicherheitskräfte gegenüber der Zivilgesellschaft in einem autoritären politischen Umfeld.[47]

Die Protestbewegungen weisen auf eine politische und spirituelle Dimension des Widerstands hin. Die von den Demonstrierenden mitgeführten Devotionalien, darunter Rosenkränze, Kruzifixe, Heiligenbilder und gelegentlich sogar Bibeln, erfüllen eine doppelte Funktion. Einerseits verdeutlichen sie die religiösen Ursprünge der Proteste, andererseits gelten sie als Schutzsymbole gegen die staatliche Gewalt, die oft mit massiver Repression auf die Proteste reagiert. Der Rosenkranz, der gemeinhin als Medium der persönlichen Frömmigkeit gilt, wurde

45 Paul Gifford, Christianity and Politics in Doe's Liberia, Cambridge 1992, 201f.

46 Vgl. Amnesty International, Justice now for Thérèse Déchade Kapangala Mwanza, https://www.amnesty.org/en/latest/campaigns/2020/06/drc-justice-now-therese-dechade-kapangala-mwanza/ (25.7.2025); Human Rights Watch, DR Congo. Security Forces Fire on Catholics Churchgoers, https://www.hrw.org/news/2018/01/19/dr-congo-security-forces-fire-catholic-churchgoers (25.7.2025).

47 Amnesty International, DRC. Rossy Tshimanga Mukendi, killed by police during a peaceful protest in DRC, https://www.amnesty.org/en/latest/campaigns/2020/06/drc-justice-now-rossy-tshimanga-mukendi/ (25.7.2025).

in diesem Fall als Mittel des politischen Protests eingesetzt. Trotz seines gewaltfreien Charakters stellte er eine gewaltige Herausforderung für das Regime dar, dessen Legitimität zunehmend verschwand und das nicht mehr in der Lage war, die Zustimmung der Bevölkerung zu gewinnen. Er erfüllt nicht nur die Funktion eines individuellen Gebetsinstruments. Gleichzeitig repräsentiert er als öffentlich wahrnehmbares Symbol die moralische Überlegenheit der Demonstrierenden gegenüber den Repräsentanten eines Staates, den sie für illegitim halten. Diese Symbolik steht im Einklang mit traditionellen Interpretationen der katholischen Marienverehrung, die Maria als Fürsprecherin der Schwachen, Unterdrückten und Mutter des Erlösers darstellt.[48]

Der Rosenkranz ist ein starkes Identitätsmerkmal im kongolesischen katholischen und politischen Milieu. Die Trägerinnen und Träger dieses religiösen Symbols beanspruchen ein Monopol auf Wahrheit, Gerechtigkeit und Moral – Tugenden, die nur in der Kirche zu finden sind. Während der Staat als Symbol für Korruption, Willkür und Gewalt wahrgenommen wurde, präsentierte sich die Kirche mit all ihren Symbolen – Rosenkranz, Kreuz, Gnadenbilder etc. – als Repräsentantin einer höheren Ordnung, die auf göttlichem Recht und spiritueller Reinheit beruhte. In diesem Sinne wird der Rosenkranz zum Symbol für den Sieg über das Böse, das sich in der gesellschaftlichen Realität der DR Kongo in Form von Korruption, Vetternwirtschaft und brutaler Polizeigewalt widerspiegelt.

6. Der Fall Vital Kamerhe – Zwischen Unschuld und politischem Widerstand[49]

Das Strafverfahren gegen Vital Kamerhe, ehemaliger Kabinettsdirektor und enger Vertrauter des Präsidenten, war einer der prominentesten Rechtsfälle in der jüngeren Geschichte der Demokratischen Republik Kongo. Im April 2020 wurde

48 Vgl. Papst Johannes Paul II., Redemptoris Mater, Vatikan 1987, N1.

49 Der folgende Bericht enthält Auszüge aus dem sogenannten 100-Tage-Prozess gegen Vital Kamerhe, einem der aufsehenerregendsten Gerichtsverfahren der jüngeren kongolesischen Geschichte. Die Auszüge geben einen Einblick in die komplexe Verflechtung von politischer Macht, Korruption und der Suche nach Gerechtigkeit in der kongolesischen Politik. Vgl. Radio Télévision Nationale Congo (RTNC), Procès de 100 jours, https://www.youtube.com/watch?v=JUehRd2kxI0 (8.8.2025).

Vital Kamerhe beschuldigt, im Rahmen des »Procès de 100 Jours« der Präsidialverwaltung mehr als 50 Millionen US-Dollar an öffentlichen Geldern veruntreut zu haben. Das Landgericht Kinshasa-Gombe verurteilte ihn wegen Korruption und Geldwäsche zu 20 Jahren Haft – ein Urteil, das weithin als möglicher Wendepunkt in der kongolesischen Antikorruptionspolitik interpretiert wurde. Das Urteil gab jedoch auch Anlass zu ernsthaften Bedenken hinsichtlich der Unabhängigkeit der Justiz.

Vital Kamerhes bewusstes Auftreten mit religiöser Symbolik zog sich durch den gesamten Prozess. Besonders auffällig war das wiederholte Tragen eines Rosenkranzes im Gerichtssaal, was in der kongolesischen Öffentlichkeit großes Aufsehen erregte. Beobachtende interpretierten diese Geste sowohl als Ausdruck individueller Frömmigkeit als auch als bewusste symbolische Botschaft, mit der er sich selbst als eine moralisch integre Persönlichkeit darstellen wollte, die zu Unrecht verfolgt worden war. Der Rosenkranz diente ihm also zur Selbstvergewisserung und Politisierung seiner Rolle als Angeklagter.

In diesem Fall erfüllte die religiöse Symbolik – der Rosenkranz – nicht nur die Funktion eines politischen Kommunikationsmittels im Sinne einer performativen Selbstdarstellung, sondern auch die eines strategischen Kommunikationsmittels zur Verschiebung der Deutungshoheit über den Prozess – als Symbol des Widerstands, der Unschuld und der moralischen Autorität. Der Rosenkranz war für ihn das Symbol für seine moralische Reinheit in einem als korrupt wahrgenommenen System und implizierte damit eine Infragestellung der Legitimität der erhobenen Vorwürfe. Vital Kamerhe verfolgte mit der Verwendung religiöser Symbole das Ziel, eine alternative moralische Ordnung zu etablieren, die im Gegensatz zu den institutionellen Narrativen des kongolesischen Staates steht. Die Darstellung Vital Kamerhes mit dem Rosenkranz in den Medien verstärkte diesen Effekt noch. Zahlreiche Nachrichtenportale, darunter »Jeune Afrique«[50] und »Radio France Internationale«[51], zeigten ihn in einer Weise, die sein spirituelles Selbstbewusstsein betonte. Visuelle Symbolik wurde so zu einer Waffe im politischen Diskurs: Der Gerichtssaal wurde zum Ort der Rechtsprechung und zur Bühne des politischen Theaters. Vital Kamerhe positionierte sich als Opfer

50 Jeune Afrique, Vital Kamerhe condamné à 20 ans de prison, https://www.jeuneafrique.com/1004046/societe/rdc-vital-kamerhe-condamne-a-20-ans-de-prison/ (8.8.2025).

51 Radio France Internationale (RFI), Vital Kamerhe condamné à 20 ans de travaux forcés, https://www.rfi.fr/fr/afrique/20200620-procès-anticorruption-en-rdc-vital-kamerhe-condamné-à-20-ans-travaux-forcés (9.8.2025).

einer politischen Intrige – eine Interpretation, die bei seinen Anhängerinnen und Anhängern und in Teilen der kongolesischen Gesellschaft auf breite Zustimmung stieß.

Im Juni 2022 wurde Kamerhe jedoch durch ein Berufungsgericht freigesprochen. Dieses Urteil wurde von vielen als Rehabilitierung im juristischen wie im politischen Sinne interpretiert. Diese Entscheidung führte nicht nur zur rechtlichen Wiederherstellung seiner bürgerlichen und politischen Rechte, sondern markierte auch seine schrittweise Rückkehr auf die politische Bühne. Die Rehabilitierung Kamerhes zeigt die ambivalente Dynamik kongolesischer Justizpraxis auf, die zwischen dem Anspruch auf Korruptionsbekämpfung und dem Einfluss politischer Interessen oszilliert. Der Freispruch markierte formal die juristische Rehabilitierung Kamerhes. Für den Betroffenen selbst gewann er jedoch eine transzendente Dimension. In seiner eigenen Deutung erschien das Urteil als ein Akt göttlicher Gerechtigkeit, durch den er – so seine Worte – von der »Schande, mit der er vor den Augen der Nation beladen war«, erlöst worden sei. Es wird von einem Wunder berichtet, das durch das Rosenkranzgebet von der Muttergottes gewirkt wurde. Dadurch wurden die Unschuld und Reinheit des Kindes offenbar gemacht. In dieser Perspektive wird die Entscheidung des Gerichts nicht allein als rechtliche Korrektur verstanden, sondern zugleich als Zeichen einer sakralen Fügung, in der sich Recht und Gnade unauflöslich verschränken. In der öffentlichen Diskussion überlagert sich die Dimension juristischer Selbstkorrektur mit einer religiösen Selbstinszenierung. Letztere interpretiert den Freispruch als Frucht des Glaubens und der Fürsprache Mariens.

Diese Ereignisse werfen zentrale Fragen zur Rolle der Justiz in hybriden politischen Regimen und zur Funktion religiöser Symbolik in der öffentlichen Meinungsbildung auf. Der Fall Vital Kamerhe zeigt eindrücklich, wie eng Justiz, Religion und Politik im Kongo miteinander verwoben sind. Dabei handelte es sich nicht um ein isoliertes Phänomen. Vielmehr ist ein strukturelles Muster erkennbar, das auf eine historische Instrumentalisierung religiöser Diskurse zur Legitimation politischer Herrschaft verweist.

7. Religiöse materielle Objekte – Zwischen Glaubensinszenierung und Opferkonstruktion

Der Fall Vital Kamerhe ist ein typisches Beispiel dafür, wie religiöse materielle Gegenstände im Kontext politischer Krisen und juristischer Auseinandersetzungen als wirkungsvolle Instrumente der Inszenierung von Glauben und der Konstruktion einer Opferidentität eingesetzt werden können. Der Rosenkranz, den Vital Kamerhe während seines Prozesses demonstrativ zur Schau stellte,[52] diente ihm als persönliches Symbol der spirituellen Erbauung und individuellen Frömmigkeit. Das sakrale Gebetsobjekt wurde auch zu einem zentralen Mittel der öffentlichen Selbstdarstellung, mit dem er das Bild moralischer Unangreifbarkeit zu erzeugen und zugleich eine breite gesellschaftliche Solidarität für seine Sache zu mobilisieren suchte. Solche Sinn- und Legitimationszuschreibungen an Dinge folgen dem, was Webb Keane als *semiotic ideologies* der Materialität beschreibt, die ikonische und indexikalische Qualitäten von Objekten in soziale Wirksamkeit übersetzen.[53]

In einem Land wie dem Kongo, in dem religiöse Symbole tief in der kollektiven Vorstellungswelt verankert sind und politische und gesellschaftliche Legitimität in hohem Maße über die Vermittlung religiöser Bedeutungen ausgehandelt wird,[54] kann der strategische Einsatz solcher Objekte eine immense symbolische Kraft entfalten, die es erlaubt, selbst schwerwiegende juristische Vorwürfe zu überblenden und alternative Interpretationen in den öffentlichen Diskurs einzubringen. Die prominente Rolle der katholischen Kirche als moralische Autorität und Mobilisierungsnetzwerk im Kongo liefert hierfür den Resonanzraum.[55]

Daher erscheint es evident, dass die vermeintliche Schutz- und Legitimationskraft materieller religiöser Objekte in einem religiösen und politischen Kontext nicht als eine dem Objekt inhärente Eigenschaft verstanden werden kann. Statt-

52 Vgl. Congo Indépendant, Programme de 100 jours, https://www.congoindependant.com/programme-de-100-jours-v-k-et-sa-ligne-de-defense-casse-gueule/ (1.9.2025).

53 Webb Keane, Semiotics and the Social Analysis of Material Things, in: Language & Communication 23 (2003), 418, https://sites.lsa.umich.edu/wp-content/uploads/sites/128/2014/07/semiotics_and_the_social-analysis.pdf (1.9.2025).

54 Vgl. Sadiki Kangamina et al., Conflict, Epidemic and Faith Communities. Church-State Relations during the Fight against Covid-19 in North-Eastern DR Congo, in: Conflict and Health 16 (2022), https://conflictandhealth.biomedcentral.com/articles/10.1186/s13031-022-00488-4 (1.9.2025).

55 Congo Research Group and Ebuteli, The Catholic Church in the DRC. A Neutral Arbiter or at the Heart of Protest? Kinshasa/New York 2022, 6f, https://cic.nyu.edu/wp-content/uploads/2022/10/report-crg-ebuteli-the-catholic-church-in-drc.pdf (1.9.2025).

dessen ist sie vielmehr ein höchst ambivalentes und kontextabhängiges Phänomen. Ihre tatsächliche Wirksamkeit resultiert in erster Linie aus der subjektiven Akzeptanz bestimmter Weltanschauungen und der kollektiven Anerkennung innerhalb einer bestimmten religiös-kulturellen Ordnung. Dieser Befund schließt an material-religiöse Ansätze an, die Religion als *Praxis der Mediation* begreifen, in der Formen (Bilder, Dinge, Rituale) nicht bloß Träger, sondern Generatoren von Bedeutung und Erfahrung sind.[56] Die als immaterielle Schutzfunktion bezeichnete Wirkung eines Rosenkranzes resultiert nicht aus einer objektiv messbaren transzendenten Kraft, sondern aus einem komplexen Zusammenspiel individueller Überzeugungen, sozialer Symbolik und diskursiver Rahmenbedingungen. Innerhalb dieser Rahmenbedingungen entfalten Objekte ihre semantische Ladung und ihre performative Wirksamkeit – genau in dem Sinne, dass »Glauben« als verkörperte Disposition und materiell gestützte Praxis zu fassen ist und nicht nur als kognitive Zustimmung.[57] Der Fall Vital Kamerhe veranschaulicht, dass die tatsächliche Wirkung religiöser materieller Objekte primär von ihrer Fähigkeit abhängt, spezifische kulturelle Codes zu aktivieren, kollektive Vorstellungswelten zu mobilisieren und bestehende Interpretationsmuster im Hinblick auf politische oder soziale Selbstbehauptung strategisch zu instrumentalisieren.

Schlussfolgerung

Betrachtet man den Rosenkranz als materielles religiöses Objekt im Kontext der Demokratischen Republik Kongo, so offenbart sich seine Transformation von einem traditionellen Gebetsinstrument katholischer Frömmigkeit zu einem hochgradig aufgeladenen Symbol politischen Widerstands. In einer von Korruption, Machtmissbrauch und sozialer Ungerechtigkeit geprägten Gesellschaft überschreitet der Rosenkranz die Grenze zwischen religiöser Praxis und politischem Handeln. Er dient Gläubigen nicht nur zur spirituellen Andacht, sondern auch als Ausdrucksmittel kollektiven Dissenses und als Zeichen moralischer Positionierung. Besonders deutlich wird diese performative Dimension im Fall des Politi-

56 Vgl. Birgit Meyer, Mediation and the Genesis of Presence. Towards a Material Approach to Religion, Utrecht 2012, 31f; David Morgan (Hg.), Religion and Material Culture. The Matter of Belief, London/New York 2010, 8.

57 Vgl. Morgan, Religion, 4.

kers Vital Kamerhe: Während seines Prozesses trug er den Rosenkranz sichtbar, um moralische Unschuld zu signalisieren und eine alternative Lesart der gegen ihn gerichteten Anklagen zu etablieren.

In diesem Zusammenhang fungiert der Rosenkranz somit als politisches Instrument, das spirituellen Schutz, moralische Stärke und soziale Mobilisierung vermittelt. Materielle religiöse Objekte sind demnach keine passiven Repräsentationen von Glaubensinhalten, sondern aktive Akteure, die in soziale und politische Prozessen gestaltend eingreifen. Ihre Wirkung überschreitet die rein symbolische Ebene: Sie werden zu aktiven Elementen im Wechselspiel zwischen Religion, Macht und Gesellschaft und ermöglichen es, hegemoniale Strukturen zu hinterfragen. Damit eröffnen sie ein fruchtbares Feld für die Analyse materieller Kultur in postkolonialen Gesellschaften, in denen religiöse Objekte als Instrumente politischer Kommunikation und des Widerstands wirken.

(Dr. Égide Pèlerin Muziazia ist Lehrbeauftragter und hatte vom 1. April bis 30. September 2025 eine Vertretungsprofessur am Institut für Religionspädagogik und Pastoraltheologie der Katholisch-Theologischen Fakultät der Universität Münster inne.)

ABSTRACT

Material objects are of central importance in African religions in particular, as they form a bridge between the visible and invisible worlds in many religious practices. They are carriers of spiritual powers that offer comfort and protection to believers, while playing an active role in social cohesion and the formation of community identity. This article examines the complex religious function of material sacred objects and their symbolic and performative presence in political contexts. The first part provides a systematic overview of the meaning, function and ritual integration of material objects in African religious systems. The focus then shifts to the rosary as a sacred object of Christianity and its representation in political protest movements and social negotiation processes.

Christliches Leben am Golf – Migrationskirchen in den Vereinigten Arabischen Emiraten

Erste Beobachtungen und Einblicke

Gregor Etzelmüller und Claudia Rammelt

Die Vereinigten Arabischen Emirate (VAE) sind ein aufstrebender, föderaler Staat, der zunehmend eigenständig politische und wirtschaftliche Interessen verfolgt. Obwohl flächenmäßig das kleinste der BRIC-Länder, erkennen Länder wie Ägypten, Brasilien und Indien längst die politische und wirtschaftliche Bedeutung der Emirate. Es ist den VAE gelungen, politisch aus dem Schatten der Regionalmächte Saudi-Arabien und Iran herauszutreten.[1] Dubai gehört zu den *leading global cities* dieser Welt. Im *Finance Global City Index Report 2024* belegt Dubai den fünften Platz. »Its strong and stable economy, ranked 2nd globally, is underpinned by its strategic role as a hub for international trade, supported by world class logistics infrastructure and its advantageous position bridging the East and West.«[2] Dubai verfügt über den zehntgrößten Containerhafen der Welt, sieht man von chinesischen Häfen ab, ist es der viertgrößte. Der Containerhafen ist einer der wichtigsten Knotenpunkte für den Seehandel zwischen China/Indien und Europa, etwa 60 Prozent des chinesischen Handels laufen über *Dubai Jebel Ali Free Zone*, die weltweit größte Freihandelszone. Fujairah ist der dritt-

1 Vgl. Dina Esfandiary, New Order in the Gulf. The Rise of the UAE, London u. a. 2023; Tobias Haberkorn, Gewinner der Globalisierung? Die Bedeutung von Dubai im Weltwirtschaftssystem, Hamburg 2010.

2 https://brandirectory.com/reports/global-city-index/2024 (28.4.2025).

größte Bunkerhafen der Welt.[3] Da sich die VAE auch erfolgreich als touristische Destination vermarkten[4] und dabei werbestrategisch auf den Einfluss von Influencerinnen setzen, gewinnen viele den Eindruck einer glitzernden Scheinwelt – eine Wahrnehmung, die das politische (auch militärische) und wirtschaftliche Gewicht der VAE verkennt. Die Arbeitskraft unzähliger Migrant*innen war für diesen Erfolg unabdingbar und bleibt es auch weiterhin. Von den 10,64 Millionen in den VAE lebenden Menschen[5] sind über 8,5 Millionen Arbeitsmigrant*innen aus den verschiedensten Ländern der Welt.[6] Mit der Arbeitsmigration[7] kamen auch Christ*innen ins Land. 2020 bekannten sich in den Emiraten 1,11 Millionen Menschen zum christlichen Glauben.[8] Diese christlichen Arbeitsmigrant*innen und ihre Gemeinden stehen im Zentrum der folgenden Ausführungen.

Unser Forschungsinteresse an christlichen Vergemeinschaftungsformen in den VAE schließt an unsere Forschungen zu Migrationskirchen[9] in Deutschland an. Aus dem von uns initiierten Netzwerk »Migrationskirchen in Niedersachsen«[10] ist ein umfassender Band zu »Migrationskirchen. Pluralisierung und Internationalisierung des Christentums vor Ort«[11] entstanden. Unsere Forschungen gehen

3 Vgl. Laleh Khalili, Sinews of War and Trade. Shipping and Capitalism in the Arabian Peninsula, London/New York 2020, speziell zu Dubai 57–69 und 94–96, zur mit dem Bau und der Operation von Häfen zusammenhängenden Migration 191–201.

4 Vgl. https://www.touristik-aktuell.de/nachrichten/destinationen/news/datum/2025/02/13/dubai-rekordjahr-fuer-den-tourismus/ (28.4.202).

5 Vgl. https://de.statista.com/statistik/daten/studie/259705/umfrage/gesamtbevoelkerung-der-vereinigten-arabischen-emirate/ (28.4.2025).

6 Vgl. https://www.globalmediainsight.com/blog/uae-population-statistics/ (28.4.2025).

7 Arbeitsmigration bezeichnet die »Migration zur Aufnahme unselbständiger Erwerbstätigkeit in Gewerbe, Landwirtschaft, Industrie und im Dienstleistungsbereich.« (Jochen Oltmer, Migration. Geschichte und Zukunft der Gegenwart, Darmstadt 2017, 30).

8 Vgl. https://www.pewresearch.org/religion/feature/religious-composition-by-country-2010-2050/ (28.4.2025).

9 Der Begriff ist nicht unumstritten. Er ist keine Selbstbezeichnung der so genannten Gemeinden und steht deshalb in der Gefahr des »othering«. Durch ihn könnten bestimmte Kirchen und Gemeinden, auch deren Mitglieder, auf ihren Migrationshintergrund festgelegt werden. Doch der Begriff hilft, darauf aufmerksam zu machen, dass es Kirchen und Gemeinden gibt, die es ohne Migration nicht gäbe. Der Begriff dient hier als Bezeichnung von Gemeinden, »die von Migrantinnen und Migranten gegründet wurden und deren Mitgliedschaft überwiegend aus Menschen mit Migrationshintergrund besteht« (Claudia Währisch-Oblau, Migrationskirchen in Deutschland. Überlegungen zur strukturierten Beschreibung eines komplexen Phänomens, in: ZMiss 31 (2005), 19–31, hier: 20).

10 Vgl. Gregor Etzelmüller/Claudia Rammelt, Forschungsnetzwerk »Begegnung mit dem globalen Christentum vor Ort. Migrationskirchen in Niedersachsen«, in: ZMiss 47 (2021), 209–214.

11 Gregor Etzelmüller/Claudia Rammelt (Hg.), Migrationskirchen. Internationalisierung und Pluralisierung des Christentums vor Ort, Leipzig 2022.

von einem polyzentrischen Verständnis des Christentums und seiner Geschichte aus.[12] Das Christentum lässt sich nur als globale Bewegung verstehen, welche die Grenzen von Nation und Kultur transzendiert, und durch die globale Ausbreitung des Christentums haben sich dessen Zentren und Peripherien beständig verschoben.

Konkret hörten wir in Gesprächen mit arabischen Christ*innen in Deutschland wiederholt, dass andere Familienmitglieder und Freund*innen an den Golf migriert seien. Als wir diesen Erzählungen nachgingen, wurde schnell deutlich, dass die Emirate auch zu einem Ziel vor allem asiatischer christlicher Arbeitsmigrant*innen geworden sind – und dass sich mittlerweile eine Migrationsroute herausgebildet hat, die in der Regel über zwei Generationen gestreckt von Indien über die Emirate neben Nordamerika auch nach Europa führt. Da wir bezüglich der Erforschung von Migrationskirchen am Golf schnell an die Grenzen von Literatur- und Internetrecherchen stießen, sind wir im Oktober 2025 zu einer Exposure-Reise in die Vereinigten Arabischen Emirate aufgebrochen. Neben intensiven Feldforschungen in Gestalt zahlreicher Gottesdienst-, Kirchen- und gelegentlich auch Schulbesuche und spontanen Begegnungen nach den Gottesdiensten konnten erste biographische Interviews mit Gemeindeleitenden unterschiedlicher Konfessionen und Denominationen geführt werden. Entsprechende Treffen hatten wir bereits von Deutschland aus vereinbart.

Aufbauend auf unseren Beobachtungen wollen die folgenden Ausführungen erste Einblicke in die Lebensumstände und Gemeinden der christlichen Arbeitsmigrant*innen geben. Dafür fokussieren wir zunächst auf die Arbeitsmigration in die VAE, bevor wir in einem zweiten Schritt die religiöse Vergemeinschaftung in Gestalt von sogenannten Migrationskirchen in den Blick nehmen. Wir wagen abschließend die These, dass sich die VAE zu einem neuen Zentrum des Christentums im Mittleren Osten entwickeln werden.

Weil zum einen die christlichen Migrant*innen am Golf bisher kaum in den Blick genommen worden sind, zum anderen aber die VAE – man kann durchaus sagen: als ein islamischer Staat paradoxerweise – zu einem neuen Zentrum des Christentums werden, hoffen wir, diese Forschungen fortführen zu können mit vergleichenden Untersuchungen zu Migrationskirchen in den VAE und der Bun-

12 Vgl. Klaus Koschorke, Religion und Migration. Aspekte einer polyzentrischen Geschichte des Weltchristentums, in: Claudia Rammelt u. a. (Hg.), Begegnung in der Glokalität. Christliche Migrationskirchen in Deutschland im Wandel der Zeit, Leipzig 2018, 57–75.

desrepublik Deutschland, mit Forschungen zur Bedeutung der VAE für die arabische Christenheit einerseits, die indischen Kirchen andererseits – und im Blick auf die Frage, wie Migrationsprozesse Theologien prägen und transformieren.[13]

1. Arbeitsmigration in die VAE

Aufgrund der wirtschaftlichen Entwicklung, der bedingungslosen Öffnung für Arbeiter*innen aus allen Ländern sowie der geographisch günstigen Lage – zwei Drittel der Weltbevölkerung leben nicht weiter als acht Flugstunden entfernt –, ziehen die Emirate Menschen aus allen Weltregionen an, sogenannte *expatriates* (*expats*). Sprachlich wird dabei nicht zwischen Einwander*innen aus dem Norden, die im Norden *expats* genannt werden, und Arbeiter*innen aus dem Süden, die im Norden als Migrant*innen bezeichnet werden, unterschieden. Beide Gruppen unterliegen den gleichen rechtlichen Rahmenbedingungen – auch wenn sich ihre realen Lebenssituationen massiv unterscheiden.

Nach einer knappen Einführung in die Geschichte der Arbeitsmigration in die VAE sollen das Migrationsregime und die Lebensbedingungen der Arbeitsmigrant*innen in den Blick genommen werden.

1.1 Migration in die VAE

Schon immer war die Golfregion eine Region des Handels, in dessen Städten verschiedene Sprachen gesprochen wurden.[14] Dennoch ist nicht von der Hand zu weisen, dass sich durch die Entdeckung der Erdölvorkommen der polyglotte Charakter der Region nicht zuletzt durch die dringend benötigten Arbeitsmigrant*innen verdichtete.[15] Schon in den 1930er Jahren trieben britische Kolonialbeamte

13 Dieser Frage gehen wir gegenwärtig in einem von der DFG geförderten Forschungsprojekt »Encountering Theologies. Theologien von Migrationskirchen« zusammen mit zwei Doktorandinnen, Pia Dieling und Dorina Treutner-Seitz, im Blick auf evangelisch-vietnamesische Gemeinden in Niedersachsen und syrisch-orthodoxe Kirchen in Nordrhein-Westfalen nach.

14 Vgl. David Commins, The Gulf States. A Modern History, London 2012, 12.

15 Aus der zahlreichen Literatur zur Arbeitsmigration in die Golfstaaten sei verwiesen auf Françoise de Bel-Air, Demography, Migration, and the Labour Market in the UAE, in: GLMM 1 (2018), https://gulfmigration.grc.net/media/pubs/exno/GLMM_EN_2018_01.pdf (28.4.2025); Hélène Thiollet, Managing Migrant Labour in the Gulf. Transnational Dynamics of Migration Politics since the

und ausländische Ölfirmen migrantische Bewegungen voran. Zwischen 1950 und 1975 kamen zahlreiche arabische Arbeitskräfte in die Region. Nach der Ölkrise in den Jahren 1973 bis 1979 lieferten die Golfstaaten große Mengen an Öl in die globalen Märkte. Das füllte die Staatskassen und ließ beträchtliche Infrastrukturprojekte möglich werden. Zu deren Realisierung war eine hohe Anzahl an Arbeitskräften notwendig. Diese kamen weithin aus arabisch geprägten Ländern wie dem Jemen, Ägypten oder Palästina, doch zunehmend auch aus Süd- und Südostasien, wo effizient arbeitende Arbeitsvermittlungsagenturen Kräfte mobilisierten.[16] Durch die anhaltende Arbeitsmigration aus den Ländern Asiens auch über die 1990er Jahre hinaus veränderten sich die demographischen Verhältnisse in der Region nachhaltig. Heute kommt die Mehrzahl der in den VAE lebenden Menschen nicht aus der Golfregion, sondern aus Indien, Bangladesch und Pakistan.[17] Aufgrund der enormen Immigration kamen auch immer mehr Christ*innen in die VAE.[18] Neben solchen aus dem arabischsprachigen Raum begegnen christliche Migrant*innen aus Indien, vor allem aus Kerala, den Philippinen und Pakistan. In den letzten Jahren verstärkte sich auch der Zuzug afrikanischer Christ*innen.

1930s, in: IMI Working Papers Series 131 (2016), https://sciencespo.hal.science/hal-01346366/document (28.4.2025); Martin Baldwin-Edwards, Labour Immigration and Labour Markets in the GCC Countries. National Patterns and Trends, LSE Research Online Documents on Economics 55239, London School of Economics and Political Science, London 2011, https://eprints.lse.ac.uk/55239/1/Baldwin-Edwards_2011.pdf (28.4.2025); Holger Simon, Die Migration indischer Gastarbeiter in die Vereinigten Arabischen Emirate, Hamburg 2009.

16 Vgl. Andrzej Kapiszewski, Arab versus Asian Migrant Workers in the GCC Countries, in: Prakash C. Jain/Ginu Zacharia Oommen (Hg.), South Asian Migration to Gulf Countries, Routledge India 2006, 1–20, hier: 6–10.

17 »As of 2019 the top countries of origin of migrants in the UAE were India (38 %), Bangladesh (10 %), Pakistan (9 %), Egypt (10 %), and the Philippines (6 %). A further 20 % came from the MENA region (excluding Iran), including from Egypt, Iraq, Jordan, Lebanon, Syria, Palestine, Sudan, Yemen, and other Gulf countries. An increasing number of migrants tend to arrive from East and West Africa.« So die statistische Übersicht der Abteilung für Migranten und Flüchtlinge des Vatikans, Migrant Profile United Arab Emirates, https://migrants-refugees.va/country-profile/united-arab-emirates/ (28.4.2025).

18 Vgl. https://www.pewresearch.org/religion/feature/religious-composition-by-country-2010-2050/ (28.4.2025).

1.2 Das Migrationsregime der VAE

Da Migration in den VAE als Arbeitsmigration gefördert und konzipiert worden ist, hat sich ein Migrationsregime[19] herausgebildet, das sich wesentlich vom deutschen unterscheidet. Während Deutschland Migrationsprozesse mit Hilfe des Codes des Rechtssystems recht-unrecht zu steuern versucht und zwischen rechtmäßigem bzw. unrechtmäßigem Aufenthalt unterscheidet, arbeiten die VAE mit dem Code des Wirtschaftssystems: Wer nicht bezahlt wird, wer also nicht beschäftigt ist, hat kein Aufenthaltsrecht. Das sog. Kafala-System, auch Sponsorensystem genannt, bedeutet konkret: Ein Arbeitgeber (»kafeel«) ist verpflichtet, die volle ökonomische und soziale Verantwortung für seine migrantischen Arbeiter*innen während deren Vertragslaufzeit zu übernehmen.[20] Wer einen solchen »Sponsor« findet und hat, erhält ein Visum für den Zeitraum des Vertrags.[21] Zumeist werden Visa für drei Jahre ausgestellt. Diese können erneut ausgestellt werden, wenn der Arbeitsvertrag verlängert wird.[22] Wer allerdings illegal im Land bleibt, riskiert nicht nur seine Ausweisung, sondern auch hohe Geldstrafen und das lebenslange Verbot einer Wiedereinreise.[23] Mit der Pensionierung müssten nach diesem System alle *expats* das Land verlassen. Doch ist ein Aufenthalt beispielsweise dann möglich, wenn die Kinder eine Aufenthaltsgenehmigung haben, Wohnraum zur Verfügung stellen und über ein entsprechendes Einkommen

19 Unter Migrationsregime verstehen wir »ein Geflecht von Normen, Regeln, Konstruktionen, Wissensbeständen und Handlungen institutioneller Akteure«, welches »die Migrationsbewegungen kanaliser[t] und die Migranten kategorisier[t]« (Oltmer, Migration, 38), zur – notwendigen – theoretischen Debatte dieses Begriffs vgl. Andreas Pott u. a. (Hg.), Was ist ein Migrationsregime? What is a Migration Regime? Wiesbaden 2018.

20 Vgl. Rohan Advani, A Realm Without Rights. Noncitizen Workers and Exclusive Citizenship in the Gulf, in: The Century Foundation (2019), 1–18, hier: 9–12; Omar H. Alshehabi, Policing Labour in Empire. The Modern Origins of the Kafala Sponsorship System in the Gulf Arab States, in: British Journal of Middle Eastern Studies 48 (2019), 291–310.

21 Vgl. Maysa Zahra, United Arab Emirates' legal framework of migration, in: GLMM 2 (2017), 1–12, hier: 5.

22 Vgl. United Arab Emirates, United Arab Emirates. Federal Law No. 13 for 1996 Concerning Aliens Entry and Residence, Amending Some Provisions of the Federal Law No. 6 for 1973 Relating to Immigration and Residence, in: National Legislative Bodies/National Authorities (1996).

23 Vgl. Zahra, United Arab Emirates, 5. Trotz dieser Regelungen leben in den VAE auch Menschen ohne Visum. Ihnen wurde durch eine Amnestie im Oktober 2024 die Ausreise ermöglicht. So berichten es die *Gulfnews* im September 2024, vgl. https://gulfnews.com/uae/uae-visa-amnesty-exit-permit-validity-extended-till-october-31-2024-1.104187937 (28.4.2025). Diese Visaamnestie soll sogar um weitere zwei Monate verlängert worden sein, vgl. https://www.damacproperties.com/en/blog/visa-amnesty-uae-2024-latest-news-today-2378/ (28.4.2025).

verfügen.[24] All diejenigen, denen diese wirtschaftliche Prosperität nicht zuteilgeworden ist, leben nicht selten mit einem semi-legalen Aufenthaltsstatus bzw. arbeiten über das Renteneintrittsalter hinaus.

Das Migrationsregime der VAE, das konsequent zwischen Bürger*innen und Nicht-Bürger*innen im Land unterscheidet, führt dazu, dass »citizens and non-nationals [grow] as two separate entities without a new, mixed, population emerging from their co-existence.«[25] Dadurch steigt die Gefahr der Ungleichbehandlung der beiden Bevölkerungsgruppen. Dass es für eine Gesellschaft problematisch ist, wenn die einen das wirtschaftliche Wachstum erarbeiten, die anderen aber gleichsam als Rentiers davon profitieren, wird in den Emiraten zunehmend erkannt.[26] Mittlerweile sind Emiratis gesetzlich zum Arbeiten verpflichtet. Indem man sie an das Arbeiten heranführt, will man dafür sorgen, dass in Zukunft mehr zentrale Stellen mit Staatsbürger*innen besetzt werden können. Gegenwärtig sind zahlreiche Leitungspositionen mit *expats* besetzt, »around 25 % of working migrants occupy managerial posts in all sectors«.[27]

1.3 Leben zwischen Luxusvillen und Labourcamps

Auch wenn die Emiratis Arbeitsmigrant*innen aus den verschiedensten Ländern der Welt herzlich begrüßen, darf nicht verkannt werden, was es für die meisten heißt, in diesem Land als *migrant worker* zu leben: Dass es sinnvoll sei, den Arbeitenden bei Arbeitsantritt den Pass wegzunehmen, erklärte uns selbst ein deutscher Unternehmer. Ansonsten würden die Arbeiter*innen, so das Vorurteil, mit den ersten beiden Monatseinkommen für zwei Monate nach Indien fliegen. Der Lohn vieler Arbeitsmigrant*innen ist allerdings gering.[28] Wird bedacht, dass monatlich für ein Bett im Mehrbettzimmer der Labourcamps knapp 100 €

24 Vgl. İdil Kıncı, Ageing, Temporary Migrants. Life beyond Retirement in Dubai, in: GIGA Focus Middle East 6 (2021), 1–10, hier: 3. So gilt für die Mittelschicht und wohlhabende Migrant*innen: Das »lack of citizenship rights in the Gulf [is] irrelevant due to their privileged socio-economic statuses or passports, which shield them against the vulnerabilities of having liminal legal statuses.« (5).

25 Vgl. Philippe Fargues, Immigration without Inclusion. Non-Nationals in Nation-Building in the Gulf States, in: Asian and Pacific Migration Journal 20 (2011), 273–292, hier: 280.

26 Vgl. Steffen Hertog, Arab Gulf States. An Assessment of Nationalisation Policies, in: GLMM 1 (2014), 1–29, hier: 20–22.

27 https://migrants-refugees.va/country-profile/united-arab-emirates/ (28.4.2025).

28 Nach Aussagen in verschiedenen Gesprächen liegt der Verdienst zwischen 600 und 1000 Euro.

zu bezahlen sind[29] und die Lebenshaltungskosten in den Emiraten beachtlich sind, können die Summen, die an die Familien im Einzelnen zurücküberwiesen werden, nicht allzu hoch sein.[30] Die Lebensbedingungen in den Labourcamps bleiben Verschlusssache. Doch lassen bereits die Anlagen die herausfordernden Bedingungen erahnen: Nicht selten sind die einfachen Wohnblöcke umzäunt und nur durch eine Schleuse erreichbar.[31] Wiederholt wurde uns berichtet, dass die Labourcamps in den letzten Jahren modernisiert worden sind, so dass die Lebensbedingungen heute wesentlich besser seien als zu Beginn des Jahrtausends.[32] Die räumlichen Lebensbedingungen der »Nannys« sind offensichtlicher. Gewöhnliche Stadtapartments sehen für sie in der Regel ein kleines, fensterloses Zimmer vor, das gerade Raum für ein Bett bietet.[33] Durch die totale Inklusion in die Familie sind die Frauen der Öffentlichkeit weithin entzogen und deshalb prinzipiell stärker gefährdet:

> »Domestic workers can face the worst situations of abuses: in particular, house confinement, workdays of up to 21 hours with no rest breaks, and, in some cases, physical and sexual assault by employers. They are excluded

29 Vgl. https://www.laboraccommodation.ae/action/rent/ (28.4.2025). Bei diesen Preisen ist es nicht verwunderlich, dass eine Verordnung aus dem Jahr 2022 verfügt, dass bei einem Verdienst unter 1500 AED die Mietkosten vom Arbeitgeber zu übernehmen sind (Ministerial Resolution No. (44) of 2022. Regarding Occupational Health and Safety and Labor Accommodation).

30 Das schließt natürlich nicht aus, dass in der Summe Beachtliches zusammenkommt: Laut Weltbank flossen 2021 20 Milliarden USD von den VAE nach Indien zurück; mehr Geld wurde in jenem Jahr nur von den USA nach Mexiko zurücküberwiesen, vgl. https://blogs.worldbank.org/en/peoplemove/bilateral-remittance-matrix-new (26.10.2025).

31 Verschiedene Studien setzen sich mit der Situation der Arbeitsmigrant*innen auseinander. Innenansichten bieten u. a. Samuli Schielke, Migrant Dreams. Egyptian Workers in the Gulf States, Kairo/New York 2020, der mit einem ägyptischen Arbeitsmigranten in einem Labour Camp in Katar gelebt hat; William Guéraiche, Transnational Filipinos in the UAE. Actors and Strategies, in: Arabian Humanities 7 (2016), https://journals.openedition.org/arabianhumanities/3139 (28.4.2025) und Laavanya Kathiravelu, Migrant Dubai. Low Wage Workers and the Construction of a Global City, Basingstoke/Hampshire 2016.

32 Vgl. https://gulfmigration.grc.net/uae-cabinet-decision-no-13-of-2009-approving-the-general-standards-manual-for-group-labor-accommodation-and-related-services/ (28.4.2025).

33 Zu den Lebensbedingungen von Arbeitsmigrantinnen in den Golfstaaten vgl. Karen E. Young, Women's Labor Force Participation across the GCC, in: The Arab Gulf States Institute in Washington (2016); Bina Fernandes, Essential yet Invisible. Migrant Domestic Workers in the GCC, in: GLMM 4 (2014), Migration Policy Centre; Human Rights Watch, »I Already Bought You«. Abuse and Exploitation of Female Migrant Domestic Workers in the United Arab Emirates, United States of America 2014; S. Irianto/Thanh D. Truong, From Breaking the Silence to Breaking the Chain of Social Injustice. Indonesian Women Migrant Domestic Workers in the United Arab Emirates, in: Thanh D. Truong u. a. (Hg.), Migration, Gender and Social Justice. Perspectives on Human Insecurity, Heidelberg u. a. 2013, 29–46.

> from labour law protections and face legal and practical obstacles to redress. Women are reported to be generally more vulnerable to these abuses than men. Along with low-skilled workers, they often come off worse when it comes to receiving the wages promised in their contracts. Women are also more likely than men to have paid unofficial fees to brokers in their countries of origin. «[34]

An der Küstenstraße und den dahinterliegenden Wohnblöcken können sich jene Arbeitsmigrant*innen Wohnraum leisten, denen es durch ein angemessenes Gehalt möglich ist, ihre Familie nachkommen zu lassen. Für diese *expats* übernimmt der Arbeitgeber zum Teil Miete und Schulgebühren wie auch eine basale Krankenversicherung. Die enormen Mietpreise und Lebenshaltungskosten setzen aber auch diese Familien unter Druck, das erarbeitete Niveau durch stetigen Fleiß zu halten. Die Angst, durch längere Krankheit auszufallen und zahlungsunfähig zu werden, ist immer gegenwärtig (Feldprotokoll 20.10.2024). Viele träumen davon, dass ihre Kinder es später nach Europa oder in die USA schaffen. Im Grunde genommen profitiert Europa von diesem Modell: Die gesuchten IT-Fachkräfte dürften in den kommenden Jahren verstärkt aus den VAE kommen. Der Rektor der *St. Mary Catholic Highschool* in Fujairah meinte, viele ihrer Schüler*innen wollten später nach Deutschland, die USA oder andere Länder des »Westens«. Dass der Schulleiter resümiert: »We speak only English at school!« (Feldprotokoll 22.10.2024), verwundert nicht. Auch an jenem Schulzweig, der dem indischen Curriculum folgt, wird auf Englisch unterrichtet.

2. Migrationskirchen in den Vereinigten Arabischen Emiraten

Wenn sich 1,11 Millionen Menschen der Bevölkerung zum christlichen Glauben bekennen, stellt sich nicht nur die Frage, welche christlichen Gemeinschaften in den Emiraten anzutreffen sind, sondern auch die nach den Möglichkeiten ihrer Vergemeinschaftung und der Gestaltung ihres Gemeindeleben. Diese beiden Punkte sollen zunächst betrachtet werden, bevor abschließend Beobachtungen aus einzelnen Gemeinden zur Sprache kommen sollen.

34 Vgl. https://migrants-refugees.va/country-profile/united-arab-emirates/ (28.4.2025).

2.1 Der Golf – ein Ort der Weltchristenheit

Aufgrund der starken Zuwanderung von Christ*innen sind heute Glaubende der orthodoxen, katholischen sowie der evangelischen Tradition in der Breite ihrer Denominationen in den Emiraten anzutreffen.[35] Das lässt sich in Dubai in Vergangenheit und Gegenwart nachzeichnen, wo sich die Christ*innen zunächst zwischen Altstadt und heutigem Flughafen getroffen haben. Hier existieren bis heute die anglikanische Kirche *Holy Trinity*, die aber auch vielen anderen evangelischen Gemeinden Raum bietet. In der Nähe entstanden fernerhin die katholische *St. Mary Church*, deren Gemeinde oftmals als größte katholische Gemeinde der Welt bezeichnet wird, aber auch die indische *St. Thomas Orthodox Cathedral* und die *Sjømannskirken i Dubai – The Norwegian seamen's centre*, vor der die Fahnen der skandinavischen Länder wehen. Ihre bauliche Nähe zum iranischen Club, zum pakistanischen Hospital und einer pakistanischen Schule verdeutlicht, dass die Gemeinden zunächst als kulturelle Einrichtungen wahrgenommen worden sind. Da die Gemeinderäume oft zu klein sind, am Sonntagmorgen aufgrund des Verkehrsaufkommens kaum mit dem Auto zu erreichen sind und sich die Stadt stark Richtung Süden und Freihandelszone ausgedehnt hat, wurden weitere Gottesdienstgebäude nötig.

Deshalb errichtete das Emirat den Church Compound in Jebel Ali. Hier lässt sich an einem Wochenende konzentriert die ganze Fülle der Weltchristenheit beobachten. Arabischsprachige Christ*innen der rum-orthodoxen Tradition feiern in der *Our Lady Of Annunciation Greek Orthodox Church*. Sie dient neben den rum-orthodoxen Christ*innen auch Gemeinden anderer östlich-orthodoxer Traditionen als Gottesdienstort. Als wir dort waren, wurde gerade eine bulgarisch-orthodoxe Gemeinde mit einer feierlichen Liturgie und anschließendem Empfang gegründet (Feldprotokoll 19.10.2024). In der *St. Mina-Kirche* direkt nebenan laden koptisch-orthodoxe Glaubende zur Liturgie ein. Indische Christ*innen syrisch-orthodoxer Tradition feiern in der *Mor Ignatius Jacobite Syrian Orthodox Cathedral*. In der anglikanischen *Christ Church Jebel Ali* kommen unterschied-

35 Literatur zu den Migrationskirchen findet sich kaum. Einige wenige Titel begegnen wie Andrew Gardner, City of Strangers. Gulf Migration and the Indian Community in Bahrain, Ithaca 2010; Stanley John, Conceptualizing Temporary Economic Migration to Kuwait. An Analysis of Migrant Churches Based on Migrant Social Location, in: Mission Studies 32 (2015), 234–249.

lichste Gemeinden evangelischer Tradition zusammen. Das Gebäude verfügt über eine Fülle von größeren, aber teilweise auch recht kleinen Räumen, die stundenweise an evangelische, auch freikirchlich geprägte und pfingstkirchlich ausgerichtete Gemeinschaften vermietet werden. Hier sind z. B. die arabischsprachigen Protestant*innen aus dem Libanon und die *Presbyterian Church of Kameroon* zu Gast. Zahlreiche Gottesdienste werden hier am Wochenende gleichzeitig gefeiert (Feldprotokoll 19.10.2024). Auch die Gottesdienste der deutschsprachigen Gemeinden fanden bei den Anglikanern in Jebel Ali statt. Weil diese aber nicht wöchentlich gefeiert wurden, war die Gemeinde keine gern gesehene Mieterin (Feldprotokoll 18.10.2024). Stärker evangelikal geprägte Gemeinden versammeln sich nebenan in dem *Dubai Evangelical Church Centre*. Geht man um die Ecke, kommt man zum Gotteshaus der *Dubai Mar Thoma Parish*. Daneben steht die *St. Francis of Assisi Catholic Church*, in der Messen in unterschiedlichsten Sprachen gefeiert werden. Davor bietet eine Fatima-Grotte den Gläubigen die Möglichkeit zur individuellen Andacht und zum Gebet. Über das Gemeindeleben und die gegenwärtigen Aktivitäten informieren neben Homepages auch Social-Media-Kanäle. Letztere stellen nicht nur die Arbeit der Gemeinde vor, sondern dienen auch der Vernetzung und Verständigung der Glaubenden. So wird uns berichtet, dass Gemeindegruppen über WhatsApp unter der Woche Kontakt zueinander halten, aber auch Bibelworte und Gedanken teilen (Feldprotokoll 19.10.2024). Zur Wirklichkeit des Church Compounds gehört auch, dass unmittelbar gegenüber der rum-orthodoxen und der koptischen Kirche – auf der anderen Straßenseite – ein Hindu- und ein Sikh-Tempel (friedlich) nebeneinanderstehen. Nicht weit entfernt vom Church Compound entfernt gibt es auch einen christlichen Friedhof.

Auch in Abu Dhabi, Mussafah, dem Industriebezirk von Abu Dhabi, und Sharjah haben sich de facto Zentren ausgebildet, in denen die Gotteshäuser der verschiedenen Kirchen nah beieinanderstehen. In Fujairah, dem einzigen vollständig am Golf von Oman gelegenen Emirat, das in seiner Entwicklung bisher nicht mit Dubai und Abu Dhabi mithalten konnte, lassen sich ähnliche Zentrierungsprozesse noch nicht erkennen.

2.2 Die rechtlich-formale Situation der christlichen Migrationskirchen

Die Emirate verstehen sich nach Artikel 7 ihrer Verfassung als islamischer Staat, in dem die Scharia als Hauptquelle der Gesetzgebung fungiert.[36] Nach Artikel 32 besteht Freiheit der Religionsausübung, wenn diese in Einklang mit den allgemein anerkannten Traditionen steht, mit der öffentlichen Ordnung vereinbar ist und nicht gegen die Sitten verstößt.[37] Christ*innen wird also grundsätzlich die Möglichkeit eingeräumt, in Kirchen ihren Glauben auszuüben. In den VAE, »a religious group desiring to practice its religious rituals can submit a request to establish and license a new place of worship or a branch of a place of worship«.[38] Dadurch unterscheiden sich die VAE etwa von Saudi-Arabien, wo die Feier nichtmuslimischer Gottesdienste durch die Verfassung verboten ist.[39] Das Verfahren ist gebührenfrei und dauert laut Auskunft der Regierung 60 Tage. Eine neue Gemeinde braucht mindestens zwanzig Gründungsmitglieder, die über 40 Jahre alt sind (Art. 6.1.a) und mindestens fünf Jahre in den Emiraten gelebt haben (Art. 6.1.e).[40] Sie müssen »of good conduct and of good reputation« sein (Art. 6.1.c) und vor allem über entsprechende Finanzen verfügen: »The Founding Members shall provide proof of the ability to bear the costs of establishing and operating the House of Worship« (Art. 6.1.h). Die Lizenz gilt dabei zunächst für zwei Jahre (Art. 11.2). Ausländische Gelder dürfen nicht angenommen werden (Art. 16.2). Von vielen wird das Lizensierungsverfahren als Ausdruck einer toleranten Religionspolitik verstanden (Feldprotokolle 20.10.2025/23.10.2025).

Zu den lizenzierten Kirchen gehören die Armenier, die Kopten, die rum-orthodoxe Kirche des Patriarchats von Antiochien, drei indische Kirchen (die *Indian Orthodox Church*, die *Malankara Orthodox Church* und die *Mar-Thoma-Church*), die Anglikaner, die »Evangelischen«, die Brüdergemeine und die Ad-

36 Vgl. https://uaelegislation.gov.ae/en/constitution (28.4.2025).

37 Vgl. https://uaelegislation.gov.ae/en/constitution (28.4.2025).

38 Vgl. https://www.addcd.gov.ae/en/Licensing-Services/Licensing-of-Places-of-Worship-for-non-muslims/Request-to-License-Place-of-Worship-branch (28.4.2025)

39 Vgl. United States Commission on International Religious Freedom, in: Annual Report (2025), Washington 2025, 36, https://www.uscirf.gov/sites/default/files/2025-03/2025%20USCIRF%20Annual%20Report.pdf (30.4.2025). Allerdings lassen sich auch hier Veränderungen beobachten: »Despite the constitutional ban on non-Muslim worship, authorities allowed Christians to gather privately – under strict conditions – and permitted stores to display Christmas and Easter holiday decorations.« (United States Commission, Annual Report). Auch uns wurde von Gottesdiensten in Saudi-Arabien berichtet.

40 Vgl. https://uaelegislation.gov.ae/en/legislations/1963/download (28.4.2025).

ventisten, in Sharjah auch die russisch-orthodoxe Kirche. Die evangelischen Kirchen stellen dabei eine Besonderheit und für die Emirate eine besondere Schwierigkeit dar, weil sie keine Konfessionskirche mit klarem Ansprechpartner, sondern eher ein Sammelbecken unterschiedlicher, z. T. auch kongregationalistischer Gemeinden sind. Hier muss – das kann auch von Emirat zu Emirat verschieden sein – ein Church Council oder ein Unternehmen gegründet werden, welches sich um die Organisation der Vielfalt und des Gebäudes kümmert. Unter der Lizenz solcher evangelischer Kirchen, Verbünde und Unternehmen können dann auch sog. Hotelkirchen ihre Gottesdienste feiern (Feldprotokolle 20.10.2025/23.10.2025). In Abu Dhabi verfügen auch die Mormonen über ein Versammlungshaus; in Dubai liegt das Angebot vor, einen Tempel zu bauen. Es gibt auch Versammlungen von Zeugen Jehovas, die toleriert werden, sofern sichergestellt ist, dass keine Muslime anwesend sind. Lizenzierte Gemeinden können eine Kirche errichten. Sie bekommen dafür von der Sheikh-Familie des jeweiligen Emirats ein Grundstück zugewiesen und überlassen.[41]

Nach Aussagen einiger Gemeinden sind diese verpflichtet, Listen mit Teilnehmenden der Veranstaltungen zu führen (Feldprotokoll 19.10.2024). Diese müssen vom Staat einsehbar sein. Ob deshalb die koptisch-orthodoxe Gemeinde den Zutritt zu ihrem Gotteshaus allein auf Glaubende ihrer Konfessionsfamilie beschränkte, wäre genauer zu untersuchen. Derartige Restriktionen wie auch das Verbot privater religiöser Versammlungen (Art. 20.6) führen aber nicht zu Beschwerden, sondern dem immer wieder begegnenden Narrativ: »Die Regierung fürchtet eigentlich nicht uns, sondern die Muslimbrüder« (Feldprotokoll 23.10.2024), »nicht uns, sondern die Islamisten«, die nicht zwischen Religion und Politik zu unterscheiden vermögen. Letztlich würden dadurch die christlichen Gemeinden von der Religionspolitik der Emirate profitieren. (Feldprotokoll 20.10.2024).

So schätzen viele Migrationskirchen die bestehende Form der Religionsfreiheit, die manche aus ihren Herkunftsländern überhaupt nicht kennen. Der Staat wird von vielen Christ*innen sehr positiv wahrgenommen. Er gewähre nicht nur Religionsfreiheit, sondern auch Sicherheit. »Die Regierung kann in drei Minuten rekonstruieren, wo Du die letzten 48 Stunden warst«, hörten wir häufiger – voller Hochachtung. Die in den VAE erlebte Sicherheit steht im Kontrast zu

41 Vgl. https://www.state.gov/wp-content/uploads/2024/04/547499-UNITED-ARAB-EMIRATES-2023-INTERNATIONAL-RELIGIOUS-FREEDOM-REPORT.pdf, 31 (28.4.2025).

Erfahrungen aus den Herkunftsländern. Ein Libanese meinte, er habe erst hier realisiert, dass man ihm im Libanon seine Jugend gestohlen habe. Hier könne er seine Kinder ohne Sorgen allein zu Freunden in der Nachbarschaft schicken (Feldprotokoll 20.10.2024). Am Ende eines dreistündigen Interviews steigert sich die Wertschätzung der Emirate bei einem anderen Interviewpartner zur Aussage: »We have the best government of the world« (Feldprotokoll 23.10.2024).

Als Ausdruck einer toleranten Religionspolitik wird auch die Errichtung des *Abrahamic Family House* in Abu Dhabi wahrgenommen. Dieser Gebäude-Komplex beherbergt eine Moschee, eine Synagoge und eine Kirche, die auch liturgisch genutzt werden. Ein Imam, ein Priester und ein Rabbiner sind permanent präsent.[42] Ein Symbol der Geschwisterlichkeit stellt auch die Umbenennung der *Mohammed Bin Zayed Moschee* in *Maryam Umm Eisa Masjid*, Maria Mutter Jesu Moschee, dar. Mit dieser Moschee, die gerade saniert wird, ist der Islam im christlichen Kirchenviertel Abu Dhabis präsent und bringt mit der Namensgebung seine Verbundenheit mit dem Christentum zum Ausdruck. In diesem Zusammenhang ist auch das »Dokument über die Brüderlichkeit aller Menschen für ein friedliches Zusammenleben in der Welt«, das als Erklärung von Abu Dhabi bekannt ist, zu nennen, welches Papst Franziskus 2019 während seiner Reise nach Abu Dhabi gemeinsam mit dem Großimam der Kairoer Al-Azhar-Universität, Ahmad al-Tayyeb, unterzeichnet hat.[43] Die Erklärung versteht sich in den Augen des Vatikans als »Markstein auf dem Weg der Geschwisterlichkeit für Angehörige aller Religionen und wendet sich ausdrücklich gegen Fanatismus, Extremismus und Gewalt im Namen Gottes.«[44]

Wie sich die Religionspolitik gegenüber den christlichen Gemeinden in Zukunft gestalten wird, wurde unterschiedlich beurteilt: Manche Christ*innen meinen stärkere Liberalisierungstendenzen zu erkennen, insbesondere nach dem Besuch des Papstes 2019, als dieser mit 120 000 Katholik*innen eine öffentliche Messe feiern durfte. Auch erlaubt das Emirat Dubai den Katholik*innen, die Gottesdiente an Weihnachten auch von außerhalb des Kirchengeländes von *St. Mary*

42 Vgl. https://www.abrahamicfamilyhouse.ae/ (28.4.2025).

43 Vgl. https://www.vaticannews.va/de/papst/news/2019-02/papst-franziskus-abu-dhabi-gemeinsame-erklaerung-grossimam.html (28.4.2025); Zbigniew Józef Kubacki, Religious Pluralism from the Catholic Point of View, in: Verbum vitae 39 (2021), 527–542; Stephan Leimgruber, Vom Koran bis zur Erklärung von Abu Dhabi. Christlich-islamischer Dialog mit Fokus auf der Arabischen Halbinsel, Zürich 2023.

44 Vgl. https://www.vaticannews.va/de/welt/news/2023-02/abu-dhabi-synagoge-kirche-moschee-abrahamic-family-house.html (28.4.2025).

zu verfolgen. Zudem stellt es an den Festtagen kostenlose Parkplätze am nahegelegenen Flughafen zur Verfügung. Manche empfinden gerade auch nach dem 7. Oktober 2023 stärkere Restriktionen, ohne diese aber zu beklagen.

2.3 Migrationskirchen als Orte religiöser Kommunikation

Die Politik der Emirate führt in Abu Dhabi, Sharjah oder in Dubai zu einer Konzentration von Kirchen an einem Ort. Im Umfeld der *Church Compounds* und in den Straßen der Kirchenviertel drängen sich am Wochenende die Autos. Parkplätze sind bis auf den letzten Platz gefüllt (Feldprotokolle 19.10.2024/20.20. 2024/27.10.2024). Wenn vorhanden, sind die öffentlichen Transportmittel voller Glaubender (Feldprotokoll 20.10.2024). Diese kommen und gehen in den Rhythmen, wie die Gottesdienste ihrer Gemeinden – in der Regel zumindest von Samstagmorgen bis Sonntagabend – gefeiert werden. Die kamerunischen Presbyterianer beispielsweise haben einen Raum im Gebäude der anglikanischen Kirche jeden Samstag von 15 bis 18 Uhr gemietet. In dieser Zeit muss der Saal hergerichtet, Gottesdient gefeiert und anschließend wieder alles in den Ursprungszustand zurückversetzt werden. Platz finden die benötigten Utensilien in einem Schrank (Feldprotokoll 19.10.2024). Weder bietet dieser Raum die Möglichkeit, Vergemeinschaftung fortzusetzen, noch wird dafür ein anderer zur Verfügung gestellt. Neben Fragen der Praktikabilität ist die Möglichkeit des sozialen Miteinanders eine Frage der Finanzen. Die anglikanische Gemeinde verlangt Raummiete, die sich an der Länge der Raumnutzung orientiert. Da die Gemeindeglieder nicht zu den gutverdienenden Arbeitsmigrant*innen gehören, war es für sie schon eine Herausforderung, die Gelder für die Miete für die Zeit der gemeinsamen Gottesdienstfeier aufzubringen. Den Raum länger zu mieten – sowohl für den Zweck der Vergemeinschaftung als auch der katechetischen Unterweisung –, sei nicht möglich gewesen (Feldprotokoll 19.10.2024).

Wer über ein eigenes Kirchengebäude mit Kirchhof verfügt, kann Menschen erlauben, sich hier frei aufzuhalten. So schaffen die Kirchen Gelegenheit zur freien Geselligkeit, das ließ sich gut in *St. Mary* in Dubai und der *Evangelical Community Church* in Abu Dhabi beobachten. Hier standen die Glaubenden nach dem Gottesdienst beisammen und wurden auch wir als vermeintliche Neuankömmlinge von einem Gemeindeglied herzlich begrüßt (Feldprotokoll 27.10. 2024). Auch in den Gebäuden der Kirchen der östlich-orthodoxen Tradition gibt es neben dem Wohnhaus des Priesters auch eines für die Vergemeinschaftung (Feldprotokoll 19.10.2024). Ebenso gibt es in den Räumlichkeiten der koptisch-orthodoxen Gemeinde in Abu Dhabi einen Versammlungsraum für besondere Anlässe (Feldprotokoll 27.10.2024). Neben Gottesdiensten werden die Räumlichkeiten besonders für religiöse Bildungsveranstaltungen genutzt. Diese werden für die Kinder in Gestalt von Sonntagsschulen angeboten. In Gesprächen wurde immer wieder darauf verwiesen, wie wichtig den Eltern ist, dass die Kinder religiös unterwiesen würden. Zumeist geschieht das nicht in der Sprache der »Heimat« oder der Liturgie, sondern auf Englisch. Über Bildungsveranstaltungen für Kinder hinaus bieten einige Gemeinden solche auch für Erwachsene an (Feldprotokoll 27.10.2024). In der *Evangelical Community Church* starteten gerade drei neue Kurse, die an den nächsten sechs Sonntagen fortgesetzt werden sollten: *Geschichte der Alten Kirche*, eine elementare *Einführung ins Christentum* und *Glaube in der Arbeitswelt*. Wir besuchen mit etwa 30 anderen den letztgenannten Kurs; dem Pastor gelang es, das Thema so aufzugreifen, dass es in verschiedene Lebenswelten hineinsprechen konnte.

2.4 Migrationskirchen als wachsende und lebendige Gemeinden

Wir sind überall lebendigen Gemeinden begegnet, die sich bewegen und bewegt sind. Beim englischen Gottesdient in *St. Mary* stehen die Leute draußen, der Kindergottesdient wird in der großen Hauptkirche gefeiert, die arabische Messe feiern 1000 Gläubige, die philippinische im Anschluss füllt die Kirche mit mindestens 1500 Teilnehmenden (Feldprotokoll 20.10.2024). Gottesdienste, Bibelstunden, Sonntagsschule, eine Vielzahl der Veranstaltungen findet nacheinander bzw. parallel statt. Nach Auskunft der stellvertretenden Gemeinderatsvorsitzenden finden die gut besuchten Gottesdiente eigentlich erst am Abend statt. Nach Ende des philippinischen Gottesdienstes ist die U-Bahn-Station überfüllt, so dass Sicherheitskräfte den Zugang regeln müssen. Im anglikanischen Church Compound feiern in mehreren Hallen nacheinander unterschiedlichste Gemeinden Gottesdienst, überall hört man lauten Gesang. Ähnliches beobachten wir in Jebel Ali (Dubai), Moussafah und Abu Dhabi.

Diese Lebendigkeit ist auch in den besuchten Gottesdiensten zu spüren. Ob mit bewegten Rhythmen im Gottesdienst der kamerunischen Gemeinde (Feldprotokoll 19.10.2024) oder den arabischsprachigen katholischen Glaubenden (Feldprotokoll 20.10.2024), Glauben entfacht Begeisterung. In den katholischen Kirchen werden Jugendgottesdiente gefeiert, Jugendtage organisiert und der Weltmissionssonntag gefeiert (Feldprotokoll 20.10.2024). In einem pakistanischen Pfingstgottesdient klatschen sich die Gläubigen rhythmisch in Ekstase (Feldprotokoll 27.10.2024). Glaubende nehmen lange Weg auf sich, um Teil dieser Gemeinschaft der Glaubenden zu werden. Auch in der Woche versuchen die Glaubenden der jeweiligen Gemeinden in Kontakt zu bleiben, zumindest über social media und Whatsapp-Gruppen (Feldprotokoll 19.10.2024). Manche Gemeinden bieten auch während der Woche Abendgebete an. An ihnen teilzunehmen, fällt vielen aufgrund des langen Arbeitstages und der langen Anfahrtswege schwer (Feldprotokoll 24.10.2024).

Die große Anzahl der Glaubenden, die zu den Gottesdiensten kommen, ließ die *Indian Orthodox Church* in Abu Dhabi ihre 60 Jahre alte Kathedrale abreißen, um einen Neubau zu realisieren. Allein das Kirchenschiff bietet jetzt Platz für 1500 Menschen. Der gesamte Neubau wurde von der Gemeinde selbst finanziert. Ende Oktober 2024 wurde noch auf die Genehmigung des Emirats gewartet, bevor die Kirche eröffnet werden konnte (Feldprotokoll 24.10.2024). Auch die koptische und katholische Kirche in Abu Dhabi sowie die armenische und die rum-orthodoxe Kirche in Mussafah haben neu und äußerst prächtig gebaut. Die stellvertretende Kirchengemeinderatsvorsitzende in *St. Mary* in Dubai beklagt, dass ihre Gemeinde nur ein Problem habe, sie seien zu viele und benötigen unbedingt mehr Platz (Feldprotokoll 20.10.2024). Man hofft, in Zukunft eine zweite Kirche bauen zu können. Jebel Ali, wo es bereits eine zweite Gemeinde in Dubai gibt, sei für viele zu weit entfernt.

2.5 Einblicke in Phänomene des Gemeindelebens einzelner Migrationskirchen

Die verschiedenen Gespräche und Besuche eröffneten interessante Einblicke in die unterschiedlichsten Phänomene des Gemeindealltags. Wir wollen im Folgenden einige hervorheben.

2.5.1 Priesterwechsel in der Syrian Orthodox Church St. Georg in Abu Dhabi

Bei der *Indian Orthodox Church* in Abu Dhabi nahmen wir an einem Abendgebet teil, das zwei Priester zusammen mit dem *Assistant Vicar* leiteten (Feldprotokoll 24.10.2024). Wir sind in diesem völlig selbstverständlich mit dem Kreuzeszeichen gesegnet worden. Im anschließenden Gespräch zeigte sich, dass die Situation insofern besonders war, als einer der beiden Priester nach drei Jahren Tätigkeit in Abu Dhabi kurz vor seiner Rückkehr nach Indien stand. Der Priester meinte, dies stelle für ihn keine Herausforderung dar, weil seine Arbeit als Priester überall auf der Welt die gleiche sei. Wir fragen uns, ob das wirklich so ist, wenn man bedenkt, dass die Sunday School in Abu Dhabi nicht auf Malayalam, sondern in Englisch gehalten wird. Der andere Priester, der gerade erst aus Indien gekommen war, verfügt bisher nur über rudimentäre Englischkenntnisse. Erst vor drei Monaten hatte er erfahren, dass er nach Abu Dhabi versetzt wird. Dass er sich dort, wo Malayalam gesprochen wird, gut einfinden kann, zeigte sich, als er nach dem Abendgebet das neue Auto eines Gemeindegliedes segnete. Wie wird es ihm auf Englisch gelingen? Durch die neu erbaute Kirche führt uns ein indischer Kleinunternehmer, Mitglied der Gemeinde, der mit seinem Unternehmen (zwölf Mitarbeitende) die Glasarbeiten in der Kirche übernommen hatte.

2.5.2 Wertschätzung gegenüber allen als formulierte Aufgabe der größten katholischen Kirche der Welt, *St. Mary* in Dubai

In *St. Mary* in Dubai fasziniert das Katholische der katholischen Kirche. Es werden Messen in verschiedensten Sprachen gefeiert, keine Gemeinde ist Untermieterin, alle sind im Pfarrgemeinderat vertreten. Auch charismatische Gemeinden haben hier ihren Raum. Wer möchte, kann die auf Englisch gefeierten Messen besuchen; auch der Kindergottesdienst wird auf Englisch gefeiert. Kinder unterschiedlichster Nationen kommen zusammen. Die Kirche bietet vielen die Chance, sich ehrenamtlich zu engagieren. Die derzeitige stellvertretende Gemeinderatsvorsitzende hat als Kollekteneinsammlerin begonnen (Feldprotokoll 20.10.2024). Als sie dann Sunday School Lehrerin wurde, musste sie, obwohl sie bereits in Indien Kommunionunterricht gegeben hatte, ein Trainingsprogramm durchlaufen. Was sie damals als eigenartig empfand, schätzt sie mittlerweile. Sie hätte in dem Programm sehr viel gelernt, vor allem didaktisch. Der Unterricht sei besser als in Indien. Die Arbeit in der Kirchenleitung nimmt sie als sehr gleichberechtigt und wertschätzend wahr. Alle sollen zu Wort kommen. »Selbst wenn der Priester Nein sagen muss, ist es niemals ein autoritäres und exklusives Nein«, resümiert sie im Gespräch (Feldprotokoll 20.10.2024). Auch will die Gemeinde allen Menschen Wertschätzung vermitteln. Auch Muslime arbeiten ehrenamtlich mit, ohne freilich zur Konversion gedrängt oder ermutigt zu werden. Sie seien dabei als Menschen, die Jesus gern haben.

2.5.3 Migration und Gottes Plan – als Pastor in der Wüstenstadt Al Ain

In Al Ain lebt Joseph, der Pastor der arabischsprachigen evangelischen Gemeinde der Stadt und Mitglied im *Board of Directors* der Evangelical Church in Al Ain, mit seiner Frau. Sie arbeitet als Seelsorgerin im *Kanad Hospital*. Da dieses Krankenhaus von einer amerikanischen Wohltätigkeitsorganisation getragen wird, ist es ihm gestattet, ein Seelsorgeteam für die christlichen Mitarbeiter*innen zu unterhalten (Feldprotokoll 23.10.2024). Als wir das Krankenhaus besuchen, sind wir überrascht, wie offen das Krankenhaus seine Vision leben darf. »Our mission is to honor God by providing whole-person healthcare with the love and compassion of Jesus Christ.«[45] Es liegen Bibeln aus und an den Wänden stehen biblische Sprüche. Hier drückt sich der Dank an die Gründer des Hospitals, Pat and Marian Kennedy, aus, die die Kindersterblichkeit in den VAE enorm gesenkt haben.[46]

Joseph und seine Frau kommen aus der Presbyterianischen Kirche Ägyptens. Joseph war zunächst für die WHO in Ägypten und dann bei Adnoc (The Abu Dhabi National Oil Company) als Vice-President der Erdgasspalte tätig. Er gab seinen prestige- und einkommensträchtigen Beruf auf, um als Pastor in den VAE zu arbeiten. Da die evangelische Gemeinde in Al Ain im Zusammenhang mit dem Kanad Krankenhaus gegründet wurde, ist ihr kleines Gotteshaus nicht Teil eines Church Compounds, sondern steht direkt neben dem Krankenhaus. Seit einigen Monaten werde die Kirche von der Polizei bewacht, ob zur Bewachung oder zum Schutz, sei unklar (Feldprotokoll 20.10.2024). Josef und seine Frau haben zeitweise auch in den USA und Kanada gelebt, sind aber »Gottes Gebot

45 Vgl. https://kanadhospital.org/about-us/ (28.4.2025).
46 Vgl. https://kanadhospital.org/our-history/ (28.4.2025).

für sie folgend« nach Al Ain zurückgekehrt. Die VAE sind heute für arabische Christ*innen durchaus eine Alternative zu den USA und Europa: Hier kann man arabisch und zugleich in Sicherheit leben – und seinen Glauben frei ausdrücken (Feldprotokoll 20.10.2024). Sein Sohn aber lebt in Europa.

2.5.4 Religiöse Bildung allein in den Kirchen

Die katholische Kirche unterhält in jedem Emirat (wie z. B. auch die armenische Kirche in Abu Dhabi) eine eigene Schule. Für diese gilt von staatlicher Seite aus das Gebot der strikten Trennung von Religion und Bildung. So wird an den Schulen nicht von Jesus geredet, doch werden sie in seinem Geiste geleitet. Diese *Policy* erklärte uns der Rektor der *St. Mary High School* in Fujairah (Feldprotokoll 22.10.2024). Er trug zwar ein Collarhemd, wollte aber aufgrund der Trennung von Religion und Erziehung nicht über Religion reden. »Wenn wir uns für Religion interessieren, sollten wir uns an den Priester von St. Mary wenden«, sagte er im Gespräch (Feldprotokoll 22.10.2024). In der Schule wird auf Englisch unterrichtet, obgleich es zwei Schulstränge gibt. Der eine folgt dem englischen, der andere dem indischen Curriculum. Beide Abschlüsse berechtigen weltweit zum Hochschulstudium. Hier begegnen wir Schüler*innen, die in Zukunft hervorragend ausgebildet (auch) nach Europa aufbrechen werden.

2.5.5 Gemeinden als Jobvermittler

Ob in den katholischen Kirchen in Dubai oder Fujairah oder in den orthodoxen Kirchen indischer Tradition in Abu Dhabi, fast überall wird in Schaukästen auf Arbeitsangebote aufmerksam gemacht. Die Gemeinden sehen es als Ziel an, Arbeitslosigkeit und damit die Ausweisung der Migrant*innen (und ihrer Familien) zu verhindern. Wichtiger als die ausgehängten Jobangebote dürften die Gemeinden dabei als Ort milieuübergreifender Zusammenkünfte sein. Hier begegnen sich, je nach Gemeinde durchaus mehr oder weniger, *expats*, die leitende Positionen innehaben (immerhin etwa ein Viertel aller Migrant*innen in den VAE), mit solchen aus dem Niedriglohnsektor. Dadurch tut sich die Möglichkeit auf, Arbeit zu finden. Es ist nicht ausgeschlossen, dass drei wartende Männer, deren Kleidung verriet, dass sie nicht zur Mittelschicht Abu Dhabis gehörten, in der katholischen Gemeinde in Moussafah jemanden treffen, der ihnen ein Jobangebot unterbreitet (Feldprotokoll 26.10.2024). Genauso ist es nicht ausgeschlossen, dass der Kleinunternehmer indischer Provenienz Arbeitende zuerst in der Gemeinde sucht (Feldprotokoll 24.10.2024).[47]

St. Mary in Dubai sieht es als bedeutenden Teil ihres Auftrags an, gerade auch für die *expats* mit geringerem Einkommen Verantwortung zu übernehmen. Diese werden zu sozial-diakonischen Veranstaltungen eingeladen. Sie sollen sich als wertgeschätzt erfahren. »Ich danke Ihnen nicht für das Essen, sondern für die Wertschätzung, die Sie mir entgegengebracht haben«, habe jüngst ein Arbeiter nach einer solchen Veranstaltung gesagt (Feldprotokoll 20.10.2024). Weil die Emirate diakonische Tätigkeiten nicht dem religiösen Ausdruckshandeln zurechnen, sind diese nicht durch die Lizenz gedeckt. *St. Mary* muss für diese Veranstaltungen deshalb einen eigenen Verein gründen, der dann die diakonische Arbeit nicht-religiös ausübt, sich also an alle Menschen richten darf, dafür aber auf religiöse Kommunikation verzichten muss.

3. Die VAE – ein Ort der Weltchristenheit. Ausblick

Im Gespräch mit arabischsprachigen Christ*innen gewannen wir den Eindruck, dass die VAE zum neuen Zentrum des arabischsprachigen Christentums avanciert. Christ*innen aus den verschiedensten arabischsprachigen Ländern unterschiedlichster Konfessionen kommen an den Golf – und erklärten uns, nicht mehr in ihre Heimatländer zurückkehren zu wollen. Doch auch aus anderen Weltgegenden strömen Glaubende in die VAE, zurzeit vor allem aus Indien und dem asiatischen Raum, zunehmend aber auch aus Afrika. Diese Migrationsprozesse wirken aber auch auf die Herkunftsländer und die dortigen Kirchen zurück: Geld fließt nicht nur an Familien, sondern auch (über die Familien) in die Kirchen und Gemeinden der jeweiligen Heimatländer. Menschen – wie der oben erwähnte Priester der *Indian Orthodox Church* –, die zurückkehren, bringen ihre Erfahrungen und neu erworbenen Fähigkeiten mit. Nicht auszuschließen ist, dass Menschen in den VAE erstmals mit dem christlichen Glauben in Kontakt gekommen sind bzw. sich nun bewusst als Christ*innen verstehen. Wie Menschen hier

47 In den Migrationskirchen in den VAE wird Sozialkapital im Sinne von Robert Wuthnows *status-bridging social capital* gebildet; vgl. zum Begriff Robert Wuthnow, Religious Involvement and Status-Bridging Social Capital, in: Journal for the Scientific Study of Religion 41 (2002), 669–684, hier: 670.

Christentum erfahren und erleben, wird auf das Christentum ihrer Herkunftsländer zurückwirken.

Dass die VAE zu einem neuen Zentrum des globalen Christentums werden, belegt auch die Gründung des *Gulf Theological Seminary* durch *The Evangelical Church* in Abu Dhabi und die *Redeemer Church of Dubai*. Diese soll dem Christentum im gesamten Mittleren Osten und darüber hinaus dienen.

> »Gulf Theological Seminary's mission is to equip pastors, church planters, and lay leaders to multiply faithful churches in the Middle East, South Asia, East Asia, and Africa. [...] We aim to see communities throughout our region transformed by the gospel of Jesus Christ working through faithful, biblical, and missional churches to make disciples of all nations.«[48]

Das Seminar hat zwei Standorte, einen in Dubai, einen in Abu Dhabi, mit etwa 250 Studierenden.

Wer sich in interkultureller Perspektive mit dem Thema »Christentum und Migration« beschäftigt, muss den Golf in den Blick nehmen. Unsere ersten Einblicke lassen erwarten, dass sich die VAE zu einem Zentrum des Christentums im Mittleren Osten entwickeln werden. Dafür sprechen nicht nur die Zahlen, sondern vor allem auch die Lebendigkeit der Gemeinden. De facto eröffnet die pragmatische Religionspolitik der VAE den christlichen Gemeinden Spielräume, die diese verantwortungsvoll und kreativ nutzen.

Interessant ist dabei, dass sich dieses neue christliche Zentrum nicht durch aktive Mission (wie im 19. Jahrhundert) gebildet hat, sondern durch vielfältige Prozesse von Arbeitsmigration. Dadurch sind die Gemeinden zum einen durch eine hohe Fluidität gekennzeichnet. Da die Arbeitsmigration in die Emirate aber voraussichtlich die nächsten Jahrzehnte anhalten wird, werden immer wieder neue christliche Migrant:innen kommen und Gemeinden ihrer eigenen Tradition vorfinden. Insofern kann man von einem stabilen, wenn auch fluidem Zentrum sprechen.

Vermutlich wird die Ausstrahlungskraft dieses Zentrums eine dreifache sein: Die VAE werden sich möglicherweise (erstens) zum Zentrum des lokalen, arabischen Christentums entwickeln. Sie werden (zweitens) ein Zentrum des asiatischen (und möglicherweise afrikanischen) Christentums werden, weil sie christliche Migrant*innen aus diesen Ländern anlocken und über Geldrücküberwei-

48 Vgl. https://www.gulfseminary.com/ (28.4.2025).

sungen, aber auch durch den Rückfluss neuer Fähigkeiten und Erfahrungen die Kirchen in Asien (und Afrika) prägen werden. Sie werden (drittens) als Zwischenetappe auf einer über zwei Generationen sich erstreckenden Migrationsroute ein entscheidender Ausbildungsort für Kinder und Jugendliche werden, deren Eltern aus anderen arabischen Ländern, Asien und Afrika in die VAE emigrieren und die dann selbst nach Nordamerika und Europa weiterziehen. Diese Menschen werden nicht einfach das Christentum ihrer Eltern im Gepäck haben, sondern jene glokale Gestalt, die das Christentum in den VAE angenommen und ausgebildet hat. Wer verstehen will, wie Migrationsprozesse das globale Christentum prägen, darf die VAE nicht ausblenden.

(Prof. Dr. Gregor Etzelmüller ist Professor für Systematische Theologie an der Universität Osnabrück, Dr. Claudia Rammelt ist Wissenschaftliche Mitarbeiterin im Projekt »Between Intensification and Relativisation. Modalities and Mechanisms of Religious Change among Muslim and Christian Refugees from Syria in Germany, Austria and Switzerland« an der Georg-August-Universität Göttingen.)

ABSTRACT

In the United Arab Emirates (UAE), a constitutionally Islamic state, more than 10 % of the resident population are Christians. It is not missionary work, but rather processes of labor migration (see 1.) that have made the UAE a new center of Christianity in the Arab world, with further influence extending into Asia and Africa. In the Emirates, one encounters migrant churches from almost all Christian traditions and denominations, which the constitution allows to practice their faith in specific and protected spaces. This granted right and the general security that many Christians have never experienced in their countries of origin lead many to have a positive attitude toward the state. The article describes the life of the migrant churches in a differentiated manner (cf. 2.) and concludes with the thesis that the UAE is not only becoming the new center of Arabic-speaking Christianity, but also a new center of global Christianity (cf. 3.).

50 Years after

Der 4. Kongress der Lausanner Bewegung in Seoul-Incheon im September 2024

Vom 22.–28. September 2024 fand im südkoreanischen Incheon in der Metropolregion Seoul der 4. Kongress der Lausanner Bewegung statt. Dieser Tagungsbericht bietet eine knappe Einordnung der Konferenz in die Historie der Bewegung, zentrale Inhalte, Konfliktfelder und Hinweise auf bemerkenswerte Entwicklungen sowie am Ende einen knappen Überblick zur Rezeption.

Entwicklungslinien

Vergleichsweise kurzfristig entschied sich die Leitung der Lausanner Bewegung unter Michael Oh, das 50-jährige Jubiläum des Gründungskongresses der Lausanner Bewegung von 1974 zu nutzen, um einen vierten großen Kongress zu veranstalten.

Nachdem sich die Bewegung der neuen Evangelikalen, die sich in den 1930er bis 1940er Jahren in den Vereinigten Staaten entwickelt und in den 1950er und 1960er Jahren globalisiert hatte, etablierte sich mit dem Lausanner Kongress von 1974 eine Plattform für deren weltweite Missionsbewegung. Dies hing auch mit den Friktionen innerhalb der ökumenischen Missionsbewegung der 1960er und 1970er Jahre zusammen, welche insbesondere im Rahmen der 7. Weltmissionskonferenz in Bangkok greifbar wurden.

So stand auf dem ersten und namensgebenden Kongress der Lausanner Bewegung 1974 unter dem Titel »Alle Welt soll sein Wort hören« die Formulierung der Grundlagen der globalen evangelikalen Missionsbewegung im Vordergrund. Schon hier zeigten sich Spannungen sowohl zwischen vor allem der Verkündigung verpflichteten und eher holistisch akzentuierten Missionsansätzen als auch zwischen nordamerikanischen Akteuren und Vertretern nicht-westlicher Länder.

Nach fünfzehn Jahren teils grundlegenden Ringens um das Verhältnis von Evangelisation und ganzheitlichem Dienst setzte sich spätestens mit dem zweiten

Kongress der Bewegung in Manila 1989 eine eher verbindende Position von Mission als Transformation in Zeugnis und Dienst innerhalb der Bewegung durch. Diese wurde auf dem Kongress unter dem Titel »Proclaiming Christ until he comes. Calling the Whole Church to Take the Whole Gospel to the Whole World« weiter entfaltet.

Nach auch organisationalen Schwierigkeiten der Bewegung in den 1990er Jahren gelang mit einer Arbeitskonferenz in Pattaya 2004 und vor allem mit dem dritten Kongress im südafrikanischen Kapstadt 2010 eine Konsolidierung. Theologisch versuchte der dritte Kongress die diversen Wirklichkeiten einer globalisierten Welt auf die theologischen Grundthemen der evangelikalen Missionsbewegung zu beziehen und dabei eine eher verbindende Rhetorik der Liebe als Grundmuster der Missionstheologie zu entwickeln. Damit einher ging eine gewisse Öffnung der Bewegung für Dialoge und Kooperationen mit dem globalen Pentekostalismus, aber auch mit ökumenischen und katholischen Akteuren.

Diese historische Entwicklung der Lausanner Bewegung bietet den Hintergrund für die thematische Ausrichtung und die Diskurse im Rahmen des vierten Kongresses in Seoul im September 2024. Fünfzig Jahre nach dem Entstehen der Bewegung und nach dem Tod aller zentralen Figuren der Gründungszeit war dieser Kongress neben der Aufnahme neuer globaler und technischer Entwicklungen vor allem durch Diskurse um eine Identitätsbestimmung und Selbstvergewisserung der Bewegung geprägt.

Rahmen der Konferenz

Der vierte Kongress der Lausanner Bewegung wurde mit Blick auf das 50-jährige Jubiläum für das Jahr 2024 terminiert. Die Wahl der künstlichen Insel Songdo mit ihren Start-Up-Hubs in der Metropolregion Seoul betont zum einen die Bedeutung der koreanischen Missionsbewegung für den globalen Evangelikalismus und unterstreicht gleichzeitig das Selbstbild als innovationsfreudig und offen für digitale Neuerungen.

Mit dem Titel »Let the Church Declare and Display Christ Together« ist einerseits der Fokus des Missionsverständnisses der Bewegung auf Wortverkündigung (*declare*) markiert und andererseits mit dem Begriff der Darstellung (*display*) eine neue Begrifflichkeit eingeführt. Diese ist vermutlich der Versuch, über die Dichotomie von Verkündigung und sozialer Aktion hinwegzukommen, indem ein stärker verkörperlichter Begriff genutzt wird. Dieser kann sowohl Zeichenhandlungen der Verkündigung, Kunst und Architektur, aber eben auch diakonisches Handeln oder prophetische Zeichenhandlungen beinhalten.

Von den 5200 Teilnehmenden waren 29 % weiblich, 16 % unter 40 Jahre alt und 28 % arbeiten nicht hauptamtlich für Kirchen, Missionsgesellschaften, caritative Einrichtungen oder andere Arbeitgeber in kirchlicher Trägerschaft. Bezogen auf den aktuellen Wohnort kamen 36,9 % der Teilnehmenden aus Asien, 25,5 % aus Nordamerika, 13 % aus Europa, 12,8 % aus Afrika, 7,7 % aus Lateinamerika, 3 % aus Ozeanien sowie 1,1 % aus der Karibik. Das Ziel einer ausgewogenen Repräsentanz der evangelikalen Bewegung und der Förderung von Frauen, jungen Menschen und Personen aus dem Wirtschaftsleben ist dabei nur teilweise gelungen. Auch auf Grund der sehr hohen Kosten für die Teilnahme wurden zu Ende der Registrierungs- und Bewerbungsphase etliche Delegierte aus dem globalen Norden nachnominiert. Daneben gab es eine größere Zahl digitaler Delegierter, welche jedoch im Kongressgeschehen vor Ort kaum vorkamen. Dies wird durch die Statistik etwas verschleiert, da diese Personen häufig für ihre Organisationen im globalen Süden tätig sind und dort wohnen, so dass die Quote von Teilnehmenden aus dem globalen Norden eher über 50 % gelegen haben dürfte.

Der Kongressablauf war von einer Zweiteilung zwischen zentralen, frontalen Gottesdiensten und Events am Morgen und am Abend sowie stärker partizipativen Arbeits- und Themengruppen am Nachmittag geprägt. Zur Mitte des Kongresses fand am Abend die Feier zum 50-jährigen Jubiläum der Lausanner Bewegung im Plenum statt.

Wesentliche Diskurslinien im Vorfeld

Von Seiten der Kongressverantwortlichen wurde die Diskussion im Vorfeld vor allem über den gut 500 Seiten langen *State of the Great Commission Report* begleitet. Dieser basiert sowohl auf Hearings von Expertinnen und Experten aus dem globalen Evangelikalismus, einer qualitativen empirischen Studie mit Leiterinnen und Leitern der evangelikalen Bewegung sowie der Arbeit einer Redaktionsgruppe. Während gerade dieser Report von vielen Seiten gelobt wurde, entfaltete sich einige Wochen vor dem eigentlichen Kongress ein kritischer Diskurs zur Programmatik.

Prominente emische Stimmen, welche im Vorfeld Kritik an Teilen der Planung und Ausrichtung des Kongresses übten, waren etwa der *Executive Director of the World Evangelical Alliance's Mission Commission*, Jay Matenga, und die

International Fellowship for Mission as Transformation (INFEMIT). Hier wurde jeweils ein stärkerer Fokus auf kontextuelle Theologien, Mission in Demut und integrale Ansätze für Mission eingefordert.

Im Vorfeld gab es auch Kritik am Veranstaltungsort. Während die Bedeutung Asiens und besonders Südkoreas für das globale Christentum von allen Seiten betont wurde, entzündete sich die Kritik daran, dass ausgerechnet eine der teuersten Regionen der Welt als Austragungsort gewählt wurde. In der Folge war es vielen potentiellen Teilnehmenden nicht möglich, die Konferenz vor Ort zu besuchen, was sich auch an der recht geringen Teilnehmendenzahl aus Südamerika und Afrika zeigte. Diese wurde durch entsprechende Nachnominierungen – meist aus dem globalen Norden – ausgeglichen, auch um den finanziellen Verlust zumindest zu begrenzen.

Zentrale Themen und Entwicklungen

Wird auf die zentralen Inhalte der Konferenz geblickt, so war diese zunächst durch den Kontext ihres Veranstaltungsortes geprägt. Die Geschichte Koreas und des koreanischen Christentums wurde in einem abendfüllenden multimedialen Event unter der Mitwirkung von bekannten Repräsentantinnen und Repräsentanten koreanischer Kirchen erzählt. Die koreanische Teilung und die Verfolgung der Christinnen und Christen in Nordkorea platzierte den Topos des Martyriums im globalen Christentum prominent. Darauf bezogen und auch darüber hinausreichend betonten Vertreterinnen und Vertreter aus Korea immer wieder die Bedeutung des Bittgebets in der koreanischen Tradition.

Wiederkehrendes Thema der Konferenz war die Bedeutung der Mission am *workplace*, wobei damit mehr als der reine Arbeitsplatz aufgerufen wurde. Wesentlich war damit christliches Zeugnis und Dienst in Wirtschaft und Gesellschaft gemeint, was auch als eine Kritik an zu ekklesiozentrischen Missionstheologien verstanden werden konnte. Dieses Thema wurde häufig mit dem der Jüngerschaft – im Evangelikalismus die geläufigere Übersetzung von *discipleship* als Nachfolge – verknüpft. Hier zeigten sich auf der Konferenz Überschneidungen, aber auch Unterschiede zu den Diskursen im Rahmen der 13. Weltmissionskonferenz in Arusha 2018.

Ein wesentlich neuer Fokus des 4. Lausanner Kongresses gegenüber den vorangegangenen Kongressen war die hohe Bedeutung, welche dem Thema Digitalisierung beigemessen wurde. Zum einen wurde versucht, Möglichkeiten der digitalen Teilnahme am Kongress zu gestalten, zum anderen gab es am Veranstaltungsort eine große Ausstellungsfläche zu dem Thema: das *Digital Discovery Center.* Auch in verschiedenen Vorträgen im Rahmen der Zentralevents und in mehreren Arbeitsgruppen wurden verschiedene Aspekte des Themas prominent aufgegriffen. Die strategische Nutzung digitaler Möglichkeiten für Evangelisation, Gemeindegründung und in Teilen auch diakonisches Handeln wurde hier sicher stärker und strategischer als in anderen Netzwerken des globalen Christentums bedacht. Kritische Stimmen zu Aspekten der Digitalisierung und Digitalwirtschaft, etwa im Sinne einer Öffentlichen Theologie, spielten demgegenüber eine deutlich untergeordnete Rolle.

Gerade zu Beginn des Kongresses wurde insbesondere die Pneumatologie als theologische Leitkategorie für Mission etabliert. Darin können eine Verschiebung und Erweiterung der zuvor stark christologisch ausgerichteten Theologie der Lausanner Bewegung gesehen werden. Die sich in den letzten fünfzig Jahren deutlich ändernden Kräfteverhältnisse des globalen Christentums finden dabei sicherlich ebenso ihren Niederschlag wie Diskurse innerhalb des Evangelikalismus zu einer Verhältnisbestimmung gegenüber dem Pentekostalismus und neueren pneumatologischen Ansätzen in der ökumenischen Missionstheologie. Wie beim Thema Jüngerschaft wurde auch in den Vorträgen zur pneumatologischen Bestimmung der Missionstheologie von Seoul kein direkter Bezug zu den theologischen Entwicklungen im Ökumenischen Rat der Kirchen hergestellt. Während noch beim dritten Lausanner Kongress 2010 der Generalsekretär des Ökumenischen Rates ein Grußwort hielt, kam es – obwohl der aktuelle Generalsekretär Jerry Pillay zur Zeit des Kongresses Termine in Südkorea wahrnahm – in Seoul 2024 zu keinem offiziellen Beitrag. Anders gestalteten sich die Kontakte zum globalen Pentekostalismus: Mit William Wilson, dem Präsidenten der *Pentecostal World Fellowship*, sprach ein offizieller Vertreter der globalen Pfingstbewegung ein Grußwort und der renommierte pentekostale Theologe Kwabena Asamoah-Gyadu hielt einen der ersten Vorträge des Kongresses. Dabei blieb in der Schwebe, ob die Beiträge als Impulse aus der Lausanner Bewegung oder als Worte von nahen, aber zu unterscheidenden theologischen und kirchlichen Strömungen des globalen Christentums verstanden werden sollten.

Ein Abschlussdokument der Tagung gab es nicht, jedoch wurde am ersten Abend der Konferenz ein zuvor von einer Arbeitsgruppe vorbereitetes theologisches Statement, das *Seoul Statement*, veröffentlicht. Dies führte zu doppelten Kontroversen. Zum einen war ein Teil der Teilnehmenden konsterniert, da sie die

Möglichkeit zu Impulsen und Feedback wie bei den vorangehenden Kongressen erwartet hatten und das Dokument nur per Mail und ohne Aussprache kommuniziert wurde. Zum anderen gab es in größerem Umfang inhaltliche Kritik am Statement. Während es für den Kontext der evangelikalen Bewegung erstaunlich wenig Debatten zum formulierten Schriftverständnis gab, war manchen der Schwerpunkt auf Evangelisation nicht klar genug ausgedrückt. Gleichzeitig forderten andere ein integrales Missionsverständnis in der Tradition besonders lateinamerikanischer Evangelikaler. Während manchen die Aussagen zu Homosexualität als zu liberal erschienen, betrachteten andere diese als ausgrenzend oder homophob. Auf dem Kongress selbst formierte sich die Kritik am Statement nach dessen Veröffentlichung in einer Chat-Gruppe und es kam zu Treffen, an welchen auch viele bekannte Vertreterinnen und Vertreter integraler Mission und des sozialen Evangelikalismus teilnahmen. Auf Grund der hier vorgebrachten Kritik wurde eine Überarbeitung des schon veröffentlichten Dokuments angedacht und im Nachgang konnten entsprechende Eingaben gemacht werden. Letztlich wurde das Dokument jedoch nicht mehr verändert, was bis heute zu Protesten, etwa der *Korean Evangelicals Embracing Integral Mission* (KEEIM) führt.

Neben diesen Themen, welche von den meisten Teilnehmenden rezipiert wurden, gab es verschiedenste Diskurse und Themensetzungen in den 25 Arbeitsgruppen des Kongresses. Diese basierten auf den 25 im *State of the Great Commission Report* identifizierten Themenfeldern (*Gaps*). Daneben trafen sich verschiedenste formelle und informelle Netzwerke der Lausanner Bewegung und aus dem Bereich des weiteren globalen Evangelikalismus.

Aushandlungen und Einordnungen

Die engagierten und teils emotionalen Debatten – eher auf den Fluren als im perfekt durchgeplanten Zentralprogramm – zeigten auf der einen Seite die Binnenpluralität der Lausanner Bewegung, aber eben auch die Friktionen, die sich nach der Zeitspanne des klassischen globalen Evangelikalismus und dem Abtreten der Identifikationspersonen der Gründerjahre ergeben. Deutlich wird das etwa an einem Vortrag der lateinamerikanischen Theologin Ruth Padilla De-Borst, in welchem diese sich kritisch mit dispensationalistischer Eschatologie und deren Auswirkungen auf globale Politik auseinandersetzte. Sie explizierte dies – aus meiner Sicht nicht immer mit sachgemäßen Analogien – am Israel-Palästina-Konflikt, was schließlich zu einer öffentlichen Entschuldigung der Kongressleitung für einzelne Aussagen führte. Dies wiederum stieß auf deutliche Ablehnung vieler arabischer, lateinamerikanischer und eher sozial-evangelikaler Teilnehmender.

Solche Diskurse sind, ohne ein profundes Wissen zur Theologiegeschichte der Lausanner und der weiteren evangelikalen Bewegung, kaum einzuordnen. Daher ist es bedauerlich, dass bisher eine journalistische und eine wissenschaftliche Auseinandersetzung mit dem Kongress und seiner Ergebnisse fast ausschließlich im innerevangelikalen Diskurs erfolgte. Eine vertiefte theologische und auch religionswissenschaftliche Analyse von Themenfeldern, Diskurslinien und Friktionen auf dem Kongress scheint mir hinsichtlich des Forschungsbereiches *World Christianity* lohnend. Zumindest mit Blick auf die Zentralveranstaltungen wäre dies durch die weitgehend – mit Ausnahme der sicherheitssensiblen Vorträge von Teilnehmenden aus Ländern wie China – zur Verfügung gestellten Vorträge möglich. Unabhängig von der je eigenen theologischen Position bietet die Rezeption eine Horizonterweiterung und einen Einblick in aktuelle Diskurse und Strategien eines zahlenmäßig bedeutsamen Teils des globalen Christentums.

Matthias Ehmann

Bericht von der Einweihung der *Pasifika Communities University* (*PCU*, ehemals *PTC*) vom 28.4. bis 1.5.2025 in Suva auf Fidschi

Seit den 1960er Jahren haben sich im Zuge der Unabhängigkeits- und Selbstständigkeitsbestrebungen von Kirchen und Staaten weltweit unterschiedliche Formen der kontextuellen Theologie herausgebildet. 1961 wurde auf einer regionalen ökumenischen Konferenz in Malua, Samoa, mit Unterstützung des Internationalen Missionsrates, der Entschluss gefasst, die Ausbildung der Pfarrerschaft für die verschiedenen Inselkirchen des Südpazifiks in einheimische Verantwortung zu übertragen. 1965 wurde durch Rev. Dr. Michael Ramsey, Erzbischof von Canterbury, in Suva auf den Fidschi-Inseln der Grundstein für das *Pacific Theological College* (*PTC*) gelegt. Die von dem Rektor Sione Amanaki Havea entwickelte Kokosnuss-Theologie, die die Kokosnuss als Symbol für den *christus praesenz* empfahl und einer Theologie des Wartens anstelle westlicher Zeitvorstellungen den Vorzug gibt, wurde 1983 bei der Ökumenischen Weltkirchenversammlung in Vancouver einem größeren Publikum bekannt. Demnach ist das Erleben der »Pacific Time« nicht von dem Gegensatz Vergangenheit-Zukunft geprägt, sondern von dem zyklischen Naturjahr. Es wird an der Reife der Kokosnuss, dem Auftauchen der Fischschwärme am Riff und der Ernte der Knollenfrüchte bemessen. Weitere Entwürfe wurden etwa von seinem Nachfolger Illaitia Tuwere als »Theologie des Landes« (Vanua) oder vom anglikanischen Bischof Winston Halapua als »Theologie des Meeres« (Moana) entwickelt. Die Betonung der Einheit von Himmel, Erde und Menschheit sowie deren gemeinschaftliche Identität ist ein gemeinsames Element der unterschiedlichen Entwürfe pazifischer Theologien. Das gilt auch für die neuesten Ansätze einer Ökotheologie im Zeichen des Klimawandels. Ozeanische Weisheiten für ein harmonisches Zusammenleben mit den Mächten der Natur gelte es wiederzuentdecken, so der Samoaner Ama'amalele Tofaeono. Allen Entwürfen ist laut Cliff Bird gemeinsam, dass sie die Interrelationalität und Interdependenz der Menschen unterstreichen.

In den letzten 60 Jahren entwickelte sich das PTC zu einem Zentrum kontextueller pazifischer Theologien. In der Bibliothek des ehemaligen PTC finden sich mehr als 100 Master- und Doktorarbeiten, in denen das Evangelium aus kontextueller Perspektive interpretiert wird. Diese befassen sich stärker mit der pazifischen Lebensweise und Kultur als mit sozio-politischer Befreiung wie sie in der Theologie Lateinamerikas vertreten wird. Allerdings standen diese kontextuellen Entwürfe in Spannung zu den Curricula der theologischen Ausbildung, die zum Teil weiterhin auf die von Missionaren eingeführten Lehrpläne zurückgingen, obwohl die Fakultät in ökumenischer Zusammenarbeit wesentliche Revisionen durchgeführt hatte. Immer wieder wurde der indigene Referenzpunkt der theologischen Ausbildung eingefordert. Der frühere Rektor Fele Nokise experimentierte in seinen Kursen mit alternativen Lehrmethoden. Einen wesentlichen Schritt weiter geht nun aber die aktuelle Leitung unter Upolu Vaai. Mit der Gründung der PCU wurde eine konsequente Kontextualisierung der Curricula vorgenommen. Grundlage ist Vaais eigener Entwurf einer »holistischen Hermeneutik«, die sich gegen die Säkularisierung der Wissenschaft im Westen sowie gegen die Ausdifferenzierung der Bereiche Religion und Entwicklung wendet und sich stattdessen für einen holistischen Ansatz der Gemeinschaftlichkeit einsetzt. Seine »Whole of Life Hermeneutik« hatte er bereits in seiner Dissertation zur Trinität auf der Grundlage samoanischer Relationalität entwickelt. In der Publikation anlässlich der Eröffnung der PCU werden die Prinzipien der »Whole of Life« Vision als ein Bildungsverständnis beschrieben, das alle Lebensdimensionen einbezieht und in der Idee des Kollektivs verwurzelt ist, die alle miteinander verbindet. Demnach existiert alles in einer differenzierten und zugleich integrierten Ganzheit, die auf der lebensspendenden Beziehung der göttlichen Gemeinschaft – Vater, Sohn und Geist – gründet. Diese Beziehung zeige sich in den lebensbejahenden Kulturen und Verwandtschaftstraditionen von Pasifika, verwirklicht in den miteinander verflochtenen Lebensweisen und erkenntnistheoretischen Zugängen, die relational geprägt sind. Diese sind zugleich harmonisch und widersprüchlich, vermittelt durch vielfältige Sprachen und Dialekte, und werden in heiligen Traditionen des Teilens, der Fürsorge, des Dienens und der Verantwortung für die Schöpfung sichtbar. Während im Westen eine auf Entweder-oder getrimmte Wissenschaftskultur vorherrsche, würde im Pazifik eine Sowohl-als-auch-Methode bevorzugt. Es ginge nicht um die Identifizierung ausschließlicher Gegensätze, sondern um sich ergänzende Gegensätze, so Vaai.

Die sechs Prinzipien der »Whole of Life Vision« für die neue Universität werden in Form eines traditionellen pazifischen Hauses mit sechs tragenden Säulen dargestellt. Diese Säulen sind:

1. Relationalität: Bildung muss relational und ganzheitlich sein.
2. Dekolonialität: Bildung muss koloniale Wissenssysteme hinterfragen und auf Befreiung und Selbstbestimmung zielen.
3. Gemeinschaftsbasiertes Lernen: Bildung muss gemeinschaftsorientiert sein und von Gemeinschaften für Gemeinschaften entwickelt werden.
4. Gerechtigkeit: Bildung muss prophetisch sein und von Gerechtigkeit geleitet werden.
5. Kontextualisierung: Bildung muss die Weisheit und Methoden der eigenen Kulturen und Traditionen anerkennen.
6. Ökumene: Bildung muss ökumenisch und interreligiös ausgerichtet sein.

Die Verwendung des Begriffs »Pasifika« im Namen der PCU soll für ein »neues Bewusstsein« stehen. Dabei geht es stärker um sozialen Wandel und selbstbestimmtes Denken als um geographische Festlegungen. Die koloniale Vergangenheit und ihr Einfluss selbst auf grundlegende Begriffe sollen nicht geleugnet, aber durch Indigenisierung (Pasifika statt Pacific) in ein selbstbestimmtes Handlungsfeld gebracht werden. Die Begriffswahl unterstreicht das Gefühl von Widerstandskraft und ist ein Weg, sich den abwertenden kolonialen oder neokolonialen Erzählungen zu widersetzen, sie zu überwinden und die (Missions-)Geschichte neu aus Sicht der Menschen vor Ort zu erzählen (*reStorying*).

Die Verwendung des Begriffs »Communities« (Gemeinschaften) macht drei Dinge deutlich:

1. Bildungseinrichtungen haben sich lange Zeit auf das dominante, koloniale, »institutionenbasierte« und »klassenzimmerzentrierte« Bildungssystem konzentriert. Dabei werden die Stimmen und Werte von Gemeinschaften – insbesondere von Basisgemeinden – oft übergangen. Die Gemeinschaften durften das Gelernte nur in den Klassenzimmern »anwenden«. Diese Universität legt hingegen Wert auf gemeinschaftsbasiertes Lernen und bringt das Lernen zurück in die Gemeinschaften, indem sie Theorie und Praxis integriert.
2. Der Fokus auf Gemeinschaften erweitert den Einflussbereich der Universität, indem er die Stimmen der Gemeinschaften in den Bildungsbereich zurückbringt.

3. Die bewusste Verwendung des Plurals »Communities« würdigt die Komplexität, Vielschichtigkeit und Beziehungsstrukturen der Pasifika-Gemeinschaften – Aspekte, die von eindimensionalen Bildungssystemen, -politiken oder -modellen oft übersehen werden.

Die PCU hat in diesem Zusammenhang ihr eigenes *Communities Research Framework* (*CRF*) entwickelt, das die ethische Verantwortung von PCU-basierter Forschung gegenüber Gemeinschaften konkretisiert, von der Selbstverpflichtung zur Einhaltung traditioneller Gastprotokolle in Dorfgemeinschaften bis zum aktuellen Thema der Datensouveränität.

Auch die Rolle universitärer Positionen und insbesondere der Lehrenden sollen in der neuen Universität überdacht und sprachlich neu gefasst werden. Professor:innen und Lektor:innen werden nun als »Facilitators of Learning« bezeichnet, also als diejenigen, die Lernprozesse ermöglichen und begleiten. Mittelfristig sollen Kurse in ausgewählten Dorfgemeinschaften von akkreditierten Mitgliedern dieser Gemeinschaften unterrichtet werden. Es wurden bereits 14 Vereinbarungen mit lokalen Dorfgemeinschaften abgeschlossen. Diese Dorfgemeinschaften sollen einerseits, ähnlich dem Programm einer Volkshochschule, von Fortbildungen durch die PCU profitieren, aber andererseits auch als Expert:innen ihrer Kultur Studierende der PCU vor Ort in einer Verbindung von Theorie und Praxis anleiten und an der Konzeption und Durchführung sie betreffender Forschungsprojekte aktiv beteiligt sein. Diese dezentralen, gemeinschaftsbasierten Kurse sollen ein wesentlicher Bestandteil der Lehre an der PCU werden. Der Begriff »University« im Namen der PCU bezieht sich daher weniger auf eine institutionalisierte Wissenszentrale, sondern vielmehr auf eine Vision und Bewegung für transformative Bildung, die die Vielfalt von Lern- und Wissensgemeinschaften anerkennt. Es wird lohnend sein zu verfolgen, ob oder wie es auf Dauer möglich sein wird, den von der PCU vorgeschlagenen Graswurzelansatz mit den akademischen Erfordernissen einer Universität in Einklang zu bringen.

Als Plattform für theologische Diskussionen mit Relevanz für die Pazifikregion und die »Whole of Life« Vision hat die PCU eine akademische online Zeitschrift initiiert, das *Journal of Contemporary Pasifika Theologies* (*CPT*). CPT veröffentlicht Forschungsaufsätze mit Peer-review sowie Buchbesprechungen und andere relevante Dokumente. Die erste Ausgabe zur Eröffnung der Universität ist in Vorbereitung und wird Beträge von Personen mit besonderer Verbindung zur PCU enthalten. Zukünftige Ausgaben sollen über allgemeine Einsendungen und Aufrufe zur Beteiligung an thematischen Sonderheften entstehen.

Neben der theologischen Ausbildung in der *Schule für Theologie und Ökumene* (*SOTE*) umfasst die Universität zwei weitere Schulen. Die Schule für Pazifische Philosophien, Bildung und Wissenschaften (SPPES) soll Bildung und Forschung fördern, die von pazifischen Philosophien und Wissenschaften geprägt sind. Dabei wird ein dekolonialisierter, ganzheitlicher Lernansatz verfolgt, der zukünftige Pädagog:innen, Denker:innen und Innovator:innen stärkt. Die *Schule für Ökologie und Resilienzförderung* (*SERD*) vermittelt Wissen und Fähigkeiten zur Bewältigung ökologischer und klimatischer Herausforderungen. Dabei sollen indigene Weisheiten, glaubensbasierte Perspektiven und gemeinschaftliche Resilienzpraktiken zugrunde gelegt werden.

Die *Schule für Theologie und Ökumene* wird weiterhin theologische und ökumenische Bildung anbieten, die Führungskräfte für Kirche und Gesellschaft ausbilden soll. Diese Ausbildung basiert auf pazifischen Werten, biblischer Weisheit und einer an Gerechtigkeit orientierten Mission. Dieser dritte Zweig ist der Einzige, der derzeit über eingeschriebene Studierende verfügt. Die beiden anderen Abteilungen setzen jedoch die Kursarbeit fort, die früher vom *Institut für Research for Social Analysis* (*IRSA*), jetzt *RILED*, verantwortet wurde. Dessen Direktor Aisake Casimira, der für die Überwindung eines ökologisch destruktiven westlichen Entwicklungsverständnisses eintritt, kann als einer der Architekten der neuen *Communities University* angesehen werden, da er seine Erfahrung als Leiter des *Ecumenical Centre for Research, Education and Advocacy* (*ECREA*) und seine Arbeit mit ökumenischen Partnern bei der *Pacific Conference of Churches* (*PCC*) eingebracht hat. Seine Erfahrung mit Drittmittelfinanzierungen kann auch für die Akquirierung von externen Finanzierungsquellen der übrigen Programme hilfreich werden, da es in Fidschi bereits andere etablierte Nichtregierungsorganisationen im Bereich der dörflichen Entwicklung gibt, wie das *Social Empowerment and Education Programme* (*SEEP*), das aus der Arbeit von ECREA hervorgegangen ist.

Durch den Universitätsstatus verspricht es aber einfacher zu werden, Drittmittel von Entwicklungsagenturen wie *UN Development*, *Tetra Tech* oder der fidschianischen Regierung, mit denen bereits Abkommen geschlossen wurden, einzuwerben. Insofern kann diese Neugründung auch als Flucht nach vorne aus der prekären finanziellen Situation des früheren PTC interpretiert werden. Dieses war ausschließlich von kirchlichen Zuwendungsgebern, ökumenischen Partnern wie der EMW und den Mitgliedskirchen abhängig, aber notorisch unterfinanziert. Da die pazifischen Kirchen inzwischen ihre eigenen Ausbildungsstätten haben, gegründet in der Regel mit von PTC ausgebildetem Personal, besteht weniger Bedarf an einer regionalen Ausbildung der Pfarrer:innenschaft, was zu einem Rückgang an Studierendenzahlen und damit Einnahmen geführt hat.

Weitere Kooperationen könnten sich mit der nur wenige hundert Meter entfernt befindlichen *University of the South Pacific* (*USP*) ergeben, einer Universität, die seit Jahren erfolgreich Studierende unabhängig von ihrem religiösen Hintergrund ausbildet. Obwohl das Christentum die am stärksten vertretene Religion in Fidschi ist, hat fast die Hälfte der Bevölkerung einen hinduistischen oder muslimischen Hintergrund. Für die PCU schließt das seit 2017 in der Region bevorzugte ökumenische Sprachbild des pazifischen Haushalt Gottes nicht nur andere Konfessionen, sondern auch andere Religionen und letztlich, im Sinne der »Whole of Life« Vision, den gesamten Kosmos mit ein. An der PCU wurde deshalb ein neues *Zentrum für Mission und Interfaith* (*MAIC*) gegründet, das die Rolle von interreligiösen Beziehungen in der Pazifikregion erforschen und verstärken soll. Anders als in Europa wird der christliche Missionsbegriff nicht als ein Hindernis, sondern – interpretiert als gemeinsame Sendung für das Wohl aller – als ein wichtiger Bezugspunkt angesehen. Zum gemeinsamen Abendmahl der PCU-Gemeinschaft sind explizit auch die muslimischen und hinduistischen Angestellten eingeladen. Über eine Öffnung geeigneter Programme für Studierende anderer Religionen wird nachgedacht, was die allgemeine institutionelle Bewegung weg von einer reinen Kirchenzentrierung hin zur integrierten Zusammenarbeit mit verschiedenen Gemeinschaften widerspiegelt. Zugleich wird hier die Herausforderung an eine theologische »Whole of Life« Vision deutlich, die allen alles sein will. Vergleichbar mit der Situation anderer ökumenischen Akteure gilt es auch für PCU, Wege zu finden teils sehr unterschiedliche Positionen zum christlichen Selbstverständnis auf glaubhafte Weise in einer Institution zusammenzuhalten. Die gilt auch für die Diversität pazifischer Kulturen, die sich nicht so leicht in eine einzige hermeneutische Konzeption einzeichnen lassen. Die angestrebte Rückwendung zur vorkolonialen Kultur, die nicht ohne Bestimmung von Kriterien auskommen wird, und die Betonung der notwendigen Indigenisierung der Curricula kann als eine Suchbewegung nach neuen Kriterien für die Ausbildung aufgefasst werden. Dabei wird sich auch die Aufgabe stellen, diese Kriterien auf nicht unproblematische Elemente indigener Herrschaftsformen oder repressiver *chiefly cultures* anzuwenden.

Am 29.4.2025 wurde die Universität im Beisein zahlreicher Alumni und Alumnae, des deutschen Botschafters, von Repräsentant:innen der Regierung sowie von lokalen Chiefs, darunter der High-Chiefin der örtlichen Rewa Region Ratu Kapu, feierlich eröffnet. Die bereits 2010 beschlossene Gründung der Universität wurde nun mit einer Yaqona-Zeremonie, in der auch in traditioneller Weise Feinmatten und Geschenke an die Chiefs überreicht wurden, einer Fahnenzeremonie sowie der Uraufführung eines Musicals besiegelt. Bei der erstmaligen Graduierungsfeier der PCU am Folgetag erhielten 168 Kandidat:innen ihre Urkunden, darunter zwölf Masterstudierende und zwei Doktoranden. Die Ehrendoktorwürde wurde an Lorine Chan Tevi, die frühere Generalsekretärin des *Pazifischen Kirchenrates* (*PCC*) sowie an den Theologen und früheren WCC Präsidenten Leslie Boseto verliehen.

Sowohl die kreativen Ideen als auch die Herausforderungen an der neuen Universität scheinen mannigfaltig. Es ist zu hoffen, dass sich für das »Home of ›Whole of Life‹ Education«, so das Motto der Universität, ein gutes Finanzierungsmodell finden wird, das den Erhalt dieser traditionsreichen theologischen Institution nachhaltig sichern kann.

» https://pcu.ac.fj/

Anton Knuth/Melanie Barbato

Klaus Koschorke/Ciprian Burlacioiu/Philipp Kuster (Hg.): **Early South-South Links in the History of World Christianity (16th - Early 19th Century)**, (Studies in the History of Christianity in the Non-Western World, Bd. 38), Wiesbaden: Harrasowitz Verlag 2024, 256 Seiten, 23 Bilder, 58,– Euro/Open Access

Zwölf Fallstudien zu Süd-Süd-Verflechtungen und sechs kommentierende Beiträge zur Konferenz der Forschungsgruppe »Polyzentrik und Pluralität des Prämodernen Christentums« (Universität Frankfurt) unterstreichen eindrucksvoll die Stärken dieses Zugangs durch das Herausarbeiten existierender christlicher »Zentren« außerhalb Europas und ihrer Verflechtungen. Es gibt inhaltliche Überschneidungen mit früheren Bänden der Serie, doch liegt der Fokus dieses Bandes auf der Vormoderne. Der Begriff des Zentrums umfasst auch Kommunikations- und Austauschräume wie den »Christlichen ›Schwarzen‹ Ozean«, den Afrikaner*innen als Sklav*innen, Remigrant*innen und Missionar*innen in alle Richtungen durchquert haben (vier Beiträge); oder den Indischen Ozean, den Thomaschristen als Händler überqueren, und der die Räume einheimischer Christ*innen in Asien verbindet (zwei Beiträge). Im 3. Teil analysieren drei Beiträge die Hagiographie von Märtyrern in Japan als Verflechtungsgeschichte im pazifischen Ozean und das Wirken dieses Narrativs in Lateinamerika. Andere Zugänge erarbeiten den formenden Einfluss z. B. kongolesischer Katholik*innen in den Amerikas und protestantischer Afro-Amerikaner*innen in Sierra Leone oder untersuchen den Einfluss des äthiopischen Christentums sowie des aksumitischen Königreichs (drei Beiträge).

Für Lesende, die in diesen Spezialgebieten wenig bewandert sind, ist vieles neu zu lernen. Die Literatur, die den Aufsätzen zugrunde gelegt wird, zeigt jedoch, dass in größerem Umfang vorhandene Forschung und wenig beachtete Aspekte in neuen Perspektiven aufgegriffen werden (das unterstreicht auch Mira Sonntag in ihrem Beitrag). In ihren historischen Studien weisen die zwölf Autoren und vier Autorinnen immer wieder darauf hin, dass in der »konventionellen« Historiographie die Perspektive einer westlichen Ausbreitung vorherrsche. Dagegen stellen sie die Wirkmächtigkeit anderer »Zentren« der Vormoderne, die *agency* einheimischer Christ*innen und vor allem die Verflechtungen, die sich dazwischen ergeben.

Über die Detailstudien hinaus leistet der Band einen Beitrag zur Konzeptualisierung globaler Christentumsgeschichte durch Kategorien wie transozeanische Räume (*seascapes*), symbolische Geographien und narrative Verflechtungen. Die Beiträge erweitern so die grundlegende und oft eher deskriptive Begrifflichkeit einer Polyzentrik des Christentums durch räumliche (transregional, transkulturell) und zeitliche (longue durée, transtemporal) Kategorien; ebenso durch das Nachzeichnen, wie Narrative entstehen, z. B. medial durch Gemälde geprägt werden, und in anderen Kontexten aufgegriffen wurden und dort formenden Einfluss gewonnen haben. Klaus Koschorke unterstreicht einmal mehr die Wirkmächtigkeit des Bildes der äthiopischen als ursprünglich »afrikanische« Kirche für andere. Stanislau Paulau zeichnet – neben einem Beitrag zum Einfluss äthiopischer Theologie auf die Reformation – in einem zweiten Beitrag nach, wie die Hagiographie des aksumitischen Königs Kaleb anderswo und in späteren Zeiten als Interpretament für das Handeln christlicher Herrscher aufgegriffen wurde. Die Beiträge von Raphaèle Preisinger, Erin Rowe und Christoph Nebgen folgen den Spuren der ersten Gruppe von Märtyrern in Japan, von denen die Mehrzahl Asiaten waren, und wie deren Geschichte im kolonialen spanischen Reich in Süd- und Mittelamerika aufgegriffen wurde.

Es ist ein Band reich an historischen Tiefenbohrungen und an Kommentaren und Rückfragen an die Beiträge und das Konzept der Polyzentrik. Das beginnt bei Fragen zum Raum (wo liegt dieser »Süden«, über den hier gesprochen wird), zur zugrunde gelegten Epocheneinteilung, die auf europäische Ereignisse zurückgeht (Christoph Marx), und danach, wie die analysierten »Christentümer« zu bestimmen seien (Birgit Emich). Adrian Hermann unterstreicht in seinem Hinweis zu einer Global History of Religions, dass die untersuchten Verflechtungen die epistemischen Voraussetzungen für das Herausbilden von Konzepten über Religion im ausgehenden 18. und beginnenden 19. Jahrhundert bilden.

Die Beiträge fokussieren auf die Amerikas, Afrika und Asien und deren Verflechtungen in der Vormoderne. Doch in deren Verflechtungen mit Kräften in Europa (katholische Kirche, Missionsorden, Papsttum, protestantische Mission etc.) wird über die Beiträge hinweg erkennbar, dass es nicht nur um Süd-Süd-Verbindungen geht, sondern um das Verflechten der unterschiedlichen Akteure auf einer globalen Bühne, für die außereuropäische Räume nicht nur exotische Kulisse sind. Gegenläufig zur Betonung der *agency* einheimischer Christ*innen fällt auf, dass nur vier Autor*innen in den Räumen leben und arbeiten, die im Band analysiert werden.

Michael Biehl

Nikita Dhawan: **Die Aufklärung vor Europa retten. Kritische Theorien der Dekolonisierung**, Frankfurt a. M.: Campus-Verlag 2024, 395 Seiten, 20,– Euro

Nikita Dhawan (Dh.), seit 2021 Professorin für Politische Theorie und Ideengeschichte an der TU Dresden, hat ein profundes Werk über Theorien der Dekolonisierung vorgelegt, in dem sie die Erkenntnisse ihrer bisherigen Forschungsarbeit bündelt. Sie schreibt aus einer ausdrücklich »postkolonial-queerfeministischen« Perspektive. Das Buch enthält nach einer Einleitung in Thematik und Gedankengang zwei Teile: Teil I: Die Geschichte der Gegenwart,

Teil II: Woher kommt die Zukunft? Sie entwirft einen weiträumigen Bogen von der Aufklärung, deren kolonial-sexistisch-rassistisches Erbe sie dekonstruiert, über die Kritische Theorie der Frankfurter Schule bis zu den Schlussfolgerungen für eine »post-imperiale Welt«.

Ihre Position hat zwei wesentliche Marker: Zum einen die kritische Distanz zu *de*-kolonialen Theorien der Dekolonisierung, die das Erbe der Aufklärung pauschal aufgrund seiner Verflechtungen mit der imperialen Geschichte Europas verwerfen. Sie berufen sich auf vernakuläre Traditionen, aus denen sie ein Gegenbild zum europäischen Imperialismus entwickeln wollen. Ihnen hält Dh. entgegen, dass auch ihr Denken nicht umhinkann, sich aus aufklärerischen Impulsen wie Gerechtigkeit, Freiheit und Demokratie zu speisen. Sie wirft ihnen eine Romantisierung indigener Traditionen vor. Ihre Vertreter:innen lehrten zumeist an Hochschulen der westlichen Welt und würden die indigenen Sprachen, auf deren Reichtum sie sich beriefen, weder sprechen noch verstehen. *Post*-koloniale Theorien der Dekolonisierung erkennen demgegenüber das emanzipatorische Erbe der Aufklärung an, das man »nicht nicht lieben« könne (so mit Spivak). Aufgabe sei es, dieses Erbe so aufzunehmen und weiterzuentwickeln, dass es zu »epistemischer Entflechtung« komme und dem Denken der ehemals Subalternen ein eigenes epistemisches Handlungsvermögen zuerkannt werde. Den rassifizierten Subjekten müsse ihre Menschlichkeit zurückerstattet werden. Auf diese Weise könne das Erbe der Aufklärung gerettet werden – vor Europa.

Zum anderen sieht Dh. ihre Position in der Tradition von Horkheimer und Adorno als eine »Kritische Theorie«, die sich dadurch auszeichnet, dass sie Affirmationen vermeidet und sich weigert, aus der Theorie vorschnell Ableitungen für die Praxis vorzunehmen. Menschen veränderten ihre Welt nicht, weil sie eine »Lehre« für richtig hielten, sondern weil ihre Situation unerträglich ist. Wie sie dies tun, muss in einem nach vorne offenen Prozess ausgehandelt werden. Dh. versteht ihre Überlegungen als Fortsetzungen eines »unvollendeten Gespräches« der ersten Generation der Frankfurter Schule, die sich ganz auf die Aufarbeitung des Faschismus als Konsequenz der instrumentellen Vernunft der Aufklärung konzentriert und ihr kolonialistisches Erbe zu wenig gesehen habe.

In den Rahmen dieser Gedankenstruktur setzt Dh. mehrere diskursive Auseinandersetzungen mit Themen und Personen. Besonders kritisch wird Habermas von ihr gesehen, weil er bis heute an der universalistischen Normativität seines Vernunftbegriffes festhält und erwartet, dass Gesprächspartner:innen aus dem globalen Süden, wenn sie auf Augenhöhe ernst genommen werden wollen, sich diesem europäischen Vernunftbegriff unterzuordnen hätten. Die Folgen der globalen Durchsetzung europäischer Normen und die Herabwürdigung nicht-europäischer Epistemologien blieben bei ihm unreflektiert.

Auch den Marxismus kritisiert Dh. mit seinem aufklärerischen Erbe. Er stelle zwar erstmals die ökonomische

Situation der Menschen in den Mittelpunkt, berücksichtige aber zu wenig die Verflechtungen der Ökonomie mit der Ausbeutung der Kolonien.

Kritisch sieht Dh. auch, dass im Zuge der Dekolonisierung oft die einheimischen Eliten bloß die Rollen der ehemaligen Kolonialherren übernommen hätten. Die revolutionären Prozesse in den Kolonien hätten zumeist in postkoloniale Albträume geführt, wie man besonders in Haiti und Liberia studieren könne.

Eine immer wiederkehrende Frage ist die nach der Legitimität von Gewalt in Dekolonialisierungsprozessen. Am Beispiel von Ghandi und seinem Gegenspieler Ambedkar führt sie diese Debatte vor Augen. Mit Butler ist Dh. der Meinung, dass Gewalt kein neutrales Werkzeug ist, das man eine Weile anwenden und dann wieder weglegen könne, vielmehr konstituiere ihr Einsatz die Welt auf nachhaltige Weise.

In den Diskursen schließt sich Dh. argumentativ vor allem Gayatri C. Spivak, Emmanuel Ch. Eze und Achille Mbembe an.

Entsprechend dem Ansatz einer »Kritischen Theorie« kann am Ende die Frage »Was tun?« nur »Nicht-Antworten« erhalten. Das bedeute aber nicht, dass man nicht handeln könne oder müsse. Die Antworten jedoch sind nicht aus Normen oder Lehren abzuleiten, sondern müssen situationsgerecht gesucht werden und für Infragestellungen offenbleiben.

Das Buch ist allen zu empfehlen, die sich vertieft mit Dekolonisierungstheorien befassen und dabei einen Überblick über die Diskurse der letzten Jahrzehnte gewinnen wollen. Zwischendurch blitzt auf, wie diese Diskurse auch aktuelle Konflikte prägen, z. B. die Debatten um Antisemitismus auf der Documenta 15 oder anlässlich der Gewalt zwischen Palästina und Israel. Dh. schreibt höchst voraussetzungsreich, deutet Hintergründe und Diskurse oft nur an. Ob die angestrebte Zielgruppe einer »allgemeinen Leser:innenschaft« erreicht wird, kann man fragen. Aber Zeit und Mühe der Lektüre lohnen allemal.

Horst Gorski

Yan Suarsana: **Globales Christentum. Studienkurs Religion**, Baden-Baden: Nomos 2024, 243 Seiten, 24,– Euro

In der Reihe *Studienkurs Religion* legt der Bremer Religionswissenschaftler Yan Suarsana mit *Globales Christentum* eine kompakte und übersichtliche Einführung in die konfessionelle Vielfalt und weltweite Verbreitung des Christentums vor. Auf nur 243 Seiten gelingt es ihm hervorragend, zentrale Entwicklungen und Strukturen christlicher Glaubensformen historisch wie systematisch zu skizzieren, stets mit dem Blick auf die Gegenwart und mit einem globalen Fokus.

Das Buch ist didaktisch sinnvoll aufgebaut: Nach einer problemorientierten und reflektierenden Einleitung, die sich kritisch mit Begriffen wie »christlich« auseinandersetzt, folgen zwei kontextualisierende Kapitel: eines zur gegenwärtigen Verbreitung des Christentums als »Religion des Südens«, eines zum sog. »älteren Christentum«. Daran schließen sich vier Kapitel zu den klassischen Kirchenfamilien (altorientalisch, orthodox, römisch-katholisch, protestantisch) an, jeweils mit derselben inneren Struktur: Gegenwartsanalyse und historische Rückblicke, die heutige Unterschiede verständlich machen. Ein abschließendes Kapitel widmet sich der ökumenischen Bewegung.

Didaktisch und sprachlich ist das Buch überaus gelungen. Komplexe Sachverhalte – etwa die altkirchlichen Konzilien, die westliche Idee des »christlichen Abendlandes« oder die Ausbreitungsdynamiken des Protestantismus – werden präzise, knapp und verständlich aufbereitet. Auch für interkulturell interessierte Leser:innen bietet das Buch viele Ansatzpunkte: Der Autor macht die Bedeutung historischer Missionsbewegungen ebenso sichtbar wie die weltweite Verbreitung charismatischer und pfingstkirchlicher Strömungen. Besonders verdienstvoll ist, dass auch weniger beachtete Themen wie (inner)christliche Gewalt oder die Verflechtung von Theologie, Macht und Politik nicht ausgeklammert werden.

Allerdings offenbaren sich bei genauerer Lektüre methodische und strukturelle Begrenzungen, die gerade im interkulturellen und postkolonialen Diskurs ins Gewicht fallen. Trotz der proklamierten globalen Ausrichtung ist das Werk in seiner Konzeption und Sprache tief in einer deutschsprachig-protestantischen Wissenschaftskultur verankert. Der Fokus liegt auf systematisch-theologischen und historischen Kategorien, während spirituelle, lokale oder politische Selbstdeutungen und Eigenlogiken nicht-westlicher Christentümer eher unterbelichtet bleiben. Zwar bemüht sich Suarsana erkennbar, koloniale Verflechtungen, Missionsbewegungen und die Rolle des globalen Südens stärker zu integrieren – insbesondere am Beispiel der Pfingstbewegung –, doch die epistemische Rahmung bleibt westlich und wird nicht problematisiert oder diskutiert. Diese Verankerung zeigt sich auch in der herangezogenen Literatur. Sie stammt nahezu ausschließlich von weißen westlichen Männern. Stimmen afrikanischer, lateinamerikanischer oder asiatischer Theolog:innen sowie postkoloniale und feministische Perspektiven fehlen weitgehend. Damit bleibt die Globalität des Christentums in Suarsanas Darstellung in erster Linie eine geographische, weniger eine epistemische oder hermeneutische. Die Herausforderung, eine auch methodisch und epistemisch pluralere Darstellung zu bieten, wird nur ansatzweise bewältigt. Gerade angesichts des gewachsenen Bewusstseins für koloniale Epistemologien und das Ringen um eine dezentrierte, plurale Religionswissenschaft und Theologie wäre mehr Mut zur methodischen Vielfalt wünschenswert gewesen. Der kritische Umgang mit dem bestehenden Kanon wäre ein erster Schritt gewesen. Die Herausforderung für zukünftige Werke besteht darin, die kartographische Perspektive mit einer methodisch und epistemisch breiteren Anlage zu verbinden, hin zu einem Christentum, das nicht nur global *verortet*, sondern auch global *spricht*.

Trotz dieser begrenzenden Faktoren bietet Suarsanas Werk eine wertvolle, klar strukturierte Einführung in die globalen Grundstrukturen des Christentums. Es vermittelt solides Basiswissen und regt dazu an, über konfessionelle und kulturelle Differenzen nachzudenken. Als Studienbegleiter in der Religionswissenschaft und Interkulturellen Theologie ist das Buch erstklassig geeignet, insbesondere dann, wenn man sich der Grenzen seines konzeptionellen Rahmens bewusst bleibt.

Dass Suarsanas Buch ausgerechnet im Vorfeld des 1700-jährigen Jubiläums des ersten Konzils von Nicäa (325–2025) erscheint, verleiht seiner Einführung zusätzliche Relevanz: Es ruft ins Bewusstsein, wie sehr christliche Identitätsbildungen seit jeher in globalen, politischen und kulturellen Aushandlungsprozessen stehen – damals wie heute.

Claudia Hoffmann

Leita Ngoy: **Prosperity Gospel Redefined. The Impact of Charismatisation of the Mainline Churches in Tanzania**, Paderborn: Brill 2025, 294 Seiten, 99,– Euro

Basierend auf einer 2023 an der Ruhr-Universität Bochum eingereichten Dissertation bietet dieses Buch eine theologisch sensible und empirisch fundierte Analyse der Charismatisierung der Evangelisch-Lutherischen Kirche in Tansania (ELCT). Ngoy konzentriert sich auf die Eastern and Coastal Diocese (ELCT-ECD), wo charismatische Gottesdienste und das *Prosperity Gospel* als Antwort auf kontextuelle Bedürfnisse – etwa den Glauben an Dämonen und böse Mächte – stark an Bedeutung gewonnen haben (3f). Ngoy, in einer lutherischen Pastorenfamilie aufgewachsen, beginnt mit einem persönlichen Bericht über ihre Begegnung mit dem Heiligen Geist in einer charismatischen Gruppe. Sie berichtet, wie sie stigmatisiert wurde, weil sie keinen männlichen Nachkommen hatte. Nachdem sie jedoch eine besondere Opfergabe dargebracht und eine Reihe von Befreiungsgebeten durchlaufen hatte, bekam sie als Wunder einen Sohn (7). Diese Erfahrung öffnete ihr die Augen für die spirituelle Stagnation ihrer Heimatgemeinde. Angesichts sinkender Mitgliederzahlen wandern viele Lutheraner:innen zu pfingstkirchlichen Gemeinden ab, um erfahrungsorientiertere Spiritualität zu finden. Ngoy argumentiert, dass die Einführung charismatischer Elemente und des Prosperity Gospel eine Antwort auf diese Nachfrage ist und zur Hybridisierung lutherischer Gottesdienste geführt hat (181f).

Im Zentrum steht das Konzept des *mafanikio gospel*, das laut Ngoy eine lokal angepasste und »neu definierte« Version des Prosperity Gospel sei. Letzteres, im Kiswahili als *injili ya utajirisho* bekannt, ist eine amerikanische Variante, die individuellen Wohlstand betont. Das *mafanikio gospel* hingegen fokussiert auf spirituelle Transformation, Gottvertrauen, frommes Leben, harte Arbeit und verantwortliche Haushalterschaft. Diese Werte fördern laut Ngoy persönliches Wohlstandswachstum, Gemeindewachstum und finanzielle Stabilität (190f). Aus sozialkonstruktivistischer Perspektive versteht Ngoy das *mafanikio gospel* als »gelebte Theologie«, geprägt von den Herausforderungen tansanischer Gläubiger. Dieses Gospel spricht laut Ngoy Menschen aller sozialen Schichten und Bildungsgruppen an (71f). Kapitel 4 zeigt anhand empirischer Daten, wie das Prosperity Gospel das Leben der Befragten auf vielfältige Weise beeinflusst (85f). Allerdings könnte der wechselnde Gebrauch der Begriffe *Mafanikio* und *Prosperity Gospel* im Buch den Eindruck erwecken, dass *Mafanikio* lediglich eine Übersetzung und keine Neudefinition ist. Die theologische Unterscheidung zwischen beiden bleibt zu dünn.

Ngoy vertritt die Ansicht, dass die Charismatisierung der ELCT nicht als Verwässerung lutherischer Identität zu verstehen sei. Missiologisch betrachtet sieht sie die Charismatisierung der ELCT nicht als Identitätsverlust, sondern als strategische und theologische Antwort auf das Wachstum der Pfingstkirchen und den weitverbreiteten spirituellen Hunger. Kapitel 4 dokumentiert das Wachstum in Gemeinden wie Mbezi, Kijitonyama und Kimara, wo charismatische Gottesdienste und Prosperity-Gospel-Lehren verbreitet werden. In diesen Gemeinden integriert die Liturgie in den lutherischen Gottesdiensten zunehmend tansanische Musik und afrikanische Motive, die viele vor allem junge Menschen anziehen, ohne die lutherische Theologie aufzugeben. Diese Entwicklung ist jedoch umstritten. Einige ELCT-Pastoren betrachten dies nicht als Wachstum, sondern als einen Transfer oder eine Bewegung der Mitglieder von einer lutherischen Gemeinde zu einer anderen. Ngoy jedoch gibt Zahlen der Mitglieder aus anderen Konfessionen und Religionen an, etwa von der katholischen Kirche und sogar vom Islam, die auf der Suche nach spiritueller Erneuerung und anderen Bedürfnissen sind (73f).

Ngoy untersucht die Verbindung von Heilungskonzepten im Prosperity Gospel innerhalb der ELCT, wo sie über den Umgang mit spiritueller Kriegsführung und afrikanischen Traditionen wie Hexerei schreibt. Sie zeigt, wie diese Elemente in der charismatischen Vorstellungskraft verankert sind und vertraute Deutungsmuster für Heilung bieten (128f). Gleichzeitig stellt sie kritische theologische Fragen zur Integration in die lutherische Praxis. Sie porträtiert charismatische Führungspersönlichkeiten wie Christopher Mwakasege, Eliona Kimaro und Willbord Mastai. Ihre Dienste verkörpern eine hybride Spiritualität, die lutherische theologische Grundlagen mit charismatischer Dynamik verbinden. Im abschließenden Kapitel unterbreitet Ngoy praktische Vorschläge, wie charismatische Erneuerung und konfessionelle Integrität miteinander in Einklang gebracht werden können – mit Betonung auf theologischer Bildung, seelsorgerlicher Begleitung und einer Neubewertung der lutherischen Berufstheologie im Licht der tansanischen wirtschaftlichen Realität. Obwohl Ngoy viele positive Aspekte des Prosperity Gospel beschreibt, sieht sie dennoch verschiedene Schwächen, wie etwa den möglichen Missbrauch von Macht und finanziellen Mitteln, die sie nicht zögert, zu kritisieren.

Neben den Vorteilen, die sie in diesem Buch bezüglich des von verschiedenen Predigern verkündeten *mafanikio gospel* und der unterschiedlichen Wege, wie Menschen – auch wirtschaftlich – profitieren, nennt, bleibt die Frage offen, ob dies ein Evangelium ist, das überall in lutherischen Kirchen übernommen werden sollte.

Dennoch ist dieses Buch ein wichtiges und provokantes Werk. Es wird zukünftig eine unverzichtbare Ressource für alle Interessierten an afrikanischer Christentumsforschung, kontextueller Theologie und die Zukunft der Mainline-Kirchen im globalen Süden sein.

Brighton Katabaro

Rudolf von Sinner: **Public Theology in the Secular State. A Perspective from the Global South**, Wien/Zürich: LIT-Verlag 2021, 270 Seiten, 24,90 Euro

Rudolf von Sinner (RvS), Jahrgang 1967, hat von 1987 bis 1993 in Basel, Edinburgh und Heidelberg Theologie studiert, in Basel promoviert (2001) und sich in Bern habilitiert (2010). Inzwischen lebt und lehrt er seit über 24 Jahren an verschiedenen Orten in Brasilien, derzeit an der *Pontifícia Universidade Católica do Paraná* in Curitiba. Mit der Evangelisch-Lutherischen Kirche in Brasilien ist er zugleich als deren Mitglied und ordinierter Pfarrer bestens vertraut. Er war Mitinitiator des 2007 gegründeten *Global Network of Public Theology*, dem aktuell 45 theologische Ausbildungs- und Forschungsstätten in allen Kontinenten angehören. Öffentliche Theologie steht in der Tradition der Befreiungstheologie der 1960er bis 1980er Jahre, ist aber seither mit neuen Problemen des gesellschaftlich-politischen Lebens konfrontiert, denen sich der Autor in den drei Teilen des Buches zuwendet. Das dabei entstandene Panorama umfasst in drei Teilen Studien zu den Begriffen »Konvivenz« (*convivência*), »Vertrauen« und »Bürgerschaft« in theologischen Diskursen Brasiliens (Kap. 1, 2 und 4), neue theologische Entwicklungen in Lateinamerika (Kap. 3), eine Auseinandersetzung mit dem religiösen Pluralismus und der Säkularisation in globaler Perspektive (Kap. 5–8) sowie kritische Überlegungen zur Verwendung des Begriffs »Volk« im Zusammenhang mit Kirche und öffentlicher Theologie (Kap. 9–12), wobei er »Volk« als Begriff und Realität gegenüber dem »Populismus« kritisch abgrenzt (Kap. 9).

Damit hat RvS zwölf zuerst teilweise als Einzelbeiträge konzipierte und in Zeitschriften veröffentlichte Texte unter dem Stichwort »Öffentliche Theologie« überarbeitet und als Sammelband zugänglich gemacht. Doch es geht um mehr als eine lose Aufsatzsammlung. Öffentliche Theologie ist im Werk des Autors teils explizit, teils implizit sein zentrales Themenfeld. Aufschlussreich dafür sind drei Beispiele:

(1) Säkularisierung: Wie RvS in vergleichender Perspektive auf gleichzeitige säkularisierende Entwicklungen in verschiedenen Kontinenten zeigt, gibt es Säkularisierung nur im Plural (Kap. 7). Obwohl sie sich hauptsächlich als Ent-Kirchlichung äussert, kommt es dadurch weder zum Verschwinden christlich-kirchlichen Lebens, noch von

Religion insgesamt (135). Die Frage nach dem Ort der (christlichen) Religion in verschiedenen Gesellschaften erhält damit eine neue Aktualität.

(2) Drei Erfahrungs- und Reflexionshorizonte: Dank der gelebten ökumenischen Existenz von RvS sind in seinen Publikationen die drei wichtigsten Bezugspunkte stets präsent: sein Herkunftskontinent Europa, Brasilien als Schwerpunktland seines Lebens und Forschens und der globale Kontext als Begegnungsorte mit vielfältigen Formen christlichen Lebens und theologischer Reflexion. Das ermöglicht es ihm, eine Süd-Süd-Perspektive auf Länder wie Südafrika und Brasilien einzunehmen und sie zugleich mit einer Süd-Nord-Perspektive zu verbinden – sei es als kritisches Korrektiv zu ökumenischen Diskursen im globalen Süden oder als Auseinandersetzung mit eurozentrischen Diskursen im Norden.

(3) Theologie in globaler Perspektive: Durch seinen Lehrer, Dietrich Ritschl, ist RvS der Ökumenischen Theologie bereits in den 1990er Jahren begegnet und hat sich während seiner Basler Promotion in ökumenischer und interkultureller Perspektive mit kontextueller Trinitätstheologie beschäftigt. 2007, während seiner Forschungen zur Habilitationsschrift am *Center of Theological Inquiry* in Princeton (wo das *Global Network for Public Theology* in eben jenem Jahr gegründet wurde), entdeckte er die Öffentliche Theologie vor allem durch südafrikanische Ansätze. Auf dieser Basis hat er sie kontinuierlich weiterentfaltet. Ihre Konturen markiert er in diesem Buch mit der Beschreibung von über 40 Facetten in verschiedenen Kontinenten und Kontexten (vgl. das Stichwort *theology* im Index, 263).

Im dritten Teil seines Buches (Kap. 9–12) geht RvS als profunder Kenner der religiösen Landschaften in Brasilien und dem südlichen Afrika (seit 2013 ist er auch *Professor Extraordinary* an der Theologischen Fakultät der Universität Stellenbosch) unter anderem den wechselseitigen Einflüssen nach, die sich zwischen Kirchen und Bewegungen auf beiden Kontinenten niederschlagen (Kap. 11). In kritischer Sicht werden etwa das »Wohlstandsevangelium« in Brasilien und seine Auswirkungen auf andere Länder erörtert, das Elemente afrikanischer Religiosität in sich aufnimmt, zugleich aber »Afrika« ins Negative wendet und afrobrasilianische Religionen dämonisiert. RvS fasst seine Beobachtungen in den vier Untertiteln des Kapitels zusammen: *Struggle for Africa*; *Fight against Africa*; *Struggle for Power and Wealth*; *Struggle against Grace*. Dieser Teil des Buches führt den zwischenkirchlichen Süd-Süd-Kontakt durch viele Details vor Augen. Das abschließende Kap. 12 befasst sich in einem historischen Rückblick mit der Reformationstheologie zwischen Migration und Mission, welche die Theologie in Brasilien geprägt und von dort aus in andere Länder und Kontinente ausgestrahlt hat.

Das breit angelegte Panorama des Buches bietet einen vorzüglichen Blick auf Öffentliche Theologie aus einer Perspektive, die sich hauptsächlich Stimmen aus dem globalen Süden – besonders Brasiliens, Lateinamerikas und

Südafrikas – verdankt. Damit ergänzt und erweitert der Autor zugleich den ihm ebenso bestens vertrauten Diskurs über Öffentliche Theologie in Europa, besonders Deutschland. Mit den Stimmen aus anderen Kontexten der Ökumene, die er zu Gehör bringt, verleiht er diesem hoch aktuellen Themenfeld den globalen Rahmen, den es verdient.

Christine Lienemann-Perrin

Hermann Hiery/Isa Scholtissek (Hg.): **Tagebuch aus dem Bismarck-Archipel. Friedrich Hoffmann in der deutschen Kolonie Neuguinea 1908–1921** (Quellen und Forschungen zur Südsee, Reihe A: Quellen, Bd. 8), Wiesbaden: Harrassowitz Verlag 2024, XIX + 264 Seiten, 68,– Euro

Das vorliegende Buch ist in der von Hermann Hiery begründeten und herausgegebenen Buchreihe »Quellen und Forschungen zur Südsee« und in diesem Fall in der Reihe »A: Quellen«, erschienen. Hiery ist auch einer der Herausgeber dieses Bandes, den er zusammen mit Isa Scholtissek veröffentlicht hat. Hiery ist ausgewiesener Historiker und anerkannter Experte zur deutschen Kolonialzeit in Ozeanien, Scholtissek ist die Urenkelin des Verfassers des Tagebuchs, des Landwirts Friedrich Hoffmann, der in seinen Aufzeichnungen die Zeit von 1908 in Deutsch-Neuguinea bis nach dem Ende des Ersten Weltkriegs 1921, als die Kolonie bereits von Australien besetzt war, beschrieb.

Dieses Tagebuch ist in seiner Art einzigartig, weil es von anderen ähnlichen Werken dieser Art deutlich abweicht, wie es Hiery in seiner umfassenden Einleitung detailliert erläutert. Die Exzeptionalität ergibt sich einerseits aus dem persönlichen Lebensweg von Friedrich Hoffmann, der von zahlreichen Brüchen, Verlusten, Entbehrungen und Neuanfängen geprägt war, und andererseits aus der Art und Weise der schriftlichen Aufzeichnungen und deren Inhalten. Der 1884 in Dresden geborene Hoffmann wanderte 23-jährig aus und verbrachte bis zum 37. Lebensjahr die Zeit in Neuguinea, zuerst in der deutschen Kolonie und – nach Ausbruch des Ersten Weltkriegs – anschließend als einer der wenigen Deutschen unter australischer Besatzungsherrschaft, bis zu seiner Ausweisung 1921. Allein schon dieser Aspekt ist bemerkenswert, weil die meisten Deutschen bereits deutlich früher von den Australiern deportiert und ausgewiesen wurden, und daher nur wenige Berichte über das Leben in der ehemaligen und dann besetzten Kolonie aus der Sicht von Deutschen existieren. Die insgesamt fünf Tagebücher (in drei Bänden; die Originale sind nicht mehr existent) behandeln mit zum Teil größeren zeitlichen Abständen zwischen den Eintragungen die wichtigsten Lebensstationen Hoffmanns, der mehrmals in seinem Leben von Grund auf neu beginnen musste, um sich eine Existenz aufzubauen, was den damaligen europäischen und weltpolitischen Entwicklungen geschuldet war. Scholtissek beschreibt in ihrem Vorwort, dass Hoffmann nach dem Verlust seiner Existenz als Pflanzer in Neuguinea 1927 ins britische Tanganyika, Ostafrika, auswanderte, um dort als Landwirt tätig zu sein. Dort wurde er, mit Ausbruch des Zweiten Weltkriegs, wieder deportiert und verlor alles, übernahm 1941 ein Gut in Polen, welches er 1945 ebenfalls verlor. Nach dem Krieg wanderte er für eine Zeit lang nach Paraguay aus, wo er schließlich 83-jährig im Jahr 1968 verstarb. Hoffmann war also jemand, der von den durch zwei Weltkriege bedingten historischen Brüchen und dramatischen Veränderungen besonders schwer betroffen war.

In dem vorliegenden Buch sind die ersten drei Tagebücher berücksichtigt, welche Hoffmanns Zeit in Deutsch-Neuguinea thematisieren. Beim zeitlich deutlich späteren Abtippen der handschriftlichen Originaleinträge durch Hoffmann selbst sind von ihm Kürzungen durchgeführt worden und er verfasste zu seinen Tagebucheinträgen zehn Jahre vor seinem Tod noch ein erläuterndes Vorwort. Darin beschreibt er Kindheitseindrücke, aber auch die Beweggründe, die ihn zu einer Tätigkeit im Dienst der Neu-Guinea-Compagnie und somit zu einer Auswanderung veranlassten. Die eigentlichen Tagebucheintragungen beginnen am 1. Januar 1908 und befassen sich mit den Vorbereitungen zur Auswanderung nach Neuguinea, den einzelnen Stationen der Anreise und seiner Ankunft in Rabaul am 31. März 1908. Die ersten Erkundungen, die landschaftlichen Reize, die Tierwelt, aber auch der erste Malariaanfall werden von ihm ebenso protokolliert wie die Arbeitsbedingungen vor Ort, seine Kontakte mit den Einheimischen und das Agieren der Weißen – Deutsche, sonstige Europäer:innen und Australier:innen –, mit denen er berufliche und private Kontakte pflegte. Hoffmann schildert seine Arbeit auf der Pflanzung Tobera, wo er für die Überwachung der Ernte und die Aufbereitung des Kaffees zuständig war, und seine Tätigkeit für das in der Nähe befindliche Eingeborenenspital. Überaus anschaulich werden von Hoffmann dessen schrittweise Erkundungen in der Umgebung, die sich entwickelnden Kontakte zu den Deutschen in der Kolonie sowie zu den vor Ort agierenden Missionaren, Beeinträchtigungen durch Malariaanfälle und Typhus, die Herausforderungen bei der Anlernung und Führung der Einheimischen für deren Tätigkeit auf den Kokos-, Kaffee- und Kautschukplantagen und Konflikte mit den Einheimischen beschrieben, denen er aber insgesamt – durchaus untypisch für die Zeit – Respekt zollt. Von besonderem Interesse sind Hoffmanns aus der Ferne erfolgte Einschätzungen der Kriegsereignisse in Europa und dessen unmittelbare Erfahrungen mit den Australier:innen ab 1914.

Begrüßenswert sind die zahlreichen und zum Teil sehr umfangreichen Anmerkungen in Form von Fußnoten, die viele angesprochene Aspekte genauer erläutern und kontextualisieren, und zahlreiche Literaturverweise beinhalten. Ein Orts-, Personen- und Schiffsnamensregister ergänzt die Inhalte sowie zwei farbige Karten, eine englischsprachige Zusammenfassung und ein separater Bildteil, der 28 Fotografien beinhaltet. Der sorgsam editierte Band ist aufgrund der gut lesbaren Darstellung der Ereignisse und Erlebnisse Hoffmanns vor Ort von einer atmosphärischen Dichte, die ihresgleichen bei Tagebüchern sucht. Das äußerst lesenswerte Buch ist somit ein Schatz, und es ist den beiden Herausgebenden nachdrücklich dafür zu danken, dass dieser Schatz gehoben und nun der Öffentlichkeit zugänglich gemacht wurde.

Hermann Mückler

Marina Ngursangzeli Behera/Michael Biehl/Risto Jukko/Kenneth R. Ross: **Hope in Times of Crisis. Reimagining Ecumenical Mission**, Eugene: Wipf and Stock Publishers 2025, 240 Seiten, 24,20 Euro

Mission ist in der Krise – nicht nur, aber vor allem in der westlichen Welt. Diese Krise stellen die Verfasser:innen des 2025 erschienenen Buches »Hope in Times of Crisis. Reimagining Ecumenical Mission« zwar nicht in Abrede, aber sie stellen ihre Überlegungen in einen umfassenden theologischen Horizont von Hoffnung. Ausgehend von den globalen Krisen unserer Welt spannt das Buch einen großen Bogen bis zu der Frage nach Ziel und Zukunft der Welt. Dabei hilft der Rückblick auf die ökumenische Geschichte der Mission und ihre Bedeutung in der Gegenwart, einen inklusiven, pragmatischen und konstruktiven Blick auf die Zukunft christlicher Mission als globales Phänomen zu entwickeln. Mission ist nach Meinung der Verfasser:innen nicht nur Mittel, sondern geradezu Aufgabe der christlichen Kirchen, um den weltweiten Krisen angemessen zu begegnen. Ihr Ziel sei es, das zu fördern, was dem Leben aller Menschen dient. Sie verbindet alle Akteure, die sich dafür einsetzen – nicht nur in christlichen Kirchen und Gemeinschaften, sondern auch die Vertreter:innen anderer Religionen und nicht religiös gebundener Positionen.

Das dringende Erfordernis angesichts globaler Krisen zu handeln, wird erkennbar an den Kapitelüberschriften: Zehn der insgesamt elf Kapitel sprechen von der »Notwendigkeit« zur Veränderung. Die Geschichte der ökumenischen Mission seit 1910 wird verstanden als Lern- und Entwicklungsgeschichte für eine Neukonzeption Ökumenischer Mission, die den gegenwärtigen Krisen wirksam begegnen kann. Es geht also nicht darum, alte Missionsvorstellungen zu transformieren oder zu transzendieren, sondern neu zu denken mit dem Ziel, eine globale Zukunft für alle zu schaffen. Die eigene Schuldverstrickung und das sich Arrangieren mit den Gegebenheiten werden dabei nicht ausgeklammert, sondern führen zu einer grundlegenden Kritik an der »Selbstgenügsamkeit« vieler Christ:innen und dem dringenden Ruf zur eigenen Veränderung.

Die ersten Kapitel beschreiben sehr drängend die gegenwärtigen Krisen der Welt: Klimakatastrophen, Kriege, polarisierte Gesellschaften, ungerechte neoliberale Wirtschaftsformen und Migration betreffen Menschen global, je nach Kontext allerdings in sehr unterschiedlicher Weise. Die verschiedenen Themenbereiche werden mit Positionen aus der Missionsgeschichte und der Ökumenischen Bewegung in Beziehung gebracht. Die Stärke dieses Ansatzes ist der globale und inklusive Blick, der Differenzen, Partikularinteressen und unterschiedliche Positionen nicht ausblendet, sie aber angesichts der Größe und Dringlichkeit der Herausforderungen für überbrückbar ansieht. Dazu müssen auch bisherige Spaltungen in der Bewegung der ökumenischen Mission überwunden werden.

Den einzelnen Kapiteln sind jeweils kurze Gespräche der Autor:innen, vorangestellt. Sie erleichtern es, die persönliche Betroffenheit der Verfasser:innen nachzuvollziehen, und regen zugleich an, die eigene Verbundenheit mit den angesprochenen Krisen wahrzunehmen und Handlungsoptionen für den eigenen Kontext zu bedenken. Da Mission als eine transformative gemeinschaftliche Kraft verstanden wird, ist das Stichwort »Gemeinschaft«, für die geforderte Veränderung von grundlegender Wichtigkeit. Insofern taucht auch der reformatorische Grundsatz des »Priestertums aller Glaubenden« hier auf. Die Rolle und Verantwortung der Einzelnen als *agents of transformation* sind von höchster Bedeutung – immer aufgehoben allerdings in der Gemeinschaft derer, die sich auf eine gute Zukunft für alle einsetzen. Dass die Verfasser:innen durchgängig als Team schreiben, also einzelne Abschnitte des Buches nicht einzelnen Personen zugeordnet werden können, ist so nur folgerichtig.

Wer etwas erfahren möchte über die Geschichte der ökumenischen Missionsbewegung wird im letzten Drittel des Buches fündig. Die Ökumenischen Missionskonferenzen, die Entwicklung der verschiedenen Stränge der Missionsbewegung und die Darstellung von besonders bedeutsamen ökumenischen Texten aus der jüngeren Vergangenheit sind der Hintergrund für die angestrebte Neuorientierung und die angemahnte gemeinsamen Vorgehensweise und Transformation missionarischen Handelns. Dabei werden Stichworte wie »holistic mission«, »reverse mission«, »mission from the margins«, »missio dei« aufgegriffen und neu bedacht. Das Buch grenzt sich klar von Mission als Konversion ab, es zielt auf eine ganzheitliche Mission, die sich – angesichts der hyperkomplexen Herausforderungen – für ein Leben in Fülle einsetzt. Die Vielfalt der Bedingungen in der Welt, der unterschiedlichen Interessen und der Verflochtenheit kirchlicher Akteure in ihr können – so die Annahme der Verfasser:innen – die kirchlichen Gemeinschaften nicht unbetroffen lassen und werden sie von innen heraus verändern.

Gottes Wirken und das Vertrauen in die Gegenwart des Geistes an allen Orten bilden die Grundlage der Hoffnung der Verfasser:innen für eine Neuausrichtung ökumenischer Mission. Das lässt sie hoffen, Verbündete überall zu finden, ohne sie christlich vereinnahmen zu wollen. Ob nicht-religiöse Akteure sich unter den so neu gedachten Begriff »Mission« subsumieren lassen wollen würden, bleibt allerdings offen. Ebenso wie die Frage, ob dieses Verständnis von Mission in einem missions- und kirchenkritischen Kontext wirklich überzeugen kann.

Die vorgestellten Überlegungen wollen Mission jedenfalls nicht als überholtes Konzept beiseitelegen, sondern den Blick weiten für ein globales kirchliches Engagement und dabei die eigene Veränderung als positive Lernerfahrung wahrnehmen. Mission ist ein Prozess, in dem spirituelle Praxis und gemeinsames Handeln miteinander verbunden sind.

Trotz ihrer unterschiedlichen Herkünfte fühlen sich die vier Autor:innen verbunden durch die gemeinsamen Herausforderungen der weltweiten Krisen und die daraus folgende Notwendigkeit, die ökumenische Missionsbewegung neu zu denken und zu einem gemeinsamen Handeln zu bewegen. Insofern ist ihr gemeinsames Buch ein Appell und Beispiel dafür, wie ökumenische Mission heute beginnen muss: Als Zusammenschluss von Menschen, die angetrieben sind von der Hoffnung auf ein Leben in Fülle. Man wünscht dem Buch viele Leser:innen und mehr noch viele *agents of change*, die diese Vision in die Praxis umsetzen wollen!

Kirsten Wolandt

Magdalena Kittelmann: **Medizin und Mission. Die Neuendettelsauer Missionsgesellschaft in Neuguinea 1886 bis 1919** (Quellen und Forschungen zur Südsee, Bd. 14), Wiesbaden: Harrassowitz Verlag 2025, 414 Seiten, 34 Abb., 4 Karten, 89,– Euro

Die vorliegende Arbeit untersucht die Anfänge der Neuendettelsauer Mission im 19. Jahrhundert an der Schnittstelle von Medizingeschichte, Missionsgeschichte und Kolonialgeschichte. Sie verfolgt die These, dass die Medizin sowohl Instrument der Missionierung als auch Feld interkultureller Aushandlung auf der Basis der Spiritualisierung von Krankheit und Heilung war.

Magdalena Kittelmann, die nach dem Abitur im Rahmen eines Freiwilligenprogramms von Mission EineWelt mehrere Monate in Neuguinea verbracht hat und heute als Ärztin am Universitätsspital Basel arbeitet, rekonstruiert mit dieser Untersuchung, die auf ihrer Dissertation am Institut für Geschichte und Ethik der Medizin an der FAU in Erlangen basiert, fachlich beeindruckend Medizin als Mittel kolonialer Selbst- und Fremdkonstruktionen.

Die Autorin arbeitet detailreich aus den Quellen heraus, wie die Mission mit ihrem gesundheitsdiakonischen Dienst eigene religiöse Ziele verfolgte. Dabei nutzte diese die noch jungen naturwissenschaftlichen Errungenschaften der modernen Medizin, um die Überlegenheit der eigenen Religion gegenüber der indigenen Spiritualität und deren Heilungspraktiken zu demonstrieren. Zwar betonten die Missionsangehörigen stets den übernationalen Charakter der Mission gegenüber der Kolonialregierung und protestierten gegen Zwangsarbeit und Kolonialskandale, das Kolonialprojekt an sich stellten sie aber nicht in Frage. Kittelmann zeigt auf, wie sich Heilkonzepte in kulturellen Aushandlungsprozessen formten, und stellt eine Wahlverwandtschaft der missionarischen Spiritualisierung von Medizin mit dem indigenen Heilungsverständnis fest, da die Erkenntnisse der Tropenmedizin religiös gedeutet wurden. So sollte das Gebet an die Stelle der Magie treten, wurde aber selbst magisch verstanden, da ausbleibende Heilung oft als Folge mangelnden Glaubens interpretiert wurde. Die Autorin ordnet das Thema in den Kontext aktueller kolonialhistorischer und postkolonialer Debatten ein und gibt auch einen Überblick zur Quellenkritik vor dem Hintergrund der Kolonial- und Missionsgeschichte Papua-Neuguineas.

Zunächst analysiert sie die Gesundheitssituation der Missionsangehörigen als auch der indigenen Bevölkerung – insbesondere im Hinblick auf Malaria, Tropenmedizin und Frauengesundheit – sowie die Entstehung von Gesundheitsstationen (Tami, Sattelberg, Wareo). Es zeigt sich eindrücklich, wie allgegenwärtig Krankheiten waren: Europäer:innen litten v. a. unter Malaria, während eingeschleppte Epidemien wie Pocken und Influenza die indigene Bevölkerung verheerend trafen. Anschließend rekonstruiert die Autorin die medizinische Versorgung der einheimischen Bevölkerung und stellt dabei indigene Heilpraktiken und Missionsmedizin einander gegenüber. Instruktiv ist der Vergleich von Wilhelm Frobenius als Missionsarzt und Johann Stößel als Vertreter einer stärker missionarisch geprägten Medizin. Das abschließende Kapitel »Medizin und Mission – Mission durch Medizin?« analysiert die religiösen und kulturellen Dimensionen medizinischer Praxis – von Heilung über Zauberei bis hin zu Tod und Sterben – und bestätigt die Hypothese, dass die Spiritualisierung von Krankheit und Heilung ein gemeinsamer Anknüpfungspunkt zur Aushandlung des Religiösen war. »Die missionarische wie einheimische spirituelle Einordnung von Krankheit und Heilung bereitet die Grundlage für religiöse Aushandlungen« (359). Während die Missionare allein durch die Verkündigung des Wortes Glauben wecken wollten, war es gerade ihr medizinisches Wirken, das Menschen zur Konversion bewegte. Abgerundet wird das Werk durch einen Anhang mit Bibliographie, Verzeichnissen und Kartenteil.

Kittelmanns Studie macht deutlich, wie stark die »Zivilisierungsmission« neben der Schulpolitik gerade in der medizinischen Arbeit verwurzelt war. Medizinische Hilfe wurde zur Konstruktion religiöser Überlegenheit missionarisch instrumentalisiert und Mission durch (naturwissenschaftlich basierte) Medizin praktiziert. Durch die Analyse von Krankheitsverläufen (insbesondere Malaria), den Einsatz von Tropenmedizin (Chinin, Untersuchungen von Robert Koch) sowie der Gesundheitssituation der einheimischen Bevölkerung gelingt eine plastische Rekonstruktion der zentralen Rolle der Medizin im Missionsfeld.

Besonders hervorzuheben ist, dass die Autorin nicht nur die europäische Perspektive nachzeichnet, sondern – mithilfe des »Gegen-den-Strich-Lesens« – versucht, Handlungsmacht und Deutungsspielräume der indigenen Bevölkerung sichtbar zu machen, so einseitig sich die europäischen Quellen auch darstellen müssen. Die Autorin geht die Missionszeitschriften, Tagebücher, Archivmaterialien sowie koloniale Publikationen akribisch durch. Dabei reflektiert sie die eurozentrische Darstellungsweise überzeugend und betont die nötige Multiperspektivität. Ob eine konsequentere Dekonstruktion der Missionsquellen durch eine Fokussierung auf die *Agency* der Menschen vor

Ort möglich gewesen wäre, müssten weitere Arbeiten zeigen. Die Verflechtung von Heilung, Macht und Spiritualität wird überzeugend analysiert und macht dieses Buch für Forschende der Missionsgeschichte, Kolonial- und Medizingeschichte zu einer unverzichtbaren Lektüre.

Anton Knuth

Pamela F. Engelbert: **See My Body, See Me. A Pentecostal Perspective on Healing from Sexual Violence.** With a foreword by Kimberly Ervin Alexander, Pickwick Publications 2024, 268 Seiten, 30 $

This book is an interesting theological exploration of healing from sexual violence within Pentecostal communities. Drawing from the lived experiences of eight Pentecostal survivors of sexual abuse and assault and the insights of five licensed Pentecostal counsellors, Engelbert carefully investigates a central question: *What does healing look like for survivors within a tradition that emphasizes divine healing?*

The book wrestles with the tension between Pentecostal expectations of miraculous, instantaneous healing through a prayer of faith, and the lived realities of survivors for whom healing is often an ongoing, multifaceted, and deeply embodied process. Rather than offering simple answers, Engelbert acknowledges the complexities and diversities of healing journeys. She proposes that healing is not always a one-time event but can instead involve a rich »conglomeration of healing factors.«

We live in a world where many no longer believe in spiritual realities or divine intervention, especially on issues as devastating as sexual violence. In this context, Engelbert's book becomes relevant, because it shows how science and spirituality can be entangled in ways that empower healing. By drawing on survivor narratives, counselling practices, and Pentecostal theology, she demonstrates that healing is strongest when communities refuse to separate psychological insight from spiritual practice. This integration offers a model for a generation often sceptical of spirituality, reminding readers that faith and science need not be in conflict but can work together toward restoration.

In chapter one, Engelbert introduces the problem of sexual violence and situates it within Pentecostal theology, acknowledging both the silences in church discourse and the theological resources available. Chapter two presents the narratives of eight Pentecostal survivors, highlighting the diversity of their experiences and the different pathways they have taken toward healing. These two chapters establish the foundation of listening, as Engelbert underscores the need for the church to hear and honour the testimonies of survivors.

In chapter three, she brings in the voices of five Pentecostal counsellors who integrate psychology and spirituality, further strengthening the act of listening by showing how professional care and theological faith can come together. Chapter four deepens the theological reflection by examining Pentecostal understandings of divine healing, raising the question of whether healing should be understood as instantaneous, progressive, or lifelong. This chapter marks the transition toward waiting, as Engelbert insists that true healing cannot be rushed or forced into neat theological categories.

The theme of waiting becomes explicit in chapter five, where Engelbert develops listening as a Spirit-led practice that honours survivors' voices, and in chapter six, which focuses on waiting as an essential Pentecostal discipline that allows space for God's timing in the healing journey. By chapter seven, Engelbert introduces the praxis of learning, calling communities to grow in wisdom, theology, and compassion as they accompany survivors. The final two chapters – chapter eight, which synthesizes the insights into a constructive practical theology of healing, and chapter nine, which concludes with a call for Pentecostal communities to embody Christ's ministry – bring the three practices of listening, waiting, and learning into full alignment, showing them as interconnected threads that guide the entire book's movement.

One of the strengths of Engelbert's book is its grounding in survivor voices, which makes the theology not only credible but profoundly embodied. The integration of theology and praxis through the framework of listening, waiting, and learning offers practical guidance for Pentecostal communities, ensuring the book is not just theoretical but actionable. Furthermore, the bridging of faith and counselling demonstrates a holistic approach that honours both spirituality and psychological science. I find the tone throughout is both prophetic and pastoral, balancing academic rigor with accessibility for pastors, counsellors, and leaders. Finally, the way Engelbert opens dialogue between science and spirituality is especially relevant for today's generation, showing how psychological sciences and Pentecostal theology can converge in addressing trauma and fostering healing.

Despite its many strengths, the book has some limitations. Its focus on Pentecostalism, while rich and detailed, narrows the scope and leaves readers wishing for broader interdenominational perspectives that might make the framework more universally applicable. The pool of participants – eight survivors and five counsellors – provides important insights but cannot capture the full breadth of global Pentecostal experiences, which could have added even more depth. Additionally, while the book aims to be pastoral and accessible, some of its theological discussions may feel dense for lay readers or those without theological training, potentially limiting its reach beyond academic or ministerial audiences.

See My Body, See Me is one among the highly recommended resource for pastors, theologians, counsellors, and Pentecostal leaders seeking to address sexual violence with theological integrity and pastoral sensitivity. Engelbert's work courageously confronts silence and shame while offering practical, Spirit-filled ways forward. By demonstrating how science and spirituality can work together, this book speaks directly to today's world one that is increasingly sceptical of spiritual intervention. Her insistence that healing involves seeing, hearing, and believing survivors as God does is both a prophetic challenge and a pastoral gift. This book stands as an essential contribution to Pentecostal theology and the broader Christian conversation on trauma, healing, and justice.

Leita Ngoy

REDAKTION

Prof. Dr. Ulrike Schröder (zusammen mit Yan Suarsana für diese Ausgabe verantwortliche Redakteurin, Rezensionen), Theologische Fakultät der Universität Rostock, Universitätsplatz 1, D-18055 Rostock, Ulrike.Schroeder2@uni-rostock.de

Prof. Dr. Yan Suarsana (zusammen mit Ulrike Schröder für diese Ausgabe verantwortlicher Redakteur), Institut für Religionswissenschaft und Religionspädagogik, FB 09 – Kulturwissenschaften, Universität Bremen, Badgasteinerstr. 1/SpT Ebene 6, D-28359 Bremen, suarsana@uni-bremen.de

Prof. Dr. Andreas Heuser, Theologische Fakultät der Universität Basel, Lehrstuhl für Aussereuropäisches Christentum, Nadelberg 10, CH-4051 Basel, andreas.heuser@unibas.ch

Dr. Alena Höfer, Referentin für Frauenpolitik und intersektionalen Feminismus, Institut für Kirche und Gesellschaft der EKvW, Fachbereich Frauen Männer Vielfalt, Iserlohner Str. 25, D-58239 Schwerte, alena.hoefer@kircheundgesellschaft.de

PD Dr. Claudia Hoffmann (peer reviews), Theologische Fakultät der Universität Basel, Lehrstuhl für Aussereuropäisches Christentum, Nadelberg 10, CH-4051 Basel, claudia.hoffmann@unibas.ch

Prof. Dr. Claudia Jahnel, Institut für Interkulturelle Theologie und Religionswissenschaft, Universität Hamburg, Fachbereich Evangelische Theologie, Gorch-Fock-Wall 7, D-20354 Hamburg, claudia.jahnel@uni-hamburg.de

Dr. Anton Knuth (Rezensionen), Missionskademie an der Universität Hamburg, Rupertistr. 67, D-22609 Hamburg, anton.knuth@missionsakademie.de

Dr. Christian Weber, Mission 21, Missionsstr. 21, CH-4009 Basel, christian.weber@mission-21.org

VERFASSER:INNEN UND REZENSENT:INNEN

Dr. Jessica A. Albrecht, Lehrstuhl für Religionswissenschaft und Interkulturelle Theologie, Jordanweg 2, D-91054 Erlangen, Jessica.albrecht@fau.de

Dr. Melanie Barbato, Pacifica Communities University (PCU), 78 Vuya Road, Suva, Fiji, melanie.barbato@googlemail.com

Dr. Michael Biehl, Hermann-Stöhr-Str. 8, D-21244 Buchholz, michael.theo@biehl-web.de

Prof. Dr. Matthias Ehmann, Jahnstr. 49–53, D-35716 Ewersbach, Matthias.Ehmann@THE.FeG.de

Prof. Dr. Gregor Etzelmüller, Universität Osnabrück, Professur für Systematische Theologie, Neuer Graben 29/Schloss, D-49074 Osnabrück, gregor.etzelmueller@uni-osnabrueck.de

Jan Gehm, Institut für Sprachen und Kulturen des Nahen Ostens und Ostasiens/Lehrstuhl für Orientalische Philologie und Islamwissenschaft, Bismarckstr. 1, D-91054 Erlangen, jan.gehm@fau.de

Dr. Horst Gorski, Ohnhorststr. 30, D-22609 Hamburg, h.gorski@gmx.net

Dr. des. Doris Günther-Kriegel, Martin-Luther-Universität Halle-Wittenberg, Franckeplatz 1, D-06110 Halle (Saale), doris.guenther-kriegel@theologie.uni-halle.de

Dr. Brighton Katabaro, Rupertistr. 67, D-22609 Hamburg, b.katabaro@missionsakademie.de

Prof. em. Dr. Christine Lienemann-Perrin, Manuelstr. 116, CH-3006 Bern, christine.lienemann@unibas.ch

Tianji Ma, Brühlstr. 12, D-35418 Buseck, tianji.ma1309@gmail.com

Prof. Dr. Hermann Mückler, Universitätsstr. 7, NIG, IV, A-1010 Wien, hermann.mueckler@univie.ac.at

Dr. Égide Pèlerin Muziazia, Kötterstr. 29, D-48147 Münster, emuziazi@uni-muenster.de

Dr. Leita Ngoy, Pavenstädter Weg 37, D-33334 Gütersloh, Leita.ngoy@ekgt.de

Dr. Claudia Rammelt, Institut für Soziologie, Platz der Göttinger Sieben 3, D-37073 Göttingen claudia.rammelt@uni-goettingen.de

Dr. Thorsten Wettlich, Institut für Religionswissenschaft und Religionspädagogik, Universitäts-Boulevard 18, D-28359 Bremen, wettich@uni-bremen.de

Kirsten Wolandt, Rupertistr. 67, D-22609 Hamburg, kirsten.wolandt@missionsakademie.de